Filming *Jungle Princess* with
Dorothy Lamour:

"Everything was set. I was lying on the
rock, Dorothy was kneeling beside me, the
cameraman was watching the clouds . . . and
then I felt the first twinge. I had to go to
the bathroom. Oh, God, I thought, not
now! Not now!! I whispered Welsh prayers.
I crossed and uncrossed my legs. Then
someone shouted, "Here it comes! Get
ready! Roll 'em! How I got through the
dialogue I'll never know. I went head first
into the pool with Dorothy after me. The
cold water of the pool did its work."

* This picture was taken at a private projection room in Holly-
wood in 1933. Among the people assembled are Hedda Hopper,
John Gilbert, Countess Dorothy DiFrasso, Cary Grant, Randolph
Scott, Jeanette MacDonald, Dolores Del Rio, Cedric Gibbons,
Myrna Loy, Alice Terry, Irving Thalberg, Norma Shearer, Lois
Wilson, Michael Farmer, Gloria Swanson, Adrian, and our boy
right down center.

Wide-Eyed in Babylon

An Autobiography by

Ray Milland

BALLANTINE BOOKS • NEW YORK

Library of Congress Catalog Card Number: 74-4016

SBN 345-24609-8-175

This edition published by arrangement with
William Morrow & Company, Inc.

First Printing: October, 1975

Printed in the United States of America

BALLANTINE BOOKS
A Division of Random House, Inc.
201 East 50th Street, New York, N.Y. 10022
Simultaneously published by
Ballantine Books, Ltd., Toronto, Canada

This is for Mal, my wife, to whom I gave, many years ago, a gold medallion on which I had inscribed:

"I married an angel."

Truer words were never spoken.

Wide-Eyed
in Babylon

chapter 1

It was a fascinating sight. Not so much the room as the people in it. I was reminded of an aviary: the beeping and twittering and rustle of pretty creatures darting about, and the occasional croaking of ravens and crows. There were the female stars, young, not so young, and the old ones and those who always try to look like Vivian Duncan. And the aggressive ones, full of hate. From a distance it is sometimes difficult to tell these actresses apart, but for an old California hand like me there are ways. The younger they are, the more fragile and diaphanous their gowns, the wider and more extravagant the gestures with their arms, and when they turn, in some small surprise, they turn only their heads. The older ones, the more mature ones, turn the whole body, and they express emphasis with their hands, or if bitchery is in the air, a slight sideways movement of the head. In confidence, you understand. In their clothing they lean toward suits. Silken suits, with trousers that hide the filled ankles and the surface veins.

Then there were the male stars, comedians and dramatic actors: the comedians serious and attentive to those speaking to them and trying to explain the meaningful democratic validity of golf tournaments sponsored by themselves. And the dramatic actors

1

expansive, somewhat noisy, and cheerful as hell. There were producers huddled in the corners with their heads together, adding, subtracting, and lying. Also a few studio heads nodding sagely while listening to a pontificating university president. There were visitors from the East and house guests from San Francisco, who all clung to one another like immigrants freshlanded. And scattered throughout the room the solitary ones, the observers, the "talented" ones, each with his driven look.

I gazed at the west wall of this lovely room, which was entirely of glass, beyond the bickering and the cheating and the decorous squeals and the uproariousness, toward the sea far below and the lights of Santa Monica. Thrusting up through it all, the golden figure of the angel Moroni, high above a temple of the Mormons, tales of whom had frightened me as a child. I turned back to the bar and motioned for a little more whiskey and asked the time. Almost ten o'clock. Oh, God, an hour before I could decently leave this glittering pastiche, this Circus Maximus, this lubricious slave market.

I've been in Hollywood forty-four years. And a star for almost thirty-nine of them. And except for a few years at the beginning, fairly competent in my profession. Once or twice I was even called brilliant. But on those few occasions it was simply a matter of opportunity. And if that last phrase isn't quite clear, ask any actor to explain it. He will probably add that if *he* had been given the same opportunities he wouldn't be in the hole he is today, working for Universal.

Tonight is envoi. I feel a touch of frost, and I have had enough, and Gomer Jenkins is dead. May I tell you about him, Gomer? We called him Caesar; he was the principal, or headmaster, of Gnoll Hall, my primary school in Wales. He introduced me to Perseus and Theseus and the Minotaur and the Gorgon's head and all of Charles Kingsley, for which I loved him. And Shakespeare, for which I hated him. He looked like the Emperor Trajan: tight curly gray hair and pale blue eyes and that high-bridged Roman nose. And always immaculate. He sometimes used the cane on us, but most often his fists, and those only when we deserved them, which was fairly frequently. To this day no amateur can hit me with a right hook due to my constant study of Gomer's feet. He was our father, and now he is dead. So I'm going home to help bury him. In a month he would have been ninety-three years old. My bags are packed and sitting on the front seat next to the driver of a rented limousine that waits in the courtyard outside. I look at my watch. Just a half hour more and then to the airport. Free.

"Do you actually know all these individuals?"

He was a little man with a Napoleonic haircut, black loafers, a dinner jacket with a vent in the back, and a defiant Bucks County accent.

"I'm acquainted with most of them," I replied, "but I know only a few."

He looked puzzled for a moment, and then barged ahead. "What? Oh . . . er, yes, yes, of course. But I imagined everyone in this sort of place . . . uh, well anyway . . . would you mind briefing me on some of them? I find them quite interesting. A little obvious, but interesting."

I looked at the supercilious little sod and felt a twinge of pity. He was so aggressively Eastern, so self-consciously Brooks Brothers. So ill-mannered. So dull. I smiled in my drink for a moment, and then asked, "Anyone in particular?"

"No," he said, "not actually; just curious."

I launched into an outrageous description of those nearest us, giving them outlandish names and ascribing to them all sorts of exotic aberrations. He loved it. Then he gestured toward the far end of the bar, where a man was standing alone. A man of middle height, graying, a look of latent mischief sneaking out of eyes that were very watchful.

"And who is he?"

"Ah," I said, "there you have me. I don't know his name, but I have seen him once before. It was a combination nightclub and house of joy in Guayaquil, Ecuador. I think he was the manager or procurator-general, or whatever it is they call that type."

He gave me an odd look and asked, "What in the world would he be doing here?"

"Oh, I don't know," I said. "Looking for talent, I expect."

With an expression of dawning disbelief and the beginnings of anger, my little friend sidled away.

I took a long pull on my Scotch and soda and turned to look at the man at the end of the bar. He was Billy Wilder, the writer and director. A genius whose talents have been recognized and sought after from his very beginnings. With one exception.

My mind began to drift, back more than forty years, to Munich and the Regina Palast. I had been skiing above Garmisch, on a mountain called the Zugspitze. I had gone with an English sports club outing. You know the sort of thing, "fourteen days all inclusive," which meant sleeping six to a room, boiled sloppy dinners and one-egg breakfasts, day and night drinking songs, and always those goddamned accordions—all for about fifty-five dollars. After six days I bolted and went down to Munich, which was roughly fifty miles away, just to get warm and to take a bath all by myself for a change.

One afternoon I went into the Regina Palast for tea. It was a typical European *palais de danse,* with a fairly large ballroom floor surrounded by small dining tables now set up for tea, and at one end of the room a bandstand with about a ten-piece orchestra, usually pretty good. Three or four tables were set aside for professional female dance partners, and a couple of tables for professional male partners, always in "Smoking." These "professionals" were all very presentable and attractive people, half of them really amateurs who just needed a little extra money, in some cases actually to keep from starving. This was the Germany of 1933.

After I had seated myself and ordered tea, I looked around at the rather sparse attendance and the three or four couples on the floor. One girl attracted me instantly; she danced with that lovely flowing English style that marked her as a professional. Her partner was also good but not quite up to her standard. When the music ended, I watched them leave the floor, and, sure enough, the man took her to the professional area and, with a stiff little bow, left her. I got up, bought tickets for four dances, and walked over to her table. I asked if she was free and would she like tea. She was and she would. She accompanied me to my table, sat, and ate enough for a horse. During the course of my four dances I found out, among other things, that the man I had seen her dance with first was a young Viennese writer, at the moment financially shorted out. He was also a temporary professional.

Years later, I was playing in the first picture Billy Wilder ever directed, and because something about him bothered me, I mentioned the incident.

"Yes," he confessed, "it was me."

He then proceeded to tell me the time he sold his first screen story and he swore it was all true.

It seems that at the time he was living in one small room in one of Munich's not too elegant rooming-houses. In the room next to his lived a girl of somewhat generous morality, who was kept by the owner of the most notorious nightclub in the city; a man a little tight with a dollar. Her name was Hilla.

Now, in order to make a little extra scratch, Hilla would occasionally bring home a gentleman acquaintance for an hour or so; he would always be out of there by midnight, on account of her protector would usually show up about two. One night, while our hero was sitting miserably in his room trying to heat a glass of milk with a light bulb, he heard Hilla come in and he knew by the footsteps that she had someone with her. He peeked outside the door and saw she had a large, mature man in tow, and, hail Caesar, the sign of affluence: he was smoking a cigar! For an hour or so there were silences interspersed with fruity rumblings and giggles. Suddenly there was a scream of brakes outside the house, and a slight crash, followed by a loud and impatient altercation. Billy looked out of the window and saw to his horror that it was the nightclub owner, who in his hurry to get out of the car had knocked a pedestrian into a garbage can. Billy thereupon rushed into Hilla's room and imparted the news that her boyfriend was outside with blood in his eye. Hilla said two words.

"Help me!"

Billy immediately grabbed the man's clothes, then shoved this stark-naked bladder of lard out into the passage and into his own little elegant nest. And there they sat, hardly daring to breathe, while Hilla's boyfriend stomped and roared. He knew that she had someone up there, that he would find the son-of-a-bitch, and when he did would strangle the bastard with his own menagerie! Then he started in on Hilla. Ah, it was lovely! In a little while things quieted down while Hilla tried to explain. Meanwhile, back in his room, Billy was staring at his guest while the large man got dressed. Suddenly Billy recognized him! He was Max Galitzenstein, managing director of a picture company in Munich called Maxim Film.

With a smile worthy of Bela Lugosi, Billy said, "Excuse me, Mr. Galitzenstein, but I happen to have just finished a screen play for a most exciting picture which would be ideal for Maxim Film."

The man looked at him. "You know me?"

"But of course," said Billy. "You are Galitzenstein. *Besitzer* of Maxim Film."

"And SOLE OWNER!" bellowed Galitzenstein.

"Yes, yes, of course, sir; though you must admit the mistake is excusable under the circumstances. But when you read this screen play you will want to buy it immediately."

"Very well," rasped the nervous tycoon. "Bring it to my office in the morning and I'll read it."

At that moment, in the other room, the antlered German roared as he again belted Hilla with what sounded like a chair. Sadly, Billy looked at his victim and said, "No, Mr. Galitzenstein, not tomorrow. Now!"

After a moment or two, a strangled voice asked, "How much?"

"Just three hundred dollars, sir," Billy said.

Sadly, Galitzenstein reached for his wallet.

After the enraged lover next door had left, spewing out frightful promises of what he would do to the despoiler of his Brünnehilde, Billy let his victim out with a great show of care and conspiracy. When Galitzenstein was safely gone from sight, Billy shot over to Hilla's room and tapped on the door. An apprehensive voice said, "Yes?"

Billy stuck his head inside. "Hilla, tomorrow night, *please,* Erich Pommer?"

"Must be pretty funny, Mr. M."

I looked up to find Nacho watching me. He was a bartender I'd known over the years who worked for Dave Chasen, this affair being catered by Chasen's. It was being given for an expatriate American countess and her hairdresser, so that they could meet the elite of the film world. Which meant that there were very few television people present.

"Recuerdos, Nacho, *recuerdos.* What's the time?"

It was eleven. Time to go. I began to look around for my hostess to thank her and say good-bye, and so started easing my way through the room toward the staircase, which in this house leads upstairs to the main hall. I also remembered that there was a powder room at the top, and my bladder, due to my intake of refreshments, was beginning to whimper for relief.

"You're not leaving?"

The speakers were a couple of house faggots from

Beverly Hills, so I smiled   a little sadly, told them
I hated to leave but had a plane to catch, and passed
on. I warily circled a trio of chic and notorious executives' wives, those lean and hungry predators who
know the sexual capabilities of half the men in the
room. And of some of the women. Then on up into
the hall, where I saw my charming hostess, a charming
woman who mumbles. I kissed her cheeks, thanked
her, and went out to the car. We were halfway down
the hill before I realized I hadn't gone to the bathroom.
I told the driver to stop at an address out on Sunset
on the way to the airport. It was the home of the
only actress I have ever really loathed—rather secluded,
and fronted by a beautiful lawn. It now has the biggest
yellow spot in town. Or will have.

chapter ii

The flight to London was uneventful. After a night in a hotel, I set out early in the morning, in a rented car, on the pleasant drive to Wales. From London it's about a hundred and fifty miles to the town of Neath, where I was born; you travel west, through Berkshire and Gloucestershire, across the Severn and into Monmouthshire, past the brooding Norman Castle of Chepstow on the Wye, and on into Glamorganshire, into Wales proper. A land of music and mountains and mystery. The land of the ancient Brythons or, if you prefer, Britons.

Have you ever talked with a witch? Been fascinated and entranced by one? I have. Because in every Welsh village there is a witch. And people go to the witch for the fulfillment of strange and devious desires. For the Celtic mind in its lonely moments is a tumbling sea of love and compassion and romanticism and neurotic hates.

I was born on a mountain called Cymla, above the town of Neath on the west coast of Wales, and given the name Reginald Alfred John Truscott-Jones. The name of our witch was Bronwen Madoc. She was old when I was six. As old as Glastonbury.

That night, after we put Gomer in the ground,

I asked about old Bron. The mourners looked at me in their strange and silent way and one said, "Yes, she still lives on the marsh."

"Still?" I asked, with wonder in my voice.

"Still," said the man.

Suddenly I couldn't wait to leave this house of relished grief, and in hurried but properly hushed tones, I bade the mourners good-bye. As I left, their eyes were as bright as coal, alive with the possibility of delicious gossip. For them, I would always be the boy on the hill with the fey mother and the three wild sisters. And the salt of their life is gossip and intrigue; in Welsh villages, you will always see a curtain move as you pass. I drove my little car the mile or so down the lane that led to the marsh, and got out. And there was her house, the roof thatched with reeds just as I knew it, but oh, so much smaller than I had remembered, the tiny windows with the center of the panes like the bottom of beer bottles. As I approached her door, I felt again the frightened fascination of my first visit.

It was a December night with a quarter moon, and I wanted assurance from someone wiser than parents that death was not inevitable. A little while before, my father had taken me to hear a famous Welsh revivalist speak on some high field, and one phrase, "Death comes to us all!" had shocked and terrified me. I looked up at my father, beseeching him to tell me this was not true. He shrugged so slightly but didn't answer. You must remember I was only seven years old. That night sleep escaped me, and all through the next day the thought stayed with me. Who would know the truth? Then I knew. Bron! Old Bron!

Now, in Wales in the winter it is dark at four o'clock, and by the time I got out of school and started my long walk home the stars were already showing; by the time I got to Bron's house it was dark. I was afraid to knock, because until now all we had ever done was to shout insults and throw stones and then run away. But I knocked, and a quiet voice said, *"Duwchymmer, bychan."*

She spoke only the Welsh tongue. I went in and saw her sitting on the hob, with a little black kettle whispering, ready for tea. She was old and in black, and she smelled of mushrooms and wet leaves. Before my courage died, I shouted to her, "Bron, must I die?"

She looked at me quietly and said, "Death will come when you are ready for her."

Then I ran. Even today, when I think of death I always see someone like Theda Bara.

Now I was before her door again, and many years had passed. I knocked, and again the voice said, *"Duwchymmer, bychan bach."*

I noticed that she used the diminutive for boy, the word *bach.* And also that the voice was thinner and higher. And again, with instant nostalgia the smell of mushrooms returned as I entered and saw her sitting by the tiny fire. She looked just as old, the eyes a little blacker, her body a little smaller, and her hands like a bird's feet.

She said, "Life in the new world becomes you."

I thanked her and told her a little of my house and my family but that I would always have an ache in my heart for Gwlad, which is the Celtic word for Wales. She was silent for a moment or two, but her eyes never left me. Then she said, "You want to know of Gwyneth, isn't it?"

Suddenly I knew why I had come. Gwyneth, who was fourteen years old when I was fourteen. To whom I had never spoken, but who had looked at me once and had run with my world in her hands. I nodded like someone admitting a sin, remembering that I had come to Bron in my misery and had begged for a love potion. But I also remembered that she hadn't smiled but had looked at me in serious fashion and said, "Go home, *bychan,* and think only of me."

I did, desperately. And slowly Gwyneth faded. Until this night. I looked at her and said, "I am now a man, but still young enough to have curiosity and romantic thoughts; is Gwyneth still?"

"She is still," Bron replied.

If the foregoing puzzles you, please remember we were speaking Welsh. I hadn't spoken it for forty years and I am still astonished. I asked Bron where Gwyneth lived and she told me. Three miles along the river toward the sea, with a husband and one child. Then she asked me if I thought it wise to rekindle a fire so long dead. What if she had become a sloven, with fat arms and eyes like pewter? I smiled and said, "Not Gwyneth."

I left her and got into my little car and drove along the sea road until I came to the house. I got out of the car and walked as slowly as I could to the door and then knocked. In a moment it opened, and a girl of about seventeen stood there with lank, dead hair and one bedraggled stocking on, and I suddenly smelled old beer. I asked her if this was the road to Cardiff and she said yes, straight the way through. You can't miss it.

I didn't go to Cardiff but circled back to the main part of the town, where I had been fortunate enough to get a good bedroom with its own bath. Luxury indeed, for the town of Neath is a small one, and the Castle Hotel quite old; built during the days of Napoleon, it still maintains the personal service of those times.

After putting my car in the stable yard, which still seemed to carry the steaming aroma of hundred-year-old horses and the important bustle of post changes, I walked to the canopied door, which the night porter held open for me. For a moment we both stood and silently looked at the yard, both hearing the ghostly shouts of the ostlers and the creaking of harness and muddy coaches. Then he turned to me and with a slow smile asked, "Would you like a little supper in your room, sir?" I had had no thought of food, but I was suddenly ravenous. Hungry for the food of boyhood, cooked in the way of farmhouse kitchens unknown outside these hills of home.

"That is a wonderful idea, if it's not too much trouble; it's really quite late."

With a deprecating wave of his hand he said he was just about to make himself some tea anyway, and was there anything I would like special. "Yes," I said, suddenly remembering. "If you could possibly do it, I would like a Welsh breakfast. I know it's late and the kitchen closed, but that is what I would really like."

With a fat little smile and the gentlest pat on the shoulder, he said, "Then you shall have it, sir. And perhaps a pint of Cadoxton beer to go with it? You will sleep well, sir."

"Ah, yes, the Cadoxton brewery, Evans and Bevan it used to be called when I was a child. I remember they bought my wonderful dog Gypsy after he became troublesome to the neighbors and people passing by and when he came to dislike the milkman and Thomas the Post. But that was a long time ago. Anyway, if you'll just draw the beer, I'll take it up with me and have a tub while you're fixing the supper." And with that I left him and climbed the staircase to my room.

I sat in the hot tub sipping beer and feeling strangely depressed. I would have stayed there for an hour had I not heard the porter come in and start rattling dishes on the small table. I hauled myself out and dried myself and put on one of those heavy towel bathrobes they have in old, good hotels and walked into the bedroom. He was standing there with a chair drawn back and a knowing smile on his face. I seated myself and, with the conspiratorial air of an old gossip, he slowly lifted the cover to reveal what is to me the most appetizing dish in the world. It had smoked country bacon, and mushrooms fried in the bacon fat, a slice of Caerphilly cheese cooked and toasted until it was crisp on the outside, and in the middle of the plate the pièce de résistance, a hot black dollop of laver bread to lightly powdered with barley flour. I must explain laver bread to you. It is an ancient food made from a special kind of seaweed found only on the Welsh coast and certain parts of Japan. When it has been processed and made ready for eating, it is black and looks like the dregs from the crank case of a twenty-year-old Morris. Laver bread is an acquired taste but, once acquired, it becomes an absolute delight. On a separate small dish were two slices of fried homemade bread. These are supposed to be cooked in the same pan after all the other ingredients are done. A little water added to the hot fat ensures that the bread will become light and crisp and will retain the flavor of the things that were there before. I ate the lot.

The porter meanwhile had busied himself filling a fresh hot-water bottle, turning down the bed and poking up the fire in the small iron grate. He came to the table to gather up the dishes.

"Didn't like it much, did you?"

"What does it look like?"

"Aye, 'tis a good meal. Tell me, sir, who was at the funeral? Many that you knew?"

"Very few. Most of them were old ones, and in front of them I still felt like a schoolboy. Old James the Baker was there, Williams the Police, Davies the Butcher, oh, and Blethin Parry, the under-manager from Bedwas. Only two of my schoolmates showed up, Idris Llewellyn and Iorwerth Brunt. Very few spoke to me; they made me feel like a foreigner.

"It seems a lot of them have died one way or another. I *would* like to have seen Benny Johns though, and perhaps Lalla Reed and a few others. Ah, well. Maybe tomorrow."

He looked at me, and then in a comforting, almost crooning voice said, "Yes, maybe you'll find some of them tomorrow. Although, I would have thought Trevor and Cyril Walters would have been there and Howell Jones. Funny, isn't it?"

I considered him for a moment and thought him

to be at least three or four years older than myself. Then I asked, "Did you go to the Gnoll?"

He looked down at the floor and smiled and said, sheepishly I thought, "No sir, no. I went to the Maera, Catholic, you see. But we did have some great old stone fights against the Gnoll after school, didn't we, *bach*?" And with that he picked up the tray and left, closing the door quietly.

I sat there slowly finishing my beer until sleep began its gentle nudging. Then I crawled into the high feather bed and put out the light and lay there for a while, pushing back the mists. Once again I was catching shrimps in the tidal pools of the marsh, and watching Gyp chasing ducks, and shouting to Dai Beynon and Donald Hope and Levi Bowater and Lalla and . . .

chapter iii

I was awakened by Gyp whimpering and scampering in a furious little dream beside me on the other pillow. He always slept in my bed. I was seven years old.

It was still dark, but I noticed it was strangely silent and I hardly dared hope . . . could it have snowed through the night? I listened, hardly breathing, for the sould of wheels or the milkman's horse trotting by or a workman's early footsteps. But nothing, just silence. I scrambled out of bed and ran across the cold linoleum floor to the window and saw that it was frosted white. I breathed on it as hard as I could until a small patch cleared and I looked out. Everything was white! I gazed across the valley to the Bedways pithead and saw a slow stream of tiny flickering lights coming down the white breast of the hillside. It was the night shift going home, which meant it was six o'clock in the morning. I opened the lower window pane and listened to the voices. Three hundred men and boys singing "The Dream of Gerontius." I heard the deep frightening voices of the older men, the clarion tones of the younger ones, and the sweet clear voices of the apprentice boys. Even Gyp beside me was quietly whining, his little potbelly straining. He thought he was singing. Gyp was a full-blooded bull terrier, about three months old, which my father had given me a month earlier. He already showed promise of great strength, long powerful jaws and deep-chested; even now showing signs of fearlessness and rollicking courage. But, like me, he also felt the cold and loved his comfort, so we scrambled back into the warm bed. I lay there thinking and anticipating the day before me.

School did not start until nine o'clock, and it was a three-mile hike down the mountain. I mentally kicked myself for not wetting my coat and hanging it on the fence the night before for it to freeze. The idea was that one would spread the frozen coat on the hill and career hell-for-leather down the hill for over a mile before one came to the crossroad. But how was I to know it would snow? Oh, bugger, today I would steal a cattle-pan and use that and drag it home in the evening. They were really better, because they were made of galvanized iron and were about the size of a small shallow bathtub. They were used to hold winter feed for the cattle—cowcake, which was made of chopped-up hay and chaff and barley, held together with black, hard molasses. We youngsters would often eat it. It was delicious, and we never had stomach trouble.

So this morning, that was how I got to school. I had forgotten something, though. Today was choir practice and we were doing the last part of *The Messiah,* which meant that long after dark I would be dragging that damn pan all the way up the hill again. I didn't mind too much; I liked the choir and almost all the people in it. We practiced two nights a week in the winter, and quite a large choir it was too. Almost two hundred and fifty voices, all male. I am blessed with a love of music and cursed with perfect pitch.

Now you may wonder why I say "cursed," so I'll tell you. It is absolute agony for me to attend a concert or go to an opera and hear a note sung even so much as an eighth sharp. I remember once when my parents took me to hear Dame Clara Butt in *Il Trovatore*. Sheer bloody torture! She flatted and farted all over the stage, and when she got to the "Miserere" she sounded exactly like a heifer giving birth to its first calf. I deliberately stuck my finger down my throat and was carted out of there retching all the way up the aisle. I have a feeling the tenor would have liked to leave with me. When we got to the lobby I was told to go into the men's cloakroom and wash out my mouth and clean myself up generally and wait there until the performance was over. Then we went home and I was given a good dose of castor oil to "clean me out."

My mother was a great believer in castor oil and senna tea. According to her, what with the muck we put in our stomachs all day it was a wonder half the children in town weren't in Llantwit graveyard. She had a point. For instance, I had a friend named Benny Johns whose older brother worked in a local chemist's shop and used to pinch jars of Horlick's Malted Milk Tablets, which we would chew by the gross. Didn't affect us one bit. And there was a sweet-shop down by the school that sold dried carob beans, which I loved, and sweet licorice root. There were paper bags of sherbert powder into which we put just enough water to make it foam; then we would eat the foamy paste with a spoon. Of course we belched a lot, but even that was fun. We would compete to see who could belch the loudest, and die laughing.

About this time my devious little mind evolved a way to increase my pocket money fivefold. Every Saturday morning I had to take piano lessons from a teacher called Professor Balaclava Evans. He was born during a period when it was fashionable to name children after famous battles and heroic generals. There was even a kid in our school named Khartoum Harris. But to get back to my pocket money: The arrangement was that I would show up at Evans's house at eleven o'clock every Saturday morning with two and sixpence, in those days worth exactly half a dollar. He would pocket the cash and seat me at the piano, whereupon I would unroll my music case and set up the piece I was working on in front of me, in this particular case a frolicsome gallop called "The Fairy's Wedding." I had been working on it for weeks and at this point looked upon it with absolute loathing. He would listen to me for about five minutes, nodding his head, and then sneak a look at his watch, give a great start and say, "I forgot something. I'll be back in five minutes. Keep practicing." And that would be the last I would see of him till the following Saturday. He was off to the Carpenter's Arms with my half-crown.

Then and there I got my brilliant idea. I could practice this dreadful habanera, together with another fulsome dirge called "The Maiden's Prayer," at home for a month and nobody would be the wiser. I would then be two and sixpence a week richer. This worked wonderfully for three weeks, until Balaclava, missing his extra beer-money, came to see my father to enquire if I was ill or perhaps dissatisfied with his teaching. When I came sauntering in, tired but happy just before supper, they were waiting for me. Balaclava got up with a lot of bustle and said good night and left. My father in his silent way just pointed to the stairs. It was harrowing. I slept on my stomach for three nights.

My father was not a cruel or a harsh man. Just a very quiet one. I think he was an incurable romantic and consequently a little afraid of his emotions and perhaps ashamed of them. To me, he was a rather tall man, very handsome, with black hair and eyes the color of sherry. His nose was aquiline and thin, and he wore a fierce cavalry moustache; he had in fact been a young hussar in the Boer War and had been present at the relief of Mafeking. He never held long conversations with anyone, except perhaps with me, possibly because I was the only other male in our family. The household consisted of my mother, a rather flighty and coquettish woman much concerned with propriety and what the neighbors thought, my three sisters each exactly one year apart, and Mary Catherine, our housekeeper and laundress. She was also the maid, the cook, and our comforter and shield. I think she was a relative of sorts on my father's side, but it was a relationship never spoken of, shadowy and secretive.

I know that my grandfather, a huge black-bearded man, had been married twice, a state which in Wales is looked upon rather like leprosy. On top of that, *his* mother had been a Spaniard, which in our county made us all rather suspect. In all he had ten children, two girls by the first wife and eight sons by his second. My father was the seventh son. He was christened Alfredo, which he never admitted. My father's half-sisters were Emma and my wonderful Aunt Luisa. Each of my father's brothers had four or five children, so you know that Wales is just crawling with my relatives. Emma had one child, a daughter, but Luisa remained a spinster and operated a business that made wagon wheels and ran a large farm where she bred horses. Good hackneys and Welsh cobs. That farm was my private paradise. It was where I learned horsemanship, and I learned it well. Not only a proper seat and how to post and take fences and walls, but the entire world of equitation. Years later Luisa died from a kick she received while helping to shoe a nervous mare and most of my youth went with her.

It was getting close to Christmas, that most wonderful and exciting time of gifts and expectation, a white and quiet world, where it seems to me the only sounds one heard were the voices of children. We would go bucketing down the hills after school in the moonlight in tin washtubs, homemade sleds, feed pans, anything that would slide. My favorite was an old Welsh coracle, a sort of fishing boat made to hold one man. It was constructed of long thin hazel wands woven like a basket and heavily tarred on the outside. Almost circular, they were used mostly on the great salmon rivers like the Usk, and the Severn and the Dee. In those days mine was not a polluted world but a world where gypsies camped and pheasants flew. And where children still believed in Santa Claus.

Above all, Christmas was the time of the Panto. Pantomime is a theatrical institution peculiar to Britain. The show is always based upon some legend or fairy story, like "The Sleeping Beauty" or "Cinderella" or "Jack and the Beanstalk," which is transformed into a glittering musical extravaganza. There is always a Prince Charming and he is invariably played by a girl, while the parts of the older females are played by men. Most of England's great comedians and tragedians have also played "dames" at some time or other. Indeed, they've looked forward to it with a great deal of relish. Three of the best in my memory were Sir George Robey, Sir Seymour Hicks, and George Jackley, all veterans and all stars. There was one stocky, bulletproof old gal called Maisie Gay, whose specialty was playing a policeman on beat. She had one routine where she would arrest an overly made-up young man, obviously "cruising," for spitting on the sidewalk. The ensuing garbled interrogation, the *entendres doubles,* the frustrated glares at the audience which, when I think of them, still send me cackling to the floor.

Yes, the "dames" had a high old time on the stage, but I'm sure they would never be tolerated in any American family theater today, even in this present age of permissiveness. Fifty percent of the material would be blue-penciled. The Pantos were about the bluest shows ever performed. And still are. But we children saw only the romantic and the glamorous, the tumbler and the occasional wicked magician. The bawdiness and ribald carrying on went right over our heads. The adults went home with a chuckle and we with stars in our eyes.

As Christmas Day grew closer, anticipation sharpened. By eight or nine o'clock we would be in bed, my sisters and I. But sleep was harder to come by; even with the bolster against the door I could hear them whispering and giggling, and then the carolers would come. I would quickly pop out of bed, rush to the window, and there they would be with a candle or two. Five or six young people singing *"Ar Hyd Y Nos"* or "Good King Wenceslaus" and singing it very well, too. For in Wales every child is taught music in some form or another from the first day he starts school. In each of the little residential streets in my village there was at least one house with a highly polished brass plate fastened at the side of the front door, with an inscription like "Madame Blodwen Davies. Lessons in Piano." Then the letters *L.R.C.M.,* which meant that she was a graduate of the London Royal College of Musicians. Or another sign might read "Professor Gladwyn Price. Violin." There was one I shall never forget, which said, "Mr. Idris Pritchard. Welsh Harp. L.R.C.M.," and then below in brackets, "[Failed]."

In Wales there is a preponderance of surnames beginning with the letter *P.* Now there is a reason for this. Hundreds of years ago there were no surnames in Wales. Every man was known as the son of his father, and this relationship was signified by the word *ap,* which meant "son of." Thus you got "William ap Rhys," which became over the years William Price. Or "John Pritchard," which had been "John ap Richard."

Anyway, to get back to Christmas. It was so much more enchanting when I was a child. There were no bleary-eyed Santa Clauses on every street corner shilling for some charity or another, 90 percent of which you've never heard, every one of them ringing those damn bells. No rabid used-car salesmen drumming up business in moth-eaten Santa suits, no TV and radio pitchmen yammering away at the Yuletide spirit. What happened to the Christmas spirit? I'll tell you, my friends, it went. And the world went with it. Long before Christmas comes you're sick of the sight and sound of it. Today children look upon Father Christmas as something old-fashioned and quaint. I remember once dressing up for my own children when they were six or seven years old, and I've never felt quite the same since. They accepted my performance very politely at the time, but they never *said* anything. Sadly, I came to realize that I had embarrassed them.

But we believed in Santa Claus with all our might, and when the day of the opening of the Christmas stocking finally came, we crept downstairs very slowly with our eyes as big as saucers, half hopeful, half afraid that maybe Santa hadn't reached our house after all. And then, at the bottom of the stairs, the whole magic scene burst upon us—the bulging stockings hanging from the fireplace and the toys spread beneath the tree.

To *me* England is the land of Christmas—the whole sight and sound and smell of it. And I remember the oranges, oh! the oranges; they're Spanish and very fragrant and the whole house smells of them. And there were other smells, of fruitcake and port wine and cigars. All these grownup glamorous things were brought out and passed around at Christmas. The rest of the year might be a dull bread-and-butter existence, but this, this was the day of delights.

The next day was Boxing Day, which was almost as exciting, for that was the day you dressed up in your best clothes, and went with your parents to visit all the relatives and neighbors to receive presents and eat cake and be kissed. Boxing Day goes back many years to a custom of distributing little boxes of gifts to household servants and retainers and later to people like the milkman, the postman, and the greengrocer—to all the people who served you during the year. Today that custom is very different. You give an envelope instead of a box, and you make damn sure both that you give it well before Christmas and that it contains a sufficiency of the necessary, or your services may be a little lumpy for the next few months. In England girls are still playing princes, though it's getting harder to tell, and the aging comedians are still playing dames. But are the children still as enchanted?

I was nine years old. I knew it was going to be a wonderful summer. I knew it because the Spanish onion men were early this year. They came in March, rolling up the lanes from the estuary on foot and broken-down old bicycles. They were dressed in faded denim trousers and collarless shirts of a foreign-looking blue, rope-soled espadrilles, and big black berets, and they were shrouded, covered, in strings of onions. They were draped over their handlebars and crossbars and strung from long poles balanced on their shoulders. Always cheerful, always smiling, they would spread through the town going from house to house selling their strings of spring onions and smoked fish. Sometimes I would come home from school and a couple of them would be in the kitchen, and Mary Catherine would be gossiping and giving them tea and bread and cheese. They were Basques, you see, and between the Celtic and Basque tongues there is a connection of sorts stemming back to pre-Roman times, so it was possible to communicate, although haltingly. I would listen to their tales of Spain and Normandy and Cornwall. I think it was then I got the idea of running away to sea, although it didn't actually happen for a year or more.

My friend and constant conspirator, Donald Hope, and I used to spend hours dreaming it and planning it, sitting high in an oak tree in the woods at the top of the hill. It seemed easy to us, because Donald's father was manager of the ship-breaking yard of Thomas W. Ward and Company, which was situated at Briton Ferry some five miles away at the mouth of the river. Weary old coasters and sad and rusty freighters were there waiting for the torch. And there would always be one old tramp steamer tied up, loading scrap. I think I was ten years old when Donald sneaked up to me one day in school and said there was a freighter in the yard, unloading hides, that would probably sail again the following Saturday. This was it! High tide would not be until midday, so if we met at four A.M. Saturday morning and walked fast, we could easily be there by six A.M. And that's what we did. We fortified ourselves with paper bags filled with bread and jam and seed cake and a couple of bottles of small beer and set off. We got to the yard and found the boat without any trouble. It was tied up at the small commercial wharf next to the yard, and on the stern I saw painted its port of registry. Santos! All my geography came alive. I saw trees with monkeys, unlimited bananas, pampas grass, and the wonderful smell of coffee bags.

The ship was strangely silent and deserted. So we scrambled aboard quite undetected and saw that the hatch covers were off. We picked the one amidships and quickly climbed down the iron ladder and went to the farthest and darkest corner, where we found a pile of sacking and old canvas. There we made our little nest, sat and waited, and had some small beer. And sat and waited. There was never a sound. It was Saturday. We were tired from the long walk, so we decided to sleep for a while. It must have been four or five hours later that I was awakened by footsteps on the iron deck above. I quietly climbed the iron ladder and peeked over the coaming; there were three men standing about thirty feet away from me looking forward, and I heard one of them say, "We'll get those two donkey engines off first thing Monday morning, they're worth saving, and there's a couple of generators in the engine room worth a pound or two. By the end of the week we can start cutting her up."

I went back down and walked slowly over to Donald and told him what I'd heard. I said we'd better go home. He looked at me wide-eyed for a moment and started to cry. It embarrassed me, so I started to pat him. I didn't know what else to do. I said, "It's no use carrying on like that. Tell them back at your house that we walked to Raglan Sands to look for mussels. And the tide was in so we couldn't get any. They'll never know the difference." With that, he started bawling more than ever. I whispered at him as loud as I dared, "Shut up, those men will hear you!"

Then he said, "I forgot to tell you. I left my mother a note!"

Now this properly enraged me. "You *mochen,* you *dwlben!* Now you've done it! My dada'll kill me!"

I sat down chastened. How was I to fiddle my way out of this situation? No way. Just would have to go home and face the music. There'd be plenty of it, and it wouldn't be "The Dream of Gerontius."

We sat there and ate the rest of the seed cake and drank the small beer, waiting for the men to leave and for the boat to be deserted and the yard empty again. It was almost four o'clock before we could start back, only this time the journey didn't seem so far. Our homes were approaching much too quickly. There was a small farmhouse set back from the road, its large front garden a mass of red-currant bushes, so we crawled in among them and sat there morosely, more or less trying to stave off the moment of truth. We started to eat the red currants; they were delicious, so we ate a bellyful. Then there was nothing else to do, so we set out on the last mile. When we got to the fork in the road we separated, he to his house, I to mine. Today, when I think of it, I always giggle. He looked like Stan Laurel having to do something Ollie forced him into.

When I got to my house I knocked at the door, something I had never done before. It was opened by Williams the Police. "Oh, come home, have you? Well, your father wants to see you, Reggie *bach.*" And with that he left.

I looked at my father, and *he* looked at *me* and then pointed to the stairs. As I went up I saw him reach for the wall of the passage on which hung some polished brass bedwarmers on long wooden handles, some horse brasses, and a couple of toasting forks about four feet long. His hand came away with a toasting fork.

Up in the bedroom I gave a sterling performance. My bawling had everything—pathos, agony, total abandonment, and just the right touch of Sydney Carton. I even managed to throw up a little, and at that moment in charged my mother and Mary Catherine. "What are you doing to this poor child? What sort of father are you?"

And from Mary Catherine—"You ought to be ashamed of yourself, you've even bent the toasting fork. Oh, and look! He's bleeding from the mouth! Oh, what a proper beast you are!"

My father looked at them completely distraught, and I saw tears in his eyes; his emotions were always so close to the surface. Then he stumbled out. Mary Catherine went to the washstand, wet a towel, and came back to wash the blood from my mouth. I told them not to worry, that it was only red currants. With that my mother belted me in the ear, and they both left.

I lay there sniffling for a while and then undressed and climbed into bed. No use expecting supper this night, which was all right with me. Couldn't eat anyway.

After brooding over the events of the day, I came to the conclusion that, all things considered, I got off pretty lucky. I could still have been in that hold, wrapped in cold canvas and almost retching from the stink of hides. Instead I was home in my own warm little bed. And after all, a hot bottom only lasts for about three days. I woozily began to hum a little song:

> "Now the day is over,
> Night is drawing nigh.
> Shadows of the evening,
> Steal across the sky."

Then I slept.

It was during that summer that they took Gypsy away from me, and I was heartbroken. But he had become very troublesome. He had grown big and very strong, and no dog in the neighborhood was safe from him. One day my father came to me and said he had sold him to the brewery for a watchdog; there had been too many complaints. We were to deliver him that day. Sadly we went off, but I couldn't go any further than the garden gate. I stopped and went to my knees and hugged Gyp. He licked my face and whined a little, but he was very subdued. He knew. I turned and ran back into the house, and I cried for the rest of the day. It was from that moment that I started to grow up.

chapter iv

The Summer of 1918 was a beautiful one. Warm and scented and hazy. And rumors were racing over the hills and down the valleys that the war would soon be ending, that the husbands and lovers would soon be home, and that we could get rid of the German prisoners of war who were laboring on the farms and replace them with our own men. The refugees would be going too, most of them Belgian children who had been billeted throughout the countryside for over three years. And this depressed me. For this meant that Victor would be leaving. Victor Rouvers was ten, one year younger than I, and had been living with us for a little more than a year. He had been sent to us from a refugee center on the east coast, where he had been kept for two years. Someone in authority finally came to the conclusion that it might be bad for children to be living within the sound of distant gunfire, which could be heard on quiet evenings when the breeze was right. Gunfire which was destroying their homeland.

Victor came to us a quiet, thin, withdrawn little boy who had no English, only a strange sort of French which was half Walloon. He was put in my charge. I was to take him to school, and he was to sit at my desk, I was to try to teach him English and bring him home every night. This infuriated me so much that for the first few weeks I treated him like a dog. No, come to think of it, much worse than a dog. At least a dog could understand you; you could have fun with a dog. But Victor? Ach! He it was who was the cause of my most embarrassing and painful encounter with Gomer Jenkins.

We were in English class, and it was correction time for our compositions which had been assigned the day before. The subject had been "A Storm at Sea," and Miss Griffiths, our prim and pretty teacher, was correcting our spelling and giving gentle, simple advice about paragraphing and construction, nothing very deep because we were not yet in our teens. She never corrected the spelling of the long words we ostentatiously used, only the sloppy and careless spelling of the short ones. She started by telling Benny Johns to stand up and spell *stomach*. Benny dutifully stood up and spelled out B-E-L-L-Y. That did it. We cackled, we howled, and we roared. I think I overdid it slightly when I fell out of my desk onto the floor. After a minute or two the room became quiet and we sat and looked angelically at Miss Griffiths, who hadn't moved or uttered a sound. Then she said, "Benny Johns, you will go to the blackboard and write the word *stomach* one hundred times."

It was sobering but not exactly crushing, as my next little escapade will show. She continued to call out words to the rest of the class and, as was her habit, she would throw a few simple ones to the other three refugees in the room, just to make them feel that they were no different from the rest of us, that they belonged. She was not averse to banging the refugees over the knuckles with an ebony ruler, either, if they misbehaved. But we adored her. I suppose fully half of us harbored childish romantic thoughts about her, but mine were becoming a little disturbing, they were verging on the physical. I would imagine that she would be set upon by some louts from the Catholic school on her way home and that I would happen by and wade in and rescue her, because I was tall and quite strong and handy with my fists. Then perhaps she would let me walk home with her.

"Victor Rouvers, spell the word *cake*." With a jolt, I came back to the schoolroom and realized that Victor was standing up with a look of panic on his face; he wasn't the brightest boy in the world. He looked down at me and I whispered, "Say after me." He nodded and I started. Without moving my lips, and industriously searching in my desk, I whispered the letter *C* and Victor called out "C." Then I quietly said "A," and he loudly repeated "A." Then I gave him another *C*. And then I whispered another "A." In the Welsh language the word *caca* is the same as the French word *merde,* only its meaning is more crude. Victor dutifully bawled out the last two letters, and then there was silence. Miss Griffiths was still, and then slowly turned pink. With a look of absolute innocence I looked around at the rest of the class, expecting at least a couple of chuckles, but there was nothing. Gomer Jenkins had just walked in. Miss Griffiths told him what Victor had spelled out, and Gomer looked at the class and then looked toward my desk. He didn't look at Victor, he looked at me. Then he crooked his finger and said, "Reggie, *bach,* in my study." He left and I followed him. I knew there would be no ducking and weaving this time. It was going to be the cane for sure. I had thought the whole thing brilliant. I was wrong. And I was right. It *was* the cane.

The corridor to Gomer's room ran between the partitions of other classrooms. The first four feet were of wood, and then clear glass reached to the ceiling. We called it Gomer Jenkins' Parade. He used to walk up and down at odd times, pause and look through the glass at each room. Just look. That was all that was necessary. For me the route was fast becoming my via dolorosa. I made the trip about twice a month, only this time I was more than usually morose and becoming more furious at each step. I didn't dread the prospect of the cane, for I had learned to live with it, but I was furious with my own stupidity and carelessness. It was in this mood that I sat down in Gomer's private office and waited. In a couple of minutes I heard the outer door close and he was there.

He looked at me for a few seconds, sighed, slowly shook his head, and walked to the cane rack. He had quite a collection, thick ones, thin ones, long and short ones, and with my furtive ratlike intelligence I watched to see which one he chose. I hoped for a thin one because they only stung—the thick ones bruised and stayed with you for days. But, ah, I was lucky, he'd picked a thin one. This wasn't going to be so tough after all. Then he said to me, "Three on each hand, Reggie *bach*."

I couldn't believe it! This was to be a game of wits! Because there was an unwritten rule, a sort of understanding we had with Gomer. When he said three on each hand it meant that he had the right to three slashes each and we had the right to snatch our hands back, but only after the cane had started down. Rather like balls and strikes in American baseball. But he was dealing with a pretty shifty kid, and he knew it. He committed enough balks to have sent me all the way home, but this was the Gnoll Hall School, not Comiskey Park, and he got me three times. Once on the right hand and twice on the left. On these occasions the thing to do was to tuck your hands flat under your armpits and hold them tight, not let the blood get to them and they hardly hurt at all.

But Gomer wasn't through. "Sit down, my boy, I want to talk to you." So I sat. And I wondered a little, because usually we were sent back to the classroom immediately, while the tears were still fresh on our cheeks as a sort of warning to the rest of the pack. This time he walked to the window and stood there looking out. Then he started pacing behind the desk, and without looking at me, said, "It's high time you started thinking about other people and not just your own pleasures. It's not that you're a selfish boy, just thoughtless. Now, today you embarrassed Miss Griffiths and made Victor look a fool, just for your own amusement and without any regard for their feelings. And that is unforgivable, to hurt people's feelings. To me, it's a sin and a big one. So go you now and say to Miss Griffiths that you're sorry and that you'll try to be better. And say the same thing to Victor. And I mean *say* it, not just pat him on the shoulder. You'll be amazed how good it will make you feel. But don't do it until after the class is over. And if I see you back here again it will be the bench for you. Now, back to your class."

I quietly left.

You see what I mean about Gomer? About apologizing after the class was out? He didn't want me to be embarrassed in front of my *macho* friends. Didn't want to hurt my feelings, because that wouldn't have done any good; it was the apology that mattered, something I didn't remember ever having done before. I felt very nervous and slightly afraid.

When I got back to the classroom they were just about ready to be dismissed, so I walked to my desk and told Victor to wait with me until everyone had gone. In a minute or two Miss Griffiths dismissed them and the scramble started. My friends were dying to ask me what I'd got, but they saw I was in no mood to be trifled with, so they all left. With, "Come on, Victor," I shambled up to the desk. Miss Griffiths didn't even look at me, but kept shuffling our composition papers and putting them in her schoolbag to take home for grading over the weekend. She seemed to be taking an awful long time about it, so I blurted out, "Victor, I'm sorry I did what I did, made you look silly, and I promise I'll never do it again." My voice was unnaturally loud and the silence that followed was even louder. Victor looked down self-consciously, but Miss Griffiths was very still. Calmer now,

I said to her, "I'm sorry for what I did, Miss Griffiths, and I'll never do anything like that again. I'll try to be better. I didn't think of embarrassing you." (It came out *embracing*.)

Her head rose slowly and her eyes seemed very bright, then she put her arms around me and said, "I know, I know. Now, will you two nice boys walk home with me and carry my schoolbag?" Would we? Would we? Oh, God! Please, please let some of those Maera buggers make one little mistake, just one? But nothing happened, nothing. It was like walking to church. And it was Victor who carried her bag. My hands hurt too much.

I awakened the next morning with the feeling that something good was going to happen, or had happened. By the time I'd sorted out the cobwebs, yesterday came back, and do you know? Gomer Jenkins was right. I did feel good, practically noble, and I couldn't wait for Monday morning to come so that I could get back to school and show Miss Griffiths the new me. And I was going to be nicer to Victor, the poor kid. I'll let him improve my French instead of my pounding English into him all the time, and I'll even let him keep watch while I steal apples and cherries out of Bowden's Plantation. I'll take him shrimping with me down on the marshes. But wait a minute, he can't swim very well. All right, I'll teach him. I'm going to make up for everything. And if I don't stop thinking like this I'm going to throw up. I'll have to draw the line somewhere or I'll have no time for myself. There I go again, being selfish, not thinking of others. Why not try it? If it doesn't work I can always go back to being my old self and enjoy life. But it did work, and I began to be conscious of other worlds outside my own. It was the first whisper of adulthood.

As the spring of 1919 approached, the little Belgians left us. Victor and his stringy cousin, Dominique and the rest of them gave us flowers and tears and gratitude, and we gave them small gifts and photographs and the sure knowledge that they all had a second home—and of course we gave them our tears. Afterward, the fields and lanes and school seemed strangely empty. Then most of the German prisoners who worked on the land left, except for a half dozen or so who wanted and obtained permission to stay. It would have been better if many more of them had remained, because of all the men of our community who had gone off to war, only half came back. Fully half of those were minus an arm or a leg, and some were blind. That spring a farmer's day was sixteen hours at least. And in the summer that followed, I saw a dead body for the first time.

It was toward the end of July, when school breaks up for the summer holiday, which in Wales lasts for about six weeks. I had noticed that the house had become quiet lately and had, for a house where no one whispered, acquired loud silences and a furtive, secretive air. A couple of days earlier I had come upon my youngest sister, Olivia, sniffling in her bedroom.

I asked my middle sister, Enid, "What's the matter with her?"

And Enid said, "Oh, shut up."

So back downstairs I went and ambled into the kitchen, which in our house was a large one, where my father usually hung out. He was sitting in his big wooden armchair staring at his feet, while Mary Catherine, her hands covered with flour, was busy cutting Welsh-cakes from a rolled-out piece of dough with a beer glass.

"Can I have some sultanas?" She just pointed to the jar beside her. I reached for a handful, then sat on the bench under the window and slowly ate them. Still nobody spoke. I felt strangely like an intruder and it bewildered me. So with a great show of indifference I announced that I was off to the canal to swim with the gang. I don't think they even knew I'd been in there.

When I got down to the canal there were only three or four of the gang there. On the towpath were three wheelchair cases from the soldier's infirmary with their nurses, just watching. One of my friends had brought a blown-up pig's bladder, and they were using it to play a sort of primitive game of water polo. It had about a four-foot string tied to it and you could either hit the attacker on the head with it or you could sling it to a teammate. A pretty raucous game. I quickly stripped and joined them. Now the Tennant Canal was only rarely used at this time. It saw perhaps one barge a week, towed by a patient shire horse and loaded with grain or timber or some-such. The barge was the home of the bargee and his wife and usually a couple of kids. They were always slow and kindly people. But as I say, the boats came along very rarely, and consequently the canal showed signs of neglect. The grass on the banks was very long and there were patches of weed and water crocus. Where we were swimming the canal was about twenty feet wide with an average depth of five feet, which was just right, because none of us were good swimmers. We would usually have one foot on the bottom. I am fascinated by water. I love it with a passion and can never live beyond the sight of it. But I am terrified of it. I fear it. Not the water itself, but what lies beneath. The fear and horror were born on this day.

We were laughing and yelling and slamming each other with the pig's bladder, showing off for the people watching on the bank, when one of the kids whacked me on the head. I pretended to be mortally wounded and with eyes rolling up into my head slowly sank beneath the surface. As I reached for the bottom with my foot, it touched something, something obscenely soft and cloth covered, which moved as I shot for the surface. I screamed as I reached the air and tore for the bank and climbed out shaking with horror. One of the nurses came over and asked what had happened. I pointed to the water and said, "There's something down there!"

"What?"

"I don't know, but I touched something—"

As we looked it slowly broke to the surface. In the shocked silence one of the soldiers said. "It's a body."

And it was. A bloated woman's body in a tweed coat, its face partly covered with swirling dark hair. Then the same soldier quietly said. "You kids run for the police and then go home. We'll take care of this."

I let the others go while I ran for home and the kitchen. When I got there I was shaking uncontrollably. I tried to tell Mary Catherine and my father what had happened, but I wasn't very coherent.

My father said, "Make him a Seidlitz powder and put him to bed. I'll go on down there."

It was a week before I could sleep the night through without disturbing dreams. Then the incident began to fade, but as it went it left room for the return of the depressing silences in our house, which bewildered me. One morning my father asked me if I would like to spend the rest of the summer with Aunt Luisa at the horse farm.

"The whole five weeks?" I asked.

"Yes," he said. "I have been asked to go with a group of men from the steelworks to help design and build some new annealing furnaces in northern Spain. I'll be gone until Christmas, and your mother will be taking the girls to visit some of her relatives in Cardigan. You'll be able to catch up on your riding, and you can even ride Bello once in a while."

Would I! Just to be allowed to mount that lovely stud was excitement enough. You see, my father owned a small share of the farm and he kept about three head there, good stock held solely for breeding purposes. Two Welsh cobs, both mares, and Bello. Bello was a hunter, not too big, about 15.2 hands, and he was entire, and quite a handful. I was on the train the next afternoon. I was thirteen years old.

I didn't know it then, but it was the end of my home. I was not to know another one until I got married.

I stayed with Aunt Luisa intermittently for almost six years. Her farm became my base, my *querencia* as it were. There were times when I had to go away to school, several of them. And there were times when I stayed with cousins in another valley. On two occasions I just took off and got a job, once in a coal mine and another time in a steel mill. My father found me both times and quietly talked me back to Luisa's. He was never angry on these occasions, he just seemed desolate.

But in those years I learned a lot. I learned to control my almost maniacal temper, and I learned about girls and about grownups and about cynicism. And I grew physically; by the time I was fifteen I was six feet tall but weighed only about a hundred and forty pounds, which was all to the good because it was a fine weight for hurdling and an occasional steeplechase. I had graduated to riding amateur in a few country meets, places like Usk and Llangibby and, on one glorious occasion, Chepstow races. But I never once won a race. The closest I ever came was a second at Llangibby and a third at a wide place in the road outside Birmingham. My trouble was that I charged the fences too much, wanted to get the front as soon as I could so that I wouldn't be bothered by horses going down ahead of me. By the time I got to the last furlong—in the races in which I didn't come down myself—my mount would be so wrung out and cold we could hardly make it across the line.

But I'm running too far ahead. Long before this, when I'd been at Aunt Luisa's about a week, she suggested that we take a little spin in the trap on Sunday morning after church, up to the Nightingale Inn, and that I should handle the reins. It was midday, brilliant and shining, and I felt the same way. So did the cob as she went spanking along, letting out a tight little fart every once in a while. The road was

an old one and must have been used for centuries
because it was at least six feet below the level of
the fields on either side, and the Nightingale Inn when
we got to it must have been at least as old. It was
set back from the road about fifty feet, two stories,
white-washed, and with a thatched roof. We sat outside
on a long bench and Luisa ordered homemade bread,
some cheese, a couple of mild onions, and beer. After
we had been eating for some minutes she said, "You
know, he was born here."

"Who?"

"Your father."

I looked at her in some surprise and said, "You
mean he was born in Monmouthshire?"

"No," she said, "upstairs. Your grandfather was
delivering a new wagon he had built for some millers
in Usk and Mother decided to go with him, but she
was further along than she thought. The pains started
at the bottom of this hill, so they stopped her and
your father was born upstairs in the front bedroom.
It was a hard birth because he was a big child, weighed
almost a stone. She had to stay here for a week almost. I was ten years old at the time, so I remember it
quite well."

I was silent while I tried to imagine my father
as a little baby crying in that room upstairs. But I
couldn't. Not my father. This Vulcan who worked
with furnaces and flames and white-hot steel; he was
never a baby. Then I remembered when Bello was
born, a little wet trembling foal who could hardly
stand. So I accepted it, but I didn't like the idea.

We were almost finished with our meal before Luisa
spoke again. She put her hand to the back of my
neck and rubbed it for a moment or two and said,
"You're getting to be a big boy now, so I'm going
to tell you this before somebody else does."

I looked at her in some surprise. She surely wasn't
going to tell me about sex and about how babies
were born. We were all brought up in farming country

and we knew about the mechanics of procreation
almost from the time we could walk. I turned to her
in curiosity, but she was staring down the hill, this
tall, leathery woman with black hair and luminous
eyes. Now, as I recall her I can describe her only
as a sort of imperious gypsy with a well-disguised
capacity for kindness. Then she spoke again.

"She's not coming back, you know. Your mother
I mean. They've decided to separate, or rather *she*
has. She says bearing five children in seven years was
enough. [I had a brother who was drowned when
he was three.] She's thirty-four years old and she
doesn't intend to be buried here when there's so much
more in the world. Well, she's a good-looking woman,
though a little fractious and high-spirited, and she
has a streak of wildness in her. I never liked her.
None of us did, but there it is. So your father thought
it would be best if you stayed with me for a bit. We
know you like it here. As far as I'm concerned you
can stay with me forever. Well, what do you have
to say, *bychan?*"

I had nothing to say. I was shocked and bewildered
and there stretched a great hole in front of me. We
sat there for a long time but no tears came. They
never did. Then she took my hand and said, "Get
the nosebag off the cob, Reggie, but don't give her
any water. I don't want her breaking wind in my
face all the way home." Then she drove us home,
and we never said a word on the way back.

Looking back to those days I am continually amazed
at the resiliency of the very young, and I am convinced
that God *does* look after drunks and children. I mean,
I could have become introspective and perhaps vin-
dictive and resentful. Had I been brought up in a
city I might have turned out that way, but I was a
country boy, and I was healthy, and my days were
full. For a week or so I moped around in desultory
fashion, and my nights were troubled, mainly I think
because there was no one around of my own age.
Then it was suggested that I should enroll in a school

of horsemanship about four miles away, headed by a retired cavalry major and his wife. It was not the ordinary run-of-the mill riding school only for children, but a serious operation for people who wanted to be professional about it. They were all older than I, except for three—two boys of about my age and a girl about a year older. I was a little more advanced than the boys. But not the girl.

Oh, certainly not the girl. Penelope Herbert, I think her name was. She was big and limber and had a sort of derisive look about her, and she immediately set about trying to make me look like the lout she thought I was. She had her own mount, as most of them did, while I and a few others used stable hacks. Pretty good ones though. It was that kind of stable. I took it for about a week and then I brought Bello. One day was enough. He was rising seven years and was really feeling his oats. That morning I had sand-papered his hoofs and had rubbed his coat down with a paraffined cloth. He looked magnificent and he knew it. He walked sedately enough into the middle of the manège and looked around and then he snorted and stopped and looked right at Penelope Herbert's mare.

She looked at me, screamed, "Get that bloody stud out of here, this mare's coming in season!"

Well, there was no way out but through the gate, which I was blocking. Now Bello was starting to rear and began prancing and side-passing toward her. The manège was completely closed in by a fence of solid boards about four feet high. The major and his groom came running out of the stable madly flapping horse blankets and yelling, the other riders scattering and shouting advice. Then Penelope howled and set her mare at the fence and cleared it, and that did it. Bello took off.

I hadn't set his curb chain very tightly that morning, so there wasn't much I could do. He just took that fence as if it wasn't there—we were off. Penelope was about a hundred yards ahead of me and heading for

a hawthorn hedge bordering a field where there was
a huge duck pond, where they kept geese and ducks
and assorted poultry. She cleared the hedge and headed
for the pond, the bottom of which was about two
feet deep in duck shit. Now Bello was not a very
fast horse, but he was all heart. What he couldn't
get over he went through, and he went through the
hawthorn. Well, he must have caught his cock in the
hedge, because he suddenly slowed, and I finally got
him turned and brought him to a stop. I looked around
and there was Penelope just coming up. Covered.
I didn't laugh, but I knew that if I didn't get away
from there I would bust a blood vessel, so I gave
Bello an unholy belt and left Penelope there.

I stayed away for the next few days but knew I
would have to go back eventually and make my
apologies. Bringing a stud like that into such a sedate
and well-ordered operation was sheer bravado and
stupidity. That's what I told the major and the rest
of them. Then I got Penelope alone and told her
the same thing. She just stared off into the distance,
very aloof. "I must say you handled him beautifully."
Then she looked at me and suddenly she grinned,
and I grinned back at her, and in seconds we were
both howling with laughter. "I wonder," she said,
"what would have happened if you'd caught me."

It was a sobering thought and brought with it a
series of mental images that surprised me because
they were strangely exciting and provocative. I gargled
something and maddeningly started to blush. This
wouldn't have happened two years before, but I was
growing up, you see.

"Look here," she said, after a few moments, "would
you like to come to our place a week from Saturday?
My parents are giving a sort of going-away party
for my brother, who is going up to Cambridge soon.
It's just for young people. Would you like that?"

I said that I would, very much.

"Of course," she said, "there'll be a few stuck-up

ones in their twenties, but a lot will be our age, so you'll be all right."

I didn't dare tell her that I wasn't quite as old as I looked, still short of my fifteenth birthday. This was going to be my first taste of high life, and I didn't intend to blow it. She gave me instructions about how to get there and the time. It wasn't far, about five miles from Luisa's, and I knew she'd let me borrow the trap, especially if I was going to see the Herberts, who were looked upon locally as being almost nobility, although it was rumored that they were originally from Herefordshire and therefore English and somewhat flawed.

As country-house parties went, I suppose this one wasn't too bad until about ten o'clock, when I got waylaid by a determined blonde who was years older than I. She must have been at least seventeen. She had been sticking pretty close to me all evening, making sure I had plenty of food from the buffet, lots of punch, and so on. At ten she slid up with two glasses of port and the suggestion that I might like to see the stables. Simple Simon said yes, and off we went.

The stables consisted of five loose boxes, the one in the middle being used for storing feed, bales of hay, bags of oats, corn, and linseed meal. By the time we had looked at the four head we had finished the port, and I was feeling grand. Just grand. Then she undulated into the loose box and whispered, "Come on!" Well, it was simply no contest, I didn't have a chance. It was the slaughter of the innocents all over again. I went in there like a young Robin Hood and came out as trembly as Maid Marian. I *really* had postcoitus melancholia, and I felt somehow degraded. I didn't want to see these people again, so I quickly got into my trap and bolted for home. By the time I had unharnessed the cob and wiped her down, I began to feel calmer, so I went to bed. I was *so* sleepy.

chapter v

That autumn I was sent to a small school in the Taff Vale called Radyr, which I thoroughly enjoyed, perhaps because I seemed to learn more quickly there. Whether it was because the teachers were better, the curriculum more challenging, or because I was blessed with a fantastic memory, I forgot nothing. Even today I can read ten pages of a script and in five minutes know it perfectly. I am not particularly intelligent; it's just that I am insatiably curious. And I have a memory. Perhaps my deflowering brought me to full bloom. Whatever it was, I was deemed bright.

At this time I lived with my mother and youngest sister, Olivia, in a suburb outside Cardiff. On Friday afternoons and Saturdays I worked as an office boy in the offices of a small shipping company owned by some cousins of my mother, in the wild and perilous dock area known as Tiger Bay. Ships from every port in the world put in there, and the streets were thronged with Lascars, Malays, Greeks, and Arabs, people of every kind and color. But there was an odd thing; all the engineers seemed to be Scottish. It never failed.

The company I worked for operated three small tramps that never plied farther than Lebanon and all the countries bordering the Mediterranean. Whenever one happened to be in port, one of my jobs would be to run down with manifests and bills of lading. Just a ten-minute trot, but it always took me an hour. It was because of the smells. I would walk around the wharves and read the names of each stern. Santos, Río de la Plata, Wei-Hai-Wei, Hong Kong, and Sydney. I imagined I could see the Seven Cities of Cíbola, Golconda, and far Mauritius. A romantic, you say? Oh, you would be so right, and I wouldn't have it any other way.

If you want something badly enough it will come to you; that summer proved it. My holidays at Radyr would last two months, and it was arranged that I would spend them going as far as Piraeus, the port of Athens, on one of the tramps and then pick up another for the return along the northern coast of Africa. But I was to work my way, after a fashion, as an assistant to the first mate, who doubled as the purser. Checking cargo lists, entering advances to the crew in the paybook when they needed money to go ashore. Not too difficult, and it left me plenty of time to explore Cádiz, Palma, Barcelona, and Marseilles, the latter a confusing and miserable place, I thought, possibly because it rained the whole two days we were there. Anyway, I've never been back there. Then Genoa and Naples and finally Piraeus. I said good-bye to Mr. Justin, the mate, who then handed me over the the firm's agent, who put up with me until the time came for me to board the other vessel for my return voyage. It was due in five days. In that time I saw the Acropolis, took a small day-steamer to the islands in the Saronic Gulf, Aegina, Hydra, Poros. It was glorious, but terribly hot, it seemed. Little did I know what lay ahead.

The other boat finally docked a day late. I was taken aboard and introduced to the captain, who turned me over to the first mate, Mr. Lintermans, who showed me the small cubbyhole where I was to sleep. The next evening we pulled out. Our first stop

was to be Palermo, and then Alexandria. That night
it seemed to get hotter, so about three o'clock in
the morning, unable to bear my little cubbyhole any
longer, I got up and went out on deck and walked
forward, hoping to take advantage of the breeze caused
by our motion through the water. But no luck. We
were only doing about ten knots, and we had a following wind of about the same. I saw someone sitting on
the forward hatch wiping himself with a towel. It
was a man named Fife, the second engineer, and
he had just doused himself with a bucket of water.

I sat down beside him and said, "It's so hot in
that place where I sleep, it's like a coffin."

He said, "Aye," and then went on slowly drying
himself.

I noticed in the dim light that his upper body seemed
strangely lined and blotched, and as he went to dry
his legs and feet I looked more closely at his back.
There were animals crawling there! I leaped up in
shock and backed off a few steps. He stopped wiping
himself and turned his head and looked at me in
surprise.

I said, "Mr. Fife, your back, there's something
on your back!"

He seemed puzzled for a moment, and then he
quickly laughed. "What's the matter, sonny, haven't
you ever seen tattooing before? Come on over to the
desk light and I'll show you some of the best work
ever done to improve the human body."

He went and stood under the desk light so that
it hit his chest. It was awesome and fascinating. From
the waist up he was quite hairless, so that the designs
stood out colorful and distinct. Around his neck was
tattooed a necklace of emeralds with a pendant ruby,
and over each breast was an Indian Turban, the right
one green and the left one red.

"Port and starboard, y'see, sonny."

From his breastbone almost to his navel was a
palm tree, and around his waist a belt such as would
have been worn by Robert the Bruce, studded with

emeralds, rubies, and a sort of yellow filigree. In between these designs it was all delicate lacework, spotted here and there with small flowers. It was really a sight. And then he turned his back. I looked for a few moments and then started to laugh. On each shoulder blade was a running foxhound heading downward; lower on his spine was another with his jaws wide, and then, just disappearing between his buttocks was a fox's brush.

I was still giggling when he said, "And here's some more." And with that he dropped his dungarees completely. "Had these put on in Samoa. Quite the fashion down there." From his hips to about halfway down his thighs were tattooed what looked like lace drawers, all very intricate and done in blue. I was absolutely amazed, and I asked him if it didn't hurt to have all that done.

"Well," he said, "you don't get it all done at once, this lot took about ten years all told. But no, it doesn't hurt, stings a little bit, yes, but doesn't really hurt. Of course, you have to go back once in a while to get the colors touched up, because they fade, you see."

"Mr. Fife, I'd like to get a tattoo. Just a little one. In Alexandria maybe? Do you think I should?"

He thought for a minute and then said, "Well, I'll tell you one thing, sonny, you get tattooed and you'll never get the clap. Now, I think you'd better turn in, the wind has changed and it's getting cooler."

With that I left him and went back to my bunk and tried to sleep. But I kept wondering what in the world was clap?

It was only four days before we got to Alexandria, and my opportunity came on the evening of the first day we docked. One of the deckhands showed me to a hole-in-the-wall where tattooing was done, and God, it was hot. A real sinkhole. The man who did the work was a wog of some sort, and his face was tattooed from below his eyes to his chin in what seemed to be a kind of veil. The walls of the little place were covered with choices. Bleeding hearts, dancing girls, animals, birds and flags, everything. I wanted something unusual, something different. But nothing took my fancy. Finally he showed me a book, and there on the frontispiece was the very thing. It was a human skull, full on, and there were drops of blood dripping from it. Underneath, and disappearing up through the neck, was a snake done in green, yellow, and red, which reappeared out of the right eye socket and sat coiled on the top of the skull. I pointed to the skull and said, "Yes?"

And the man said, "Yes. Sit down."

I wanted it done on the outside of my upper right arm. He just shrugged and dragged over a small table which held some jars containing different colored inks and what appeared to be a bunch of goose quills and went to work. Oh, yes, it stung all right. He was stabbing me at a rate of a hundred and fifty times a minute and in between wiping off the blood with a rag that was none too clean. Then he slapped a piece of gauze on my arm with sticking plaster and held out his hand for payment, and I went back to the ship. It had taken an hour.

The next day was occupied with unloading some mixed cargo and taking on bales of cotton. The heat was almost unbearable, and I couldn't get relief by sluicing myself with a bucket of water because I had to keep my arm dry. The tattoo artist was very insistent upon that. When I turned in that night, I felt a little feverish. We pulled out about noon the next day and there was some relief, although I didn't fall asleep until almost three A.M. When I awakened the next morning, I felt as if I was on fire. My arm was swollen and ached abominably. I thought I'd better see Mr. Lintermans, who had charge of the medicine chest. When I told him how I felt and showed him my arm, he was furious and asked me who had taken me to have it done. I said I had gone on my own. With that he went to get the captain, who, when he arrived, became quite agitated, either because he thought I was more ill than I figured or because I was related to the owners; I wasn't sure. They quickly uncovered my arm and after a few moments decided to bathe it with a solution of bicarbonate of soda and water. Then they redressed it, made me take a couple of powders in a glass of water, and told me to get back in bed and stay there. They would look in on me in an hour or so. I don't remember much after that except nightmares, and pain, and people, and commotion. And then silence.

Why was everything so still? So quiet? I opened my eyes to a world that was gray and as soft as a cloud. Was I dead? I glanced to my left and I saw a shuttered window, then I slowly looked to my right. There was a woman sitting in a white woolen gown with a hooded head covering, and she was asleep. She must have felt me staring at her, for she suddenly opened her eyes and gently smiled and reached over to feel my forehead. Then she put her finger to her lips and left the room. She came back almost immediately with a short dark man who wore glasses with a black ribbon on them. He went around to the left side of the bed, felt my neck and forehead and the pulse in my left wrist. Still holding my hand, he said, "You are with us again. You are feeling better?"

I croaked, "Yes, but where am I? What's happened to me?"

He patted my hand and said, "Later. I will tell you later. But you are quite all right, only now, you must sleep more. Please drink this, it is very pleasant."

He watched me while I drank some pinkish liquid through a tube and while the woman bathed my face with a wet cloth. Then he left. The woman sat again and watched me. She never said a word. After a while I closed my eyes and slipped away.

When I awakened again it was dark, but there was a dim light to my right, and I saw the woman still sitting there. She was reading what seemed to be a Bible, which she immediately closed. She bent over me, smiling. I wanted desperately to go to the bathroom but felt too weak even to move my legs, so I asked her to help me. She looked uncomprehending for a moment and then said something in what I took to be Spanish. I began to feel a little panic, because I didn't think I could wait another second, so I pointed to my stomach. Thereupon she reached under the bed and came up with a chipped white enamel jug and a big matching pan and gently, oh, so gently slipped them under and stood and waited. And I couldn't go. I was too embarrassed. So she turned and quietly left the room. I had never peed lying down before and certainly not on my back. It was quite a performance. And one-handed, remember. There was a little knock on the door, and she stuck her head in with an inquiring look. I nodded. She came and just as gently took the jug and pan out of the room. She was back in about five minutes with a bowl of soup and some soft bread and she spoon-fed me. I was surprised at my hunger. The next thing I remember, it was daylight again.

And that's the way it went for the next two days. I awoke on what I think was the third morning, feeling wonderful except my right arm looked like a bandaged haggis with tubes sticking out of it. The doctor was there, looking very pleased. He told me that I was in a small hospital on the outskirts of the city of Almeria on the southeast coast of Spain. It was run by a religious order, and he was the chief physician, and his name was Cantu. It took me a little time to get my tongue around his first name. It was Hermenegildo. He went on to say that I had been brought there by the captain and mate of a small cargo steamer, who explained who I was and what the circumstances were. He found that I was suffering from a bad case of septicemia in my right arm and shoulder. I was lucky, he said, not to have lost my arm. The ship had left five days before, and this was now my tenth day in the hospital. My family had been notified that I was well on the road to recovery and that there was nothing to worry about. He said I would have to remain in the hospital for another week and would then be removed to his own home for a few weeks of convalescence. He had three children about my own age and thought I would be much happier there. And besides, the hospital needed the bed. Did this appeal to me? I am afraid I cried a little as I thanked him. I was still pretty weak.

After a minute I said, "Dr. Cantu, I'd like to ask you something. What is clap? Is it worse than this?"

"What is what?"

"Clap."

He looked puzzled, and then a light dawned. He hitched his chair closer and began to paint a picture of what he called social diseases that was so horrifying that I can remember it to this day practically verbatim. When he had finished he asked me if I understood him, and if I was quite clear about the consequences.

I said, "Yes, doctor, and I'm quite sure about something else, too."

"And what is that?"

I replied, "I think I'd like to become a nun."

Then we both laughed.

I spent a month at Dr. Cantu's house, which was about a mile from the hospital, his family consisting of his wife, two daughters and a son. Ariadne, the older daughter, was seventeen; Cesar, the son, was fifteen and Maria, the youngest, was fourteen. The household help amounted to five: a cook, three maids, and a gardener with a flock of kids of his own. The entire establishment behaved as if they were just one family. I learned more Spanish in that one month than I learned in the next ten years. When the time came for me to leave, I felt uprooted and lost, and when I was put upon a boat at Algeciras for my journey to Cardiff, I was terribly depressed. It was as if I had to start all over again. A song I had heard before.

By the time I got to Cardiff I was in much better spirits. The week's voyage, including a stop at Lisbon, had done wonders. Luisa met me, because my mother and sisters had flown the coop again. The minute I stepped ashore she grabbed me in her arms and for the first and last time in her life, she kissed me, and then examined me from head to foot in the most minute fashion. Then she said, "You're thinner," and bustled me off to the train for home.

The first thing she did when we got back to the farm was to get the boiler going. "You're going to have a hot bath and get some decent clothes on, and then I want to take a look at that arm." When I presented myself about an hour later she told me to take my shirt off. The tattoo was quite discernible and in gorgeous color. She stared at it as if she'd seen a chicken with two heads and said, "Good God!"

I began to mumble something about wanting to have something a bit different, something that nobody else had.

She said, "Well, you've certainly got it, and all I can say to you is, if you ever get married be sure and tell your intended a month before the service. Otherwise on opening night she's liable to bolt. And another thing, you're going to have to live with this for the rest of your life. And for God's sake don't show this thing to any of my friends. The disgrace would kill me." She never mentioned it again. From then on she seemed more affectionate, or as much as she could be without appearing to be soft, as she termed it. To her, showing one's emotions was a sign of weakness.

When autumn came, Aunt Luisa decided that it was time I learned something practical, so I was enrolled at King's College, Cardiff. It was a small establishment which, in addition to the usual standard courses, gave about four hours a week of typewriting, shorthand and bookkeeping. I liked it for two reasons: a student named Dorothy Taylor, who was blond and very wise, and Miss Bassett. Miss Bassett taught shorthand and typing and I suppose was about forty years old. But it didn't matter much to me. I was almost sixteen, going on twenty-five. Between the two of them, King's College was a roaring success, and, not surprisingly, in the year I was there I got up to eighty words a minute in shorthand and forty a minute in typing and lost about ten pounds in weight. A well-rounded scholastic year.

When winter came, it was back to the farm and more work, more racing. With the last came disillusionment and the knowledge that adults, whom one had been taught to respect, could have feet of clay and a touch of the poltroon. The county fair was held in early spring, and one day was always set aside for racing, all strictly amateur, but still rather pretentious and somewhat haughty. There were three Galloway races on the flat and two point-to-points with hurdles and a hedge or two. I was entered in one of them with Bello. Just before the start, while I was checking him over before getting up, I was approached by a so-called "gentleman farmer" very much respected locally.

"You know that Hereford horse," he said, "the one that's favored, name's Pilot or something. Well, I would not like to see him win, you know. If you could just bother him a little, clip his heels now and then, nothing serious you understand, all in the general rough-and-tumble that goes on in these things, I would appreciate it. It might be worth a couple of quid to you."

This was all said with a kind of ho-ho-ho geniality and a pat on the shoulder as he walked away. I looked after him in amazement and not a little shock. Then came disgust. Why did he come to me? Did I look dishonest? Or was it because I did not come from a so-called "county" family and was therefore more amenable to chicanery? The brazen bogus bastard! With mounting fury I got up on Bello and cantered to the starting line. As we were milling around waiting for the starter to get us straightened out, I went up to the fellow who had the ride on Pilot. I told him

of the conversation and to keep his eyes open. I didn't
mention any names, just keep his eyes open.

He grinned at me and said, "Don't worry about
it, son. Happens all the time."

As luck would have it, at the first turn there was
a hedge and a sharp turn to the left. Pilot's rider
and I took it side by side, and where we landed was
mud, grass and thin mud. After one stride Pilot's
legs went out from under him and he was down. When
the race ended I was about fifth. I went back to the
unsaddling area and while I was unfastening the girth
this same individual came up, shook my hand with
a great show of camaraderie, and left a pound note
in it. I stared at it and then slowly tore it up. He
suddenly looked like a beetle and said, "Not enough?"
And then I hit him and kept on hitting him. When
they pulled me off him I found that I was the shitty
end of the stick. From that day on I was persona
non grata in local racing circles, and the area kept
spreading.

At the end of summer I asked Luisa if she minded
my sitting for the entrance examination for the
University of Wales, which had a branch at Cardiff.
She said anything would be better than to have me
moping about the place the way I had been. And
she was right. Lately things didn't seem to have much
point. I felt dissatisfied and restless. I wanted to *go*
somewhere, *do* something, anything that was different.
So I went down to Cardiff and sat for the examination,
which took three days, staying at night with some
cousins in the Taff Vale. Ten days later the results
were out and I was in. I remained at Cardiff until
the following summer. I did quite well, but I didn't
want to go back.

Then came a year of aimlessness. I got a job as
a junior clerk in the offices of a steel mill, living in
the meantime with my father's youngest brother,
Frank, who had a son my own age. It was a year
of complete self-indulgence. We went dancing at small
local dance halls and chased girls. We drank beer

and chased girls. We took up boxing, seriously, at a gym run by the brother of Jimmy Driscoll, The Nonpareil. And we chased girls. And then it began to pall. The dreary monotony of our activities, the viciousness of the little gossipings, the small horizons all came to a head the beginning of that June. Our local dentist, a pillar of the Church, furtively dropped his hand onto my crotch while he was examining a wisdom tooth that had been bothering me. In shock and horror, I lashed out and kicked him in the stomach and ran out of there. In my ignorance I was terrified; it was the canal all over again, something beneath the surface, something obscene and horrible. It was my first brush with a homosexual. It was not to be my last.

Within an hour I had packed my bag and was on my way to visit my father, whom I hadn't seen for over a year. He still lived in the same house, being looked after by my eldest sister and, of course, Mary Catherine. They were all glad to see me. *"Duws,* how tall you are, and how nice-looking," Mary Catherine said. "Oh, the girls will be having a high old time with you, they will. But you're so thin! Never mind, we'll soon put some meat on your bones. Sit you down now." And off she went to the kitchen. I was eighteen years old, six feet two inches tall, and I looked like a tuning fork.

I stayed in my father's house for three weeks, but I found I couldn't talk to them. They were just as narrow and just as parochial as the rest of the people I knew. And talking to my father was not much help. He seemed to have become even more remote and withdrawn. I had been there two weeks when I told him I would like to join the cavalry. He just went on filling his pipe. Then after a little time had passed, he said:

"Before the war it wouldn't have been a bad idea. Three or four years in the cavalry would put a lot of manhood in any boy, but now, I don't know. Most of the cavalry have been dismounted, they're putting them in tanks, driving lorries, mechanizing 'em. I think there are a couple of Lancer mobs in India still. But you wouldn't want that. Then over here there's the Horse Artillery, a pretty group, kind of fancy, Aldershot Tattoos, that sort of thing still have dress uniforms for special occasions. Then there's the Inniskilling Dragoons. But they're a kind of scruffy bunch, mostly Irish."

He thought for a minute or two and then continued, "But there's one mob here that would be perfect for you. Household Cavalry. There are two regiments, the Horse Guards, who are called The Blues, and the Life Guards. Now what you want to get into are The Blues. They're a little more elegant, have a little more class. But I hear they're hard to get into. Why don't you write to that Major Ramsey who ran that riding school you went to near Usk? He could probably help you. You're the right size, your education is all right, you're healthy, and you look well when you're up. Why don't you do that?" It was the longest speech he'd ever made to me.

I went upstairs and wrote a rather long letter to Major Ramsey, who had always been very decent to me, a kind man. I told him I wanted to get into the Household Cavalry. Not the Life Guards, but The Blues, and could he help me? By the time I was halfway through the letter the thought of The Blues had become a burning desire, so I put a lot of other stuff in the letter too. I went out and posted it that afternoon. Many years later Major Ramsey showed it to me, he had kept it, and as I reread it I felt an ineffable sense of loss, of despoliation, a mourning for the death of innocence.

A week later I got a reply. Yes, he thought my decision not a bad one and he had written a rather glowing letter to the colonel of The Blues, "naturally, knowing you, I had to lie a little, ha, ha." He also advised me that if accepted, I should sign for four years' active service and eight in the reserve, that one's minimum term of service was twelve years split three different ways. Four and eight, five and seven, or eight and four. He thought that after four years I might want to go on to something else. God, what a wise man!

I was like a cat on hot bricks until I got a reply. It asked if I would present myself at the barracks of The South Wales Borderers in Newport, Monmouthshire (it was only about thirty miles away), for a physical examination. If that was satisfactory, would I report to Albany Street barracks in London one week later for a comprehensive interview and examination which would take three days. If accepted, I must be prepared to stay.

This was a long time ago and the intervening war has changed a lot of things, not only The Blues. I was accepted.

I had only one slight problem: the horse they gave me for the riding test. God, what a big bastard he was. Seventeen hands, jet black, a mouth like Marie Dressler and a mind of his own. I noticed he had on both a big, curling bit *and* a bridoon. I wondered why. Then I got up on him, and I found out. It was like trying to maneuver an express train. We were in an indoor riding ring, about two hundred feet long by about a hundred wide and covered in tanbark. There were two obstacles down the center, a low wooden wall and a moth-eaten piece of hedge. No wings. The riding master was Corporal-Major Dawkins, a big stern-looking man, and his assistant, Corporal-of-the-Horse Robinson, was a thin, dark, elegant fellow who wore black Hessian riding boots. They told me to trot this juggernaut twice around the ring on the left rein, then change and canter around twice in the other direction and come to a stop. The trot? No problem. But the canter was a ride on Leaping Lena. It took me three times around instead of two before I could bring him to a stop, and when I did, he stood there as quiet as a mouse. I thought I'd broken eight fingers. The two riding masters stood there grunting and mumbling for a few seconds, then

Corporal-Major Dawkins said, "Line him up in the center and take those two obstacles and come out on the right rein. Quietly now." Not without some trepidation, I put him at the wall, which he took without breaking stride. The hedge he went right through. There were three strides left before we came to the riding ring wall and that's where we parted company. I was already leaning for a turn to the right, but he had another idea. He turned to the left. I picked myself up from the tanbark and looked at the two instructors. Robinson, the elegant one, smiled and said, "Don't feel too badly, son. He's quite a handful. He needs a little work and so do you. But we'll take care of that. You did quite well."

I asked if the horse had a name. No, not officially, they had numbers. This one was B 63. From B Troop in B Squadron.

The next eight weeks were a nightmare. In order to describe it, which I think I should, I must give you a picture of the accomplishments necessary to become a full-fledged trooper in the Household Cavalry, at least in those days. You had to be competent in the use of lance, saber, and thrusting sword; proficient in the use of rifle, machine-gun, and signals—which meant single-flag Morse; heliograph, lamp, and landline signaling. You had to do all this while mounted on a seventeen-hand horse with a mind of his own. You also had to know infantry drills, marching, and map reading, and you were responsible for the care and feeding of one, or often two, horses, along with the upkeep of two sets of harness, both field and ceremonial. Then there was your own personal equipment, which consisted of four uniforms: stable dress (utilitarian), active service uniform, dismounted dress uniform, mounted ceremonial uniform, sundry cloaks, great-coats, caps for different occasions, gold and silver helmets, horsehair plumes, great black jackboots that came halfway up your thigh and weighed a ton, white buckskin riding breeches, swan-necked spurs, heavy buckskin gauntlets that came almost to your elbow, steel breastplates and backplates, sword belts, sword knots, cartouche boxes, and cuirass straps. And because we rode with a practically straight leg, a damn good jockstrap. The aforementioned eight weeks were spend learning the fundamentals of all those activities. Next came a four-week period of polishing up the weak spots.

Then the day of "Passing Out"! The day you become a Household Cavalryman. The week before I had been devoted to the humdrum things, dismounted drill, musketry, foil épée and saber, etc. But this was the *day!* Mounted and in full regimental regalia, with saddles covered in black sheepskin, gold stirrup buckles, silver neck chains, breastplates, and pipe-clayed surcingles, the horses shining and prancing. Ah, we could have taken Samarkand! There were seven of us.

The exercises were to take place in the large outdoor manège. A small set of bleachers had been set up for the colonel and the squadron officers and our instructors. There were also a few invited guests, wives, and so on. The colonel was Lord Innes-Ker, known to us as Mad Jack. There was Corporal-Major "Tich" Horrocks, who taught dismounted drill, a mighty man whose voice could be heard in the outer Hebrides. The gentlemanly Corporal-Major Harrod, who taught gymnastics and fencing, and our riding masters, Dawkins and Robinson. And there was also the fearful figure of Regimental Corporal-Major Twydle. What a name for a man who could bite a rifle in half with his bare teeth. By the way, there are no sergeants in the Household Cavalry, they're all corporals of some degree or other. Considering our highly nervous condition, the exercises went off very well. The precision riding, equitation, and school exercises were a success, I thought. Actually, the horses knew them better than we did. Only in the jumping was there one flaw, which was extraordinary considering the equipment we were carrying. "Wurpits" Watson, a chawbacon from Gloucestershire, went down coming off the table jump,

God knows how, he managed to get his spurs hung up in his sword sling. He lay there like a trussed Christmas turkey ready for the oven. As it was the last event of the day, Mad Jack got up and said, "Put that man out of his misery." Then he headed for his quarters.

That night we gave ourselves a little party in the mess to celebrate "Passing Out," the day we were ordained, as it were, the day we became full-fledged troopers in His Majesty's Household Cavalry. To our party we invited our instructors, who, strangely enough, turned out to be human. Even Twydle came rambling in, drank a half gallon of beer, pinned up our assignment order, and left, muttering that he didn't know what the regiment was coming to and thanked God there wasn't a war on otherwise he hated to think what would happen to the country if it were up to us to defend it. Then with a shattering roar, "Tich" Horrocks read out the assignments. My name came sixth on the list, and while I waited I didn't take a breath. I wanted so much, I wanted . . . "JONES! B Squadron, B Troop. Watson . . ." I'd got it! I'd got it! B Troop, with whom I'd been quartered all through my training, oh, great, just great!

Twelve young men, all over six feet, ranging from twenty to twenty-eight years of age, and not a lemon in the bunch. Now, with the addition of Watson and myself, the troop would be at full strength, fourteen.

And the best of these was George Gillam. He was four years older than I and had been delegated as my "old soldier." He'd been in the regiment three years and was wise in its ways. It was he who taught me how to make my bed, and how to unmake it. How to fold the blanket and sheets—and it had to be done just so. How to hang and clean my weapons and equipment. He taught me how to avoid the pitfalls and the mistakes so easily made by a young rookie, and above all, never be caught dead with anybody from A Squadron. He had a wicked and subtle sense of humor, yet I rarely knew him to laugh out loud.

He remained my closest friend for thirty-five years.
Until the day he dropped dead on London Bridge.

Then there was Porky. His name was Percival Poole,
and he came from Bristol. We had met once before
when he was a student at Clifton, a large private
school, referred to with true English reverse snobbery,
as a "public school." They had a fairly good boys'
Rugby team, and when I was at Radyr we played
them. And beat them. But only just, because Porky
was their hooker, the biggest kid on the team. He
had been a member of B Troop for almost a year,
having made it one jump ahead of a paternity order,
brought by a girl he said he wouldn't have touched
with a barge pole. But his family was wealthy and
he was wild. Stranger things have happened. He was
built in a series of ellipses: he had round blue eyes,
a round head, muscles that bulged, arms that curved.
Even his legs were slightly bowed. The only straight
thing about him was his hair, which was smooth and
straight and blond. He walked like a man trampling
through a pond. He was always smiling and always
thinking of things to do that were slightly illicit. He was
not crooked, mind you, just a little nefarious, but a
great companion.

Then there was the mysterious Billings, moody
Price, a strange fellow named Hudson, who is now
the Baron de Hadeln and lives in Florence. There
was Eric Dunbar, a devout Scotsman, the scruffy
Hall, an electrical and mechanical wizard, and the
elegant Casey, a true libertine of whom we were very
proud. Besides he had the largest civilian wardrobe
in the troop, from which we could always borrow.
To put it mildly, fourteen individualists. There was
not another troop like it in the whole Brigade of
Guards and from what I see of the youth of today,
there's not likely to be one again.

There was just one very slight flaw. "Wurpits"
Watson. Try as we would, we could never make him
anything but what he was: a chawbacon from
Gloucester. But he was good-hearted; stupid, but

good-hearted. For instance, if one of us had a hot
date and at the same time found ourselves scheduled
for Whitehall guard duty, a twenty-four-hour gig,
Wurpits could always be counted on to take our place,
not on the date, but at Whitehall. God, Wurpits on
a date was like watching a bear trying to peel a banana.
Boy, was he ever lacking! Know what he's doing now?
He's the head of one of the biggest companies on
the Eastern seaboard of the United States. They make
brassieres and girdles and tricky female underwear,
by the million. That's how stupid *he* was. As I said,
it was a nice troop, something for everybody.

chapter vi

I had seen her somewhere before, but for the life of me I couldn't remember where. She stood on the outer edge of the sidewalk looking foreign and mysterious in a leggy Hungarian sort of way. Her eyes I thought were blue and heavy, and they held a touch of some secret amusement. She kept looking at me. At my face, at me. Not at the steel breastplates, or my horse, or the huge black jackboots. She had none of the usual tourist appurtenances, no camera, no guide to London or Whitehall in her hands. She had only a square black calf-skin purse and a tall slim French umbrella. She was delightful. Suddenly I remembered! I had seen her the day before.

Now, here I must digress and be a little informative. When the reigning monarch is in residence at Buckingham Palace, there is a changing of the guard at Whitehall, which is called a "full guard," complete with Royal Standards, trumpeters, the lot. It always draws a tremendous crowd of sightseers and tourists, who pack the sides of the small courtyard between Horse Guards Parade and Whitehall itself to watch the taking over from the previous guard. I noticed her immediately. She had had a hat on the day before, a black hat with one rose on it, which

63

hung directly over one eye. I had no more time to inspect her, for I had been designated number two of the first half-section, which meant that I was one of the first two mounted guards posted. As I entered the small stone sentry arch facing Whitehall and settled B 63 into position, I wondered if she would come out with the rest of the crowd and watch for a moment. But she didn't. So, with a feeling of regret I prepared for the two hours of immobility and boredom.

Now it was the next morning, and here she was again! She looked about my own age, nineteen. But it's hard to tell with Continentals. After a minute or two of studying she very deliberately took a pencil and notebook from her handbag and started writing. Then she tore the leaf out of the book, folded it, and started walking toward me. Oh, please, I thought, don't speak to me, because I can't answer. And don't try to give me anything because I can't take it.

Fortunately, she did none of these things. She simply walked toward me and tucked the note into the top of my jackboot and went away. I tried to sense whether anybody had seen or noticed. No, everything appeared to be normal. B 63 stood magnificently to attention, feet nicely together, neck beautifully arched. Sound asleep. The other guard on his side of the entry gates had that peculiar Yorkshire stare in his eyes which told me he was on Ilkley Moor and would be until we were relieved. There was just one more place to look. A window on the second floor of the War Office directly across Whitehall. In 1649 a scaffold had been erected before this window and through it walked Charles the First and was there beheaded. Behind the same window there now sat a piddling little War Office Clerk, whose greatest joy in life was to report to the Officer of the Guard the slightest infraction in deportment on the part of the mounted sentries on duty. We loathed the little bastard. But at this moment even he wasn't there. I became reassured and began to speculate, somewhat lecherously, on what the note could possibly say. The thought that she might have been a whore occurred and was instantly dismissed. She was too pretty, too elegant, too young. And then there was that secret look of amusement she had. But the thought persisted that I had seen her before, not just yesterday, but before . . . before.

Now if you want to know how long eternity is, I can tell you. It begins with the chiming of a clock in Whitehall Palace and ends two hours later with the same sound. On this particular morning because we had been the first sentries posted the day before, we had only to sit in the box for one hour before being relieved by the new, incoming guard for that day. Then, without dismounting, we joined the troop for the long trot back to Albany street. It seemed interminable and even after we arrived there, we still had to attend to our horses' unsaddling and watering, wisping and feeding. (Don't puzzle over the word *wisping*, it's authentic, I assure you.) A full two hours had passed since the time she had slipped the note in until I got that goddam jackboot off. Then I couldn't find it. It must have worked out somehow on the long ride back! I sat on my bed frustrated and fuming. And then I saw it! I had slipped down inside my sock. It gave a telephone number; the writing was European. The ones were like sevens, the sevens like F's. It said, "Please call and ask for me. My name is Dominique. It is necessary that I thank you for something."

Good God! How could I have ever done something for a vision like that and not remember her? Then set in the depression of having been mistaken for somebody else. But wait a minute . . . Dominique? I fought and fought but nothing came. Well, don't just sit there, you clod, get on the blower and find out! I quickly got dressed in slacks and tunic and went down to the guardroom, where the telephone was. It rang four times with that particularly unfriendly English double buzz that seems to say, "You're wasting your time," when someone answered.

"Dominique?" I asked.

"One moment, please."

There was a wait, then another voice, "Hallo?"—a much younger one this time.

I said, "Is this Dominique?"

There was a pause, then very tentatively, "Yes, but who is calling, please?"

I took a deep breath and said, "This is the trooper to whom you gave a note this morning."

"Oh, how enchanting!" she replied.

And then a tumble of words from me, the gist of which was "Why?"

The conversation finally dissolved into an agreement to have dinner together that evening. (I happened to be quite flush that week.) We arranged to meet at a place called Quaglino's in Bury Street. But downstairs, because it was shadowed and frequented by people who gave the impression that they shouldn't be together. Just a little clandestine. I got there fifteen minutes ahead of time, ordered a drink, and sat staring into it, still trying to understand the situation.

I didn't know she had arrived until I sensed a hush of curiosity. I looked up to see the other people staring with typical English insolence at the foot of the small staircase behind me. I turned and there she was, dressed in a black velvet suit, tawny hair, no hat, white gloves, and a small silk purse. She was absolutely stunning. As I stumbled to my feet she came toward me in a delightfully unaffected way and sat in the chair I was wildly waving at and said she would like a Dubonnet. I, being almost twenty, ordered another brandy and soda. After some very self-conscious small-talk on my part, I suggested we move into the dining area and have something to eat. Still no explanation from her, just that look of secret amusement. It was a smallish room with a five-piece orchestra and a tiny dance floor. After we were seated, the waiter came and stood quietly mesmerized while she ordered, in French, a meal fit for a robin. I forgot what I ordered. When the waiter had gone I turned to her and said, "Now tell me."

"My name is Dominique Rouvers," she explained. And then the dawn came up like thunder. "You and your sisters used to call me Nicky." And there, Goddamit, it was! This was stringy Nicky? Little draggle-drawers? But I could see it now, the chrysalis had really opened. Hoo!

Through dinner she told me of her life since she had left us. How she had been reunited with her parents and that her home was now in Paris, and all the while I kept seeing a picture of a lion lying down with a lamb. Halfway through our meal the dance floor began filling up, and I asked her if she would care to dance. She would love to. And damned good she was, which didn't help my romantic turmoil a bit, on top of which the piece they were playing was "Just a Memory."

During the dance I elicited the information that she was staying in London at a friend's flat for two weeks in order to have her teeth attended to. That was a bit of a shocker. I couldn't imagine anyone coming to England to have his teeth attended to. This was the country where people's teeth, when they had any, were always slightly tinted with verdigris. And *her* teeth looked beautiful, along with the rest of her. The music stopped, and we returned to the table, and, as it was midnight, I cannily suggested that it was perhaps time I took her home. She quietly smiled agreement, whereupon I got a slight touch of the trembles. Without losing too much of my man-about-town air, we got out of there and got a taxi. During the ride to the flat I asked her how she found me. It seemed that in one of my sister's letters to her she had been told of my whereabouts and activities. So she had decided to watch the changing of the guard the day before, on the off-chance that I would be on duty. I was. And here we were. At that point the taxi pulled to the curb in front of the place where she was staying, and we got out. I was just about to pay him off when she said no, that I had better keep it because it was most difficult to get another one in that area after midnight. Then she put out her hand and began to thank me for a wonderful evening. All restraint left me and I bent to kiss her. She gracefully turned her cheek and that's what I got. I frantically asked if that was the way people kissed in France.

"But of course! How else would one kiss one's sister? To me, *tu es comme mon frère!*" And with that she left. Slowly the rocket's red glare subsided, the sun sank quietly into the sea, and gradually I became conscious of the taxi's engine idling at the curb. I climbed inside and flopped.

"Albany Street bloody barracks," I snarled.

I inserted the foregoing vignette to show some of our duties and some of the pitfalls we faced. Upon reflection I think it also shows a certain lack of moral fiber, a touch of the callous—but remember, I was barely twenty and life to me was one big pastry shop. Our evenings and every other weekend were free, and we were stationed in London. As long as we were back in barracks by six A.M. for morning stables and did our work and duties efficiently, our time was our own after six P.M. And we made full use of it.

That summer we were due for a month's field maneuvers under canvas, and for that the entire regiment moved out to a place called Pirbright in Surrey, about thirty miles distant, and we did it in the saddle with all our equipment on pack horses. We set out at four A.M. on a lovely summer morning and, in fairly easy stages, made it to the grounds at midday. It was a wonderful spot, a huge grassy area, gently sloping and about a mile square. There were woods all around it and here and there clumps of gorse and individual stands of trees. At one end was a small lake, used for watering the horses. That afternoon and far into the night we worked setting up the horse lines, watering and feeding the animals, digging sanitation facilities, setting up our sleeping tents, mess tents, and marquees. By the time we spread our ground sheets and crawled between the blankets it was almost midnight. As a special concession, morning stables would be an hour later. Magnificent gesture! That month I acquired a skill that was to prove the turning point of my life. To be taken out of a sane, pleasant, and carefree life with almost no responsibilities and dropped into a frantic, hysterical, and often vicious one was quite bewildering. And to me, even after forty-odd years of the theatrical profession, I still find it slightly bogus. But, I'm running ahead of myself, I still have a few things I'd like to remember before I describe that existence, such as *how* I got into it.

Our month at Pirbright was dedicated to practical soldiering. Night exercises in signaling, using only lamp. Day exercises using both heliograph and flag, also C.W. landline. Then map reading, which meant sending out troops in all directions and having them meet up with each other in predetermined spots using only contour maps or ordnance maps. I only got into one spot of bother on these jaunts. It happened on one of the all-night signaling exercises. Porky Poole was in one section and I in another. We were supposed to get into communication with each other across a valley about a mile wide, and God must have been with us that night because we made contact. After a very dull hour of regulation sending and reading, Porky suddenly opened with:

> *There was a young lady of Corry,*
> *Who went for a ride in a lorry . . .*

and then went on to finish a very dingy limerick. Not to be outdone, I started sending one back:

> *There was once a Bishop of Buckingham,*
> *Who stood on the bridge of Uppingham . . .*

> *Sorry, Porky, forgotten the last two lines, they're very tricky. Anyway, it's time to pack up. See you in camp.*

By the time we turned in, it was four A.M., which meant that we didn't have to get up until time to go to midday stables, the most important hour of the regimental day. Horses to be watered and groomed, lines cleaned, equipment polished and saddle-soaped. And Squadron Office. Oh, yes, Squadron Office. It was there that all business for that day was attended to, guard lists made out, duty assignments, problems attended to, and punishments meted out. I was sponging out B 63's dock when someone tapped me on the shoulder. I looked around and it was our troop Corporal-of-Horse, old Con Andrews. I knew something was wrong because he was smiling.

"Get your jacket on," he said. "You're for Squadron Office, me lad."

"Me?" I said.

"You," he said.

I called to Gillam to give B 63 his feed and snaked into my jacket. All the way to the office, my mind was clicking like a computer. Where had I slipped up? What had I done that I'd forgotten to cover up? I couldn't think of a damned thing. But, wait a minute! It couldn't be that they were thinking of . . . no, they wouldn't be thinking of making me an Acting Lance-Corporal-of-Horse? No, they couldn't be. I'd refuse it. Why, I would lose all my friends. No sir, thank you, sir, it's very flattering and all that, but, no sir. Mind firmly made up, I presented myself to Corporal-of-Horse Wiseman at the tent-flap. He took me in and announced me to the Officer of the Day, who happened to be Major A. C. Turnor, M.C. This was the officer who led the last cavalry charge ever made by the British army. It happened in the First World War. Quite a man. He considered me for a moment, his eyes like glass doorknobs, and then without preamble and with diamondlike diction, he recited:

"Watching the stunts of the cunts in the punts,
And the tricks of the pricks who were fucking
*   them."*

I stood absolutely shocked. I mean, to hear a man like Major Turnor, a man we all admired, using such gutter words was quite unbelievable. I felt as if I had lost something. And then he said, "Trooper Jones, that is the proper couplet, is it not?"

I gaggled and waffled and then said, "Yes, sir, I er, I think that's right. It's a little tricky, but I think you've got it right. Yes, sir."

"Good. I'm glad, and you've got five days confined to camp. On your way back to the lines, send Trooper Poole to me immediately. Dismiss."

When I got outside the tent, Corporal-of-Horse Wiseman, with a smile of great unction, took out a notebook and said, "I wonder if you'd mind my taking down that entire limerick? I think it's *awfully* clever."

I could hear him cackling halfway back to the lines. I went up to Porky and said, "Squadron Office, on the double."

"Me? What happened?"

"You'll find out, you stupid clod!"

And there went one of the greatest weekends we'd ever planned. There'd be no Fat Fan's tonight. At that moment, B 63 decided to take a nip at my left buttock, and in my rage I belted him in the nose. He reared, broke his headstall, lashed out with both feet and took off. I chased him for half an hour before I rounded him up and got him back. On top of everything, it cost me an extra night of stable guard. And all Gillam did was to look at me and say, "Tantrums! Tantrums!" Aaaagh!

In the regiment, musketry was taken very seriously, two days a week being spent on the range, which was about three miles distant. Our rifles were .303 Short Lee-Enfields, which we looked after with a care second only to that we gave our horses. They were a good weapon, and up to six hundred yards quite accurate. The only problem we ran into occasionally was the ammunition, which was govern-

ment issue and sometimes carelessly loaded. Nevertheless, I took to it like a duck to water.

As a kid in Wales I had done very little shooting,
maybe half a dozen times with a rook gun, knocking
down crows and rooks in springtime. The gun of
my childhood was a single-shot smooth-bore piece,
I suppose the closest U. S. caliber would be a .410,
but I was never enamored of the sport. Then I met
with the Lee-Enfield, and it was love at first sight.
We had been taught back in barracks how to hold
and load it, to sight and fire it, to take it apart and
care for it, but now we were really using it. I quickly
found I had a talent for shooting. The rifle felt as
if it were an extension of myself, and I was already
blessed with phenomenal eyesight, so it was practically
a marriage made in heaven.

The instructors soon noticed that I was a natural,
and I often found myself being excused from squadron
chores and taken out to the butts for extra practice
sessions. There were also four or five others in the
same situation, one of them a Canadian. I asked him
one day why the concern with so much extra practice,
and he said the Brigade of Guards musketry competition was coming up soon, and this mob had never
even come close. This time they thought they had
a chance. So, here we were.

Two days before we broke camp, the regimental
championships were held, together with a day of track
and field, a couple of horse races over obstacles, tent
pegging, and an exhibition of saber work by a retired
corporal-major named Eggleston. The final night to
be capped by the awarding of prizes. I was never
much good at field sports, with the possible exception
of jumping. In the long jump I did a little better than
nineteen feet. A lieutenant named Francis Francis,
that's right, Francis Francis, a thin, saturnine chap,
did twenty-one feet. In the high jump I did five-nine,
Francis Francis did five-ten. Comes now the mounted
obstacle race in which we were not allowed to ride
our own horses, but drew mounts by lot. And no

bits allowed, just bridoons. I drew Dunbar's pig, B 50, a mare that was always in heat, and my lovely B 63 was drawn by, that's right, Francis Francis, and I could see he was having a little trouble with him. You see, B 63 was a rig, which is to say that when he was cut, only one testicle had come down, so he still had one up inside him, and that made him just a little flighty. Also, during my year and a half with him I had taught him to answer to the name of Peter-boy, I'd got him to follow me wherever I went like a dog, a quality rare in a horse.

The race was all around the camp site, roughly a mile. It started at the Squadron Offce and went clockwise, straight for a quarter mile to just short of the lake, where we turned right, down a long backstretch to finish where we started, the whole course littered with obstacles of all kinds, walls, gates, great bales of straw, triple bars. As we were milling around at the start I saw that Francis Francis was about four horses inside of me, so I just happened to shout, "Come on, Peter-boy!" And here he came, rearing and side-passing to end up right beside me on the inside. At that moment, the gun went off and we were away. Now, Peter-boy had one white fetlock on his right hind of which he was very proud. All you had to do to get him really wild was to whisper, "You've got *shit* on it!" He'd snort and lash out and really create, but give him half an apple and he'd calm down. After we had gone a couple of hundred yards he was half a length ahead and I suddenly squeaked, "You've got *shit* on it, you've got *shit* on it!" With that, he half bucked and lashed out, and then he really took off. We didn't see them again till after the race was over. They'd made the lake all right. Yes, without a bit he was quite a handful.

The day ended with an exhibition of saber work by the expert, Corporal-Major Eggleston. Do you remember that Korean in one of the Bond pictures, the one they called Oddjob? That's what he looked like, only bigger. They had rigged up four fully grown sheep carcasses, skinned and dressed just as you see them in butcher shops. They were hung on hooks in the form of a square, with Eggleston in the middle stripped to the waist holding a cavalry saber. He announced that he would cut all four sheep in half, using a total of only four strokes. It took him three seconds. It was frightening.

To show the other side of the coin, he had another little stunt. One of our officers was a Major Coombe, whose wife was one of the most beautiful women I had ever seen, Lady Moira Coombe. She was slim and delicate and very fair. She looked like a jonquil. Eggleston asked if she would be kind enough to assist him, and she agreed. He seated her in a chair and asked her to bend forward and bare the back of her neck, which she did very prettily. He then placed an apple on her neck and stood up with the saber held in both hands high above his head. Then it suddenly flashed down and the apple fell to the ground, neatly split in two. Lady Moira got up and, smiling, shook his hand and returned to her seat. Only then did we applaud. To me, it was a sobering and strangely obscene exhibition.

The next day I was entered in four of the six events scheduled in the regimental marksmanship competition. It was our last day in camp. We would move back to London over the weekend. Of the four tests in which I competed, I won three. I think I could have won the fourth, except for a piece of stupidity on my part. It was a rundown from six hundred yards to two hundred. We were to get off five shots at each firing station; at six hundred from a prone position, at five hundred also prone, four hundred kneeling, three hundred sitting, and two hundred standing, and the whole thing within a time limit. We were allowed only twenty-five rounds. That meant five clips of five cartridges each, and to avoid accidents, you loaded only after you had arrived at a firing position. In order to gain a couple of extra seconds, I deliberately left the flap of my bandolier open on the rundown to the two-hundred-yard firing position, and halfway there, out popped my last clip and disappeared into the short thick gorse. By the time I scrabbled around and found it, the balloon had gone up. Just as I got to the firing point, the targets went down and that was that.

However, that night in the mess we celebrated. I had won enough points to get my regimental sharpshooter badge, and B Troop was cock of the walk. I had also won about twenty pounds in prize money, so the drinks flowed. Even Twydle patted me and rumbled something complimentary. But I have rarely been able to take more than two drinks without throwing up. That night I had three and passed out. I remember a very famous female star in Hollywood who, when I asked her at a party if I could get her another martini, said, "I only have one. If I have two, I'm under the table. And if I have three, I'm under the host." So I'm not alone.

We had only been back in town a week when I was told to report to Squadron Office again. I looked blankly at Con Andrews and said, "Christ, what have I done now?"

"I don't know, lad, but get your tunic on. Smartly now."

I put it on, brushed myself down, and headed for the office which was at the end of the stable block. But I needn't have worried. The squadron officer that day happened to be Lord Molyneux, a damned good type, probably the handsomest officer in the entire British army. Always immaculate and with great style. We would watch him leave barracks at night dressed in civilian clothes and we would remember every detail and slavishly try to copy him. Some of us came pretty close, but it was expensive.

I reported to Corporal-of-Horse Wiseman, who took me in and announced me. I saluted and stood to attention. Captain Molyneux very pleasantly told me to stand easy, which meant I was not in trouble. Then he said, "We would like to send you to Bisley for a few days during the next two weeks for rifle practice. You're probably aware that the army competitions are to be held next month, and according to your records we think you might have a good chance to do something. Would you like that?"

My God, Bisley! Would I? What Wimbledon means to tennis, Bisley is to shooting. It's the Grand National, the Center Court, the TOP!

"Oh, yes, sir. Very much, sir."

"It will mean, of course, that you will be taken off the guard list during this time. Transportation will be by car each day, and there will be three others going also. You will be in charge of Regimental Corporal-Major Twydle and the musketry officer. Bear in mind that this is not an order. You may turn it down if you wish, but if you *should* do that, I'm afraid Regimental Corporal-Major Twydle would be *most* disappointed."

If I'd any qualms at all, which I didn't, that bit about Twydle got rid of them. I had been skating on pretty thin ice with *him*.

Having arranged with Gillam to take care of B 63 on the Bisley days and having carefully gone over my rifle, which was a good one, I left the next morning. The other three trying out were, I think, Bosbery from A Troop, the Canadian, Ballantine, from C Squadron, and a farrier named Porter. A Captain Gollan was the musketry officer. Why, I'll never know. A most peculiar individual. We were issued special ammunition, and I noticed that the percussion centers were colored blue. When I asked Captain Gollan what it meant, he answered, "Good heavens, I haven't the slightest idea, but it *is* a lovely shade." And he slipped back into his coma. So I went to Twydle, who told me that they were a special load, absolutely uniform and therefore dependable, so if a few shots went wild the fault was yours and not the ammo's. For eight days out of the two weeks we practiced. All distances and all firing postures. I was fascinated.

There were several army instructors down there who were most helpful. The best of the lot was a Scotsman. I was shocked to learn that he was in the H.L.I. (Highland Light Infantry). But that's no criterion, after all. The Darley Arabian was discovered while pulling a milk cart in Paris. And for those who don't recognize the Darley Arabian, he, together with the Byerly Turk and the Godolphin Arabian, were the progenitors of every registered thoroughbred in the world today.

The two weeks just flew by. Then we had a ten-day hiatus before the army meet, which we used to clean up the rough spots, of which I had two. One was loading. I was always cutting my right thumb shoving the cartridges down out of the clip, hurrying to save time. The other was on the rundown, again hurrying and thereby causing the heartbeat and breathing to become heavier, which was certainly no help. In those days I was prone to excitability and more than a little impatient. I've since learned to control those traits. Or I'm getting old.

The outcome of the meet was very satisfying. Of the four competitions in which I was entered, I won two—an extraordinary feat if you remember the number of competitors and the fact that I was practically a rookie. For the next few weeks I was unbearable. Later on I started messing around with hand guns, revolvers, and the new German Luger, and there was a wonderful Belgian F.N. automatic, the barrel of which never seemed to get too hot. That's the trouble with automatic hand guns. After three or four shots the barrel gets hot and accuracy becomes nonexistent. Anyway, I developed quite a talent for marksmanship, so let's leave it for a while.

"What's the matter with Porky?" It was Gillam, and I was trying to finish a letter to Luisa when he sat down across from me.

"Why? What's he done now?" I asked.

"Oh, it isn't what he's done," Gillam replied. "It's

what he hasn't done. He's letting his equipment go. He just sits staring at his hands and he walks like a man with his feet frozen. It's not like him. No zip."

"Ah, don't worry about him," I said. "Just the wrong time of the month."

Gillam shook his head. "No, he's been like this for almost a week now. He acts puggled."

"Okay," I said, "I'll have a word with him."

I went back to finishing my letter. The next day after morning stables I had breakfast with Porky, and at one point, when I asked him to slide the sugar over he handed me a bread-roll. I said, "Perce, there's something on your mind. What is it?" You see, with Porky, in order to get him to take you seriously you had to use his proper name, Percy. Then he became very earnest.

He stared into his tea for a few seconds and then he said, "I've met this girl who's driving me absolutely crackers, I'm off my feed and I can't even get a decent night's sleep."

I made a few commiserating noises and then, "You mean you've got her in the family way."

He gave a short sharp bark. "Hell, no. I only wish to God I could. She won't even let me hold her hand. I've never even been alone with her. She's always surrounded." He lasped back into his private little misery.

Up until then I'd never been touched by the Grand Passion. Several hot and frantic desires, yes, but nothing so all-consuming as this poor bastard was going through. I asked him who she was and what she did. Apparently she was an actress, young and not very successful. He had met her at a cocktail party somewhere in Covent Garden. Porky always had a penchant for odd people, whether they were glamorous or notorious didn't matter. He couldn't tell the difference. One of his acquaintances was a man named Bobby Page, a wholesale flower merchant who owned a building in Covent Garden directly across from the main market. He lived in a large

flat above his officers and as a hobby and diversion
ran a drinking and snack club in the basement, purely
for theatrical people and a few RAF officers. He had
been in the old Royal Flying Corps as a balloon officer, and that's what he looked like. A balloon. But
very cheery and generous, completely hooked on the
theater and the people who had any connection with
it.

All this I found out later. The immediate thing
was that Porky wanted me to go with him the following night to this Bobby Page's place to see if I could
do anything to help. This dolly had agreed to meet
him there. Through the machinations of Casey, the
elegant trooper, I had acquired a couple of quite good
civilian suits, slavishly trying to emulate Molyneux.
I'm afraid, though, I looked quite the lounge lizard,
but it was very good for my ego.

I never went around with Porky much at night.
For one thing, he had a talent for getting mixed up
with the wrong kind of people. I don't mean crooked
or shady types, but people who just seemed aimless
and erratic. He was always in trouble, mainly because
he was naive and *believed* everybody, although he
was far from stupid. Also he frequented a different
pub from the one I did, the Marlborough Head. I
used the Audley Arms in Mount Street, mainly because
the racing crowd went there and I liked to keep abreast
of what was going on in National Hunt circles. That's
the governing body of all racing not on the flat. And
very helpful it was, too, in my occasional flutters with
the bookies. But let me get on with the more immediate problem, Porky's Pitiful Predicament.

We arrived at this place in Covent Garden about
ten o'clock the following evening. It consisted of two
rooms, one of which contained the bar and a few
tables, and the other a fireplace, a big gramophone,
and three or four other tables. That's all, and it was
in the basement. There were only about seven people
there, four women and three men, one of whom was
Bobby Page, who came bustling up to us with a great

deal of bonhomie. He seemed unreasonably glad to see us, I thought. "Now, before I introduce you," Page said, "You must have a drink. What'll it be?" As I was in my best civilian clobber, I ordered a brandy and soda, and Porky, with his taste for the esoteric, ordered a large rum and sparkling lemonade with a dash of bitters. While the drinks were being made I looked at the other people in the room, and immediately a feeling of inadequateness came over me, almost a shyness. It was not the men so much as the women. The men were rather insignificant, but not the four women. They were just a little too loud when they talked, very sure of themselves, and very beautiful.

At that moment Page came up with our drinks and started to introduce us. "This is Percival Poole, a dear boy, and this is a friend of his, Mr. er, Stpmfrmpf. This is Miss Phyllis Dare, whom I'm sure you know, Miss Margaret Bannerman. Miss Enid Stamp-Taylor. Oh, and yes, this is Margot St. Leger."

I didn't hear who the men were. I was poleaxed by this redheaded girl, Margot St. Leger. I had never seen anything like her. The basement became the Garden of the Hesperides. She was Diana and Atalanta and Pallas Athene. And I felt like a farmer. I never knew when Porky's inamorata came in. I was completely ensnared by Miss St. Leger. I was trying desperately to be fascinating when I felt a tap on my shoulder. There he stood holding the arm of an overblown barmaid, or so she seemed to me, but after all my standards had suddenly changed. I got up and took a closer look at her. She wasn't bad really, rather tall and sort of lush, dressed in something black and filmy, blond and with a look of martyrdom on her silly face. She had apparently been insulted by the taxi driver. She kept dabbing her eyes with what looked like a lace doily. Her name was Molly Caxton, and she was twenty-five if she was a day. Apparently she had just come from the Criterion Theater, where she had a small part. French maid I think she said.

I told Porky he should get her a drink and cheer her up. Then I dove right back to Miss St. Leger. I asked her if she knew this Molly Caxton, what sort of a type was she.

"Oh, yes," she said, "I know her. She faints a lot."

That stopped me for a moment and I thought I'd better change the subject. I asked her if *she* was an actress.

"No," she said, "not really. I'm a ballet dancer. I'm in rehearsal for the new Stanley Lupino show. I'm doing a speciality in it, but they've promised me a few lines. We open at the Gaiety in two weeks. But tell me about you? What do you do?"

"Me? Oh yes. Well, you see, I ride a lot." She didn't seem too interested, because she was watching a new arrival, a tall, very handsome man with a spoiled expression, who gave Margaret Bannerman a peck on the cheek, waved disinterestedly at the others, and went to the bar.

"Who's he?" I asked.

"Oh," she said, "that's Pat Somerset. He's married to Margaret Bannerman, but I don't think it's going so well."

"Why not?" I asked. "She's so beautiful."

"Well, in the first place, I think she's more talented than he is. Also she's a star. In the second place he's too good-looking for his own good. In the third place his father is an admiral, which for some reason he thinks should be an advantage. I don't like him."

I looked at the other people in the room, then I turned to her and asked if she would tell me about them. "For instance, who is Phyllis Dare?"

She looked at me for a moment as if I were wearing a fez. "You're joking. You've never heard of Phyllis Dare?"

"Oh, I think I've heard the name, but I don't know who she is. I'm sorry."

She looked at me rather hard and said, "Where do you do all this riding? Siberia? I think I'd better brief you on them before you *really* put your foot in it. To begin with, Phyllis Dare is one of the most famous and talented women in the British theater. That tall, hot-looking blonde talking to Pat Somerset is Enid Stamp-Taylor, a musical-comedy star very much sought after. Both on and off. Those two men talking by the fireplace, the taller one is Captain Richard Norton, society type. His wife's a great friend of the Prince of Wales. The smaller man with him is Donald Calthrop, an actor. Brilliant, but shall we say, a little erratic? You know about me, and you know about Margaret Bannerman, so just use your judgment with the rest of them. Now I've got to leave. I have a rehearsal in the morning. Good night. Give me a ring sometime." And before I could even get up, she'd gone. I felt very much alone.

I turned to find out how Porky was doing and saw that he was deep in conversation with Miss Bannerman. Miss Caxton, seated on the couch next to him, watching, was not liking it one bit. Suddenly, with a pretty little sigh, she fainted. Not on the floor. Oh, no, no. She fainted with her head in Porky's lap. Immediately most of the people in the room began fluttering about, though I noticed that a few at the bar just turned back to their drinks. But our Porky simply got up and gathered her in his arms and said, "Bobby, if you don't mind, I think I should take her upstairs to your sitting room and lay her on the couch. I'll take good care of her."

And Bobby, with a perfectly expressionless face, answered, "Yes, Percy dear boy, you do that. I'm sure she'll be as right as rain in no time. She's subject to these little spells, you know. But it's nothing serious."

With that, Porky manfully climbed the stairs with his light o' love. I'm not sure, but I think I heard a faint voice cry, "Excelsior!" I sat and talked to Margaret Bannerman for a while, but her attention was sporadic to say the least. Her eyes never left the bar. I got up and tried to circulate. But it was no use. These people were strangers. Not that they were unfriendly, far from it. They were just strange and sort of glittering, and I felt quite out of my depth. They moved with a different style, and they seemed to speak a different language. I felt tongue-tied, so I landed as nonchalantly as I could at the end of the bar and just watched. It must have been almost one o'clock when I noticed that the place seemed to be emptying. I slipped out and went back to the barracks. But it was a long time before I slept. I had seen a different world.

Over the next three months I went back to Page's club about half a dozen times. I also went to a couple of theatrical parties with Margot St. Leger, and at one of them I met a film actress named Estelle Brody, a very quiet American, who was a star in British films. It was Estelle who planted the first seed, who started a restlessness in me and the beginning of discontent. It was she, in her quiet, penetrating way, who first asked if I wanted to stay in the army the rest of my life. I looked at her in some surprise. Suddenly I was aware that I had never thought of the future, that I had never even given much thought beyond tomorrow. Life was too joyful. "Think about it, sonny, and when you have, give me a ring."

I had never been very interested in the theater. Up until that time I don't suppose I had seen more than four plays. I think the first one I ever saw was *The Only Way*, with Martin Harvey and his wife; I must have been ten years old. I can remember only boredom. And the last one was on my nineteenth birthday, at the old Bedford in Camden Town. It was *The Silver King*, with Tod Slaughter and company, who played it very straight. The audience didn't, though. They howled at the actors, offering all sorts of bawdy advice. Even a dead fish came flying out of the "gods" at one point. But it was Saturday night and they were having a high old time and so were we. Gilliam, Dunbar, Casey, and myself, we were full of beer and oysters, which at that time you could buy from the sidewalk stalls for a shilling a dozen.

Outside of these few occasions, my theatrical time
and money were spent on opera or ballet, anything
with music. And, of course, the Palladium, to my
mind the greatest variety theater in the world. I went
twice a month without fail. I loved it, the individual
brilliance of the performers, the marvelous American
humor, because fully half the bill came from the United
States. I'd ache from laughing at Burns and Allen,
Milt Britton's wild and woolly orchestra, York and
King, and the grace and beauty of Dave Fitzgibbon
and Jean Barry's dancing. Then there was Will Fyffe
from Glasgow, Billy Bennett and Albert Rebla from
London's East End. And the insane Harry Tate and
his golf sketch. But the legitimate theater? I never
gave it a thought. And while we're on the subject,
what do they mean by the term *legitimate?* Is there
an "illegitimate" theater? If there is, then it must
mean that the former is the dull one, full of posturings,
and the latter the one with gaiety. I know that if
ever I'm in a town with only two theaters, and one
is playing *A Doll's House* and the other *The Pirates
of Penzance,* you'll know where to find me. But I'd
better get on.

Over the next few months I became increasingly
restive. I began to chafe at the deadly routine of army
life, the sameness, where everything was done by
rote and tradition, and my temper became shorter.
My irritation led to one last run-in with Twydle. It
happened on the occasion of a state visit by the king
of Afghanistan. The procession was to start from
Victoria Station in full panoply, complete with the
British Royal Family and the Afghans. It was to be
a state luncheon given by the City of London at the
Guildhall. Please remember that at this time we still
ruled Inja, and the Afghans were a nice little buffer
group, so the gesture had a point. On the preceding
evening, Porky and I had gone to a party given by
Estelle Brody for some American friends of hers.
It developed into quite a bash. Since none of the
Americans had ever seen a full state procession before,

we suggested that they go down to the Guildhall the next day before noon and get settled in the bar at the Bunch of Grapes, which was an inn at the edge of the great courtyard in front of tht Guildhall. We would meet them there during our two-hour dismounted period while the luncheon was going on. They thought it was a marvelous idea and we left it at that. It was a bright, brisk autumn morning when we gathered at Victoria for the forming of the procession. The coaches being used were open landau types. I was assigned to the right side of the one carrying, among others, the Prince of Wales. I had drawn that spot several times, and the way I was feeling that morning, I almost felt on nodding terms. I had tucked a small brandy flask inside my cuirass. Earlier I had taken a couple of nips before getting mounted. I had no intention of spending five or six hours out there on B 63 all alone, because he was feeling no pain that morning either.

The procession started off promptly at eleven-thirty. We arrived at the Guildhall a little after midday. When we had dismounted and turned the horses over to the handlers, Gillam, Porky, and I repaired to the Bunch of Grapes and our friends, who were already there enjoying themselves hugely. We took off our helmets and, as it was impossible to sit normally in chairs, what with all our accoutrements and sabers, I hoisted myself on a couple of wine cases stacked against the wall. It was then that I met my first Hollywood star. She was one of the group from the night before, and her name was Constance Talmadge. She was married to a man who appeared to be the host of the party, name of MacIntosh, Alistair MacIntosh. I learned later that he was a salesman of sorts, but only of things that were very expensive, such as Rolls-Royces. One of his accounts must have been champagne, because that's all we drank that day.

I think I must have been on my fifth glass when the warning trumpet sounded, which meant that we had about ten minutes to get mounted. I slipped down from my perch and suddenly found that I could barely stand. I'd had one glass too many. On top of which, the minute I got outside I just had to get to the urinal, which happened to be a public one at the foot of a flight of stone steps. By the time I got down there and went through the complicated procedure of un-buckling, unbuttoning, unflapping, and unchucking, I barely made it. But, ah! the relief! I had just started the rebuckling process when I heard the trumpet sound "Prepare to Mount." Oh, God, I had two minutes! I'd never make it. After frantic fumblings I started up the steps, and as I reached the top my saber got caught between my legs and down I went. Now it's very difficult to get to your feet in that regalia even when you're sober. In my condition it was impossible. I twisted and turned like a gaffed pike for a couple of seconds and then someone lifted me, and it was Gillam, lovely Gillam.

"George, please! Get me mounted. Just get me on top and I'll be all right. If Twydle sees me now he'll cleave me from skull to crotch!"

Somehow Gillam got me in the saddle and sorted out my reins. I managed to jam the protruding tops of my jackboots under the saddlebags and I was safe. There was only one thing wrong. I couldn't see! Oh God! I'm blind! Blind! And me, not yet twenty-one!

Through my panicky despair I heard Gillam's voice: "Your helmet's on backwards. Turn it around quick!"

And indeed, that was what had happened. The helmet's long tailpiece was down in front of my eyes. I managed to get it turned properly, but in doing so I never got the brass chin strap on the point of my chin. It was in my mouth. While trying to correct that problem I dropped my saber, and it was hanging from the sword knot. When I savagely grabbed for the hilt I managed to give Dunbar's B 50 a nice little four-inch gash in the dock. She let fly and belted old B 63. Then he lashed out and got Con Andrews square in the chest and dented his breastplate so badly

I don't think he took a deep breath all the way back to barracks. But all was not over yet. It's a funny thing about horses. Although they are one of the dumbest animals in tht world, they're very intuitive, and B 63 was practically clairvoyant. He knew instantly that I was a little floaty, and right then and there decided who was going to be in charge.

He started off quietly enough, until we got opposite the Savoy Hotel, whereupon he decided he'd do a little side-passing, which he kept up all the way to Trafalgar Square. By this time I had had a bellyful, so I let him have both spurs, and up he went like a rampant unicorn. I belted him between the ears with my saber and that cooled him a little—that is until we got to Admiralty Arch, which is rather narrow. He made straight for the wall to try and brush me off, so I gave him another kick with my right hook and almost ended up in the landau with the Prince and his party. Up until my little contrétemps in Trafalgar Square they had had that bovine look of after-lunch boredom. But now they had chirked up quite a bit. I managed to get down the Mall as far as St. James's Place, when a hefty biddy who looked just like Bella Abzug ducked into the road from the line of cheering spectators, waving a flag and a bunch of flowers. She threw the flowers at the carriage, missed, and hit B 63 in the nose. Up he went, busted his curb chain, and that was it. I went right through the mounted band, who were helpless because their reins are fastened to their stirrups. The drum horse, who was at least nineteen years old, ended up in the memorial fountain, and I finished up in Buckingham Palace courtyard, alone and without a friend in the world.

I will now draw a merciful curtain over the outcome. Suffice it to say I didn't see the outside of the barrack walls for three weeks. Twenty-one days of barrack guards and stable guards. But I got a lot of letters written.

January 3 is my birthday, but I have never paid

much attention to it. It always seemed to get lost in the welter of Christmas and New Year festivities. But this time it was different. I received a few cards and two letters, one containing ten pounds from my father, and the other a check from Luisa for five hundred. I couldn't believe it. And then it dawned on me! I was twenty-one years old that day.

As the winter dragged on, I became more restless and dissatisfied. That the prospect of another two years was unbearable was due in no small part to my sudden affluence and to the fact that Ballantine, the Canadian, had bought himself out. In those days a soldier could obtain an unconditional discharge after three years by purchase. It meant a payment of about forty pounds and took about a month to organize. Well, I had a world to see and quite a bit more than forty pounds. I had wisely socked the five hundred in the bank, and it was still there. I remember I had gone to the Brompton Oratory, which is Roman Catholic, to hear a concert of religious music given by their choir. The program was magnificent, and I was moved almost to ecstasy, so much so that I started walking through Kensington Gardens and into Hyde Park. I went on up to Marble Arch and across Oxford Street, up Portland Place and into Regent's Park. It was a Sunday afternoon, and I don't remember seeing a soul, just dreaming. I came back to earth to find that I'd arrive at the barrack gates. I didn't want to go in. I knew what I wanted. I wanted solitude. For three years all my activities had been in a group, for three years I had slept in a room with thirteen other men, and now I wanted privacy.

That night I talked it over with Gillam, who listened to my fanatic railings against bondage with his usual quizzical expression, but he agreed with me finally and said, "I suppose trying to find a Welshman with common sense is like trying to find a bull with tits." He advised me, however, to wait until we got to Windsor in June, where the regiment was due to spend a year polishing up our field work, our duties in London to be taken over by the 1st and 2nd Life Guards. And that is what I did. I wrote my father and Luisa and told them of my intention. They were noncommittal and wished me the best. I called Estelle Brody to say I would be a free man in August and asked if she could advise me. She told me to get in touch with her the moment I got out, and in the meantime to do a lot of reading out loud, and to do it as slowly as possible, because I spoke like lightning. And to sit on my hands when I did, because I waved them about too much. I was astonished, nobody had ever told me about myself before. It was a peculiar sensation.

June came, and I made out my application. Molyneux was his usual decent self and signed it. Bobby Shaw and Sale, our squadron lieutenants, said they were sorry to see me go, but wished me luck and signed it too. But Twydle said he'd have to think about it. When I panicked and asked him why, he stared at me balefully for a few seconds and then rumbled from beneath that mighty moustache, "See me after midday stables tomorrow."

I hardly closed my eyes that night. By now I wanted my freedom so badly I was ready to make it over the wall. I talked with Gillam and Dunbar and Casey, but they just shook their heads and said they couldn't understand it. Gillam *did* say he thought Twydle really liked me and just hated to see me go. I threw a boot at him and went about my business.

When midday stables were over I went out to the stable yard, where Twydle, with his measured tread, was pacing up and down. He beckoned me over. After a few preliminary rumbles, he turned and said, "You know, the Brigade of Guards rifle competition comes up the middle of July, and in the middle of August the army meet takes place. Now I think that it would be a nice gesture on your part if you were to enter both of these events. It would be good for the regiment. After that you can go. But I warn you,

I'd like to see a little silverware. Besides, it will keep you off the streets eight weeks longer. Well?"

Well my ass! There was nothing I could do, so with true regimental fervor I said I'd be glad to, but I'd have to get in a lot of practice. He said he would arrange it, and that was that.

I won three of the four events I entered in the Brigade meet, and two out of three in the army meet. (almost twenty years later, it was 1947, I think, I took little Elizabeth Firestone to a regimental dance at Combermere barracks in Windsor. The silverware was still there.)

The first thing I did when I got out was to contact Bobby Page. He said he had a small guest room at the top of the building above his own flat and that I was welcome to use it until I found a place of my own. I stayed there a week, and it was hell. His place didn't get quiet until about one A.M., and at three A.M. the bedlam of Covent Garden market started. I still wasn't alone. I hunted around and finally I found a small bed-sitting room in Half Moon Street just off Piccadilly for three guineas a week. It had a telephone and clean linen once a week. The telephone was a pay phone, just outside in the corridor. I had two very good civilian suits which I had had made for me a few months before. When Casey wanted to flog a dinner jacket which I had borrowed previously and fitted me perfectly, I offered to do two barrack guards for it and he jumped at the chance. I was all set to go. But where? This was at the end of 1928 and the beginning of 1929.

The first person I called when I got out was Estelle Brody, but she was on location in Ireland and would not be back for two weeks, so I killed a week going to a couple of plays and popping into Page's for a drink now and again. I met one riotous gal there by the name of Norah Howard. She was going with one of the three Yacht Club Boys, Stewart Ross; the other two were Joe Sargent and Al Barney. They were American and the biggest nightclub hit in London. They remained my friends for many years. I remember Stewart's saying to me, "You in this racket, kid? I mean acting or something? What do you do?" I said I didn't do anything, that I had just come out of the army and was sort of looking around. He said, "Well, get in it, boy. You've got the build for it. It's the only way to get fat. Look at me. I can't sing and I don't read music, and here I am playing the piano and singing and making a small fortune, and my two partners are in the same boat. Don't be bashful. They'll never know the difference."

I didn't believe him, but I went home thinking that night.

I called Estelle Brody the following Sunday, and she was back. She suggested that I come down to the studio in Elstree on Tuesday and have lunch with her. Then she would have someone take me around and try to explain the goings-on. Just tell the man at the gate, and he would direct me to where she was.

I got there at midday, a half hour early, was given the directions, and immediately got lost. I found myself in a cavernous place that looked like an airplane hangar, lit up by what seemed to be at least a thousand searchlights. It was absolutely blinding. After a few moments I saw that it was a huge nightclub with about a hundred and fifty people sitting around, all in evening dress, and all very beautiful. At the foot of a staircase were standing two people, apparently rehearsing a scene. The man wore a moustache and was in tails, very handsome and sophisticated, but it was the woman who took my breath away, the most exotic-looking creature I had ever seen. I edged over to a man in overalls who sported a belt from which hung the damnedest collection of tools I'd ever seen, and I asked him what was going on.

"It's a picture called *Piccadilly*. The feller standing by the stairs is the leading man, nice type, name's Jameson Thomas. The Chink he's talking to is Anna May Wong. Why don't you move around to the other side of that rostrum? You can see better, but watch the cables."

I'm glad he told me, because the floor looked like a snake-pit. I stayed for about ten minutes, but nothing seemed to be happening, and the people sitting at all the tables looked bored to death. So I left and eventually found Estelle, and we went to lunch in the commissary. There were four other people at the table, one of whom turned out to be her director, Norman Walker, and another the studio casting director, whose name was Allen. The conversation during lunch made no sense to me, so I said very little except that I had wandered onto the set of *Piccadilly* and that nothing seemed to get done. Estelle explained to them that this was my first time in a film studio and wouldn't it be a good idea for Allen to give me a couple of days' crowd work so I could see for myself that they weren't all nutty.

Allen turned and said, "If you have a dinner jacket I can give you a call for tomorrow morning and you can work on the set you saw today. What do you think?"

Suddenly I heard myself saying that I would like it very much but that I knew nothing about makeup and that everybody seemed to be painted orange.

"Don't you worry about that. I'll tell one of the extras to make you up. Just report on the set at eight A.M. in your dinner jacket. I'll take care of the call."

It was as simple as that.

I got there promptly at eight A.M. and was approached by an aging juvenile in white tie and tails who said he was to make me up. Which he did and said I looked lovely. Then I wandered about the set waiting for someone to tell me what to do. But no one spoke to me or even approached me. I had stood around for half an hour or more when a voice in my ear said, "Could you possibly tell me what one is supposed to do? I'm afraid I'm quite bewildered." He was an immaculate-looking bird, with a toothbrush moustache, dressed as I was, in a dinner jacket. I told him that he'd asked the wrong person, that it was the first time I'd ever seen a studio. It apparently was his first time also, although he'd been in the theater for ten years. His name was Jack Raine, and he was married to a West End star named Binnie Hale. He seemed a very decent chap, so we hung onto each other like babes in the wood. The set was teeming with people, but still no one spoke to us.

Hours later we were quietly standing on the sidelines dissecting the other extras and wondering why they all looked so indescribably bored, when two men came up to us. One of them was Allen, the casting director. With him was a tall, thin man. They just looked at us, and then the thin one said, "Would you both mind turning around, slowly?" Jack looked at me and his eyebrows went up to his hairline, but we turned, slowly. The man looked at Allen and said, "They'll do." And walked away.

We went with Allen to his office and he explained. "That was Denison Clift. He's an American director shooting a picture in Scotland, and he needs a couple of house-guest types. You'll have to leave tonight for Pitlochry, which is north of Edinburgh. You'll share a sleeper, and when you get there report to the Hydro Hotel. It'll be for two weeks and the pay will be three guineas a day. Can you do it?"

I said yes, and Jack dazedly nodded his head.

The following morning I was in Pitlochry. And that ended my first day in the movies. I don't know what the picture was called, because I don't think it was ever released. The leading man was a gorgeous ham named Nigel Barrie, and he looked just like the Duke in "The Wizard of Id." We sat there for two weeks, and it pissed rain the entire time. I don't think they shot a single foot of film, so finally we all went back to London, and that was the last I ever heard of it.

For a day or so I kept to myself and did some thinking. I totted up what I had learned, and it didn't seem to be much. I had done absolutely no work,

I had spent a little over two weeks in a fine hotel in a drenched and dismal little town in what they said was Scotland, all my expenses had been paid, and I had over fifty pounds in my pocket to show for it. Surely this didn't go on all the time? I decided to call Jack Raine and ask if he would be kind enough to straighten me out on a few things over a drink somewhere. He said he would be glad to and we arranged to meet at the Café Royal. During our two weeks in Scotland, when we were not playing bridge, we had just stared out the windows at the rain. I never talked about myself or any plans I might have had for the future, because these people were just not of my world. I was at a way station, marking time.

I spent two hours with Jack while he, in his vague and bewildered way, tried to explain the theatrical profession to me. I got the impression that acting was a most insecure calling, peopled mostly by exhibitionists, but seasoned here and there with those who were touched with genius. The ones who kept the theaters open. In Jack's opinion the rewards far outweighed the risks. The upshot of our talk was that I should get an agent. If I could. The problem was that I had had no experience and so would have to lie a lot. Jack suggested two agents, one named Dan Fish and one named Frank Zeitlin.

I went to Dan Fish's office that afternoon. There was a reception room divided by a wooden rail behind which sat a secretary with cropped fair hair and an efficient manner. The rest of the room was taken up with a sofa and a lot of chairs which were filled with what appeared to be the members of a circus. The moment I walked in everyone seemed to freeze and they glared at me, then with great disdain went back to whatever they had been doing. I felt like a leper. When I went up to the girl behind the desk and said I would like to see Mr. Fish, she turned a pair of frosty blue eyes on me and proceeded to examine me from head to toe. I wanted desperately to see if my fly was open.

"And what is it regarding?"

I stammered out something about wanting Mr. Fish to be my agent, that he had been recommended to me.

"Oh, *really?*"

I'm afraid I blushed, because the frost seemed to melt a little. "Got your pictures?"

"I beg your pardon?"

Then, with the slightest touch of exasperation, "Have you brought your pictures, your stills?"

"Oh. Well, you see, I didn't bring any."

She very patiently looked down at her hands and said. "It's no use coming in here without your pictures. Call me when you've got them and I'll see if I can get you an appointment. My name's Connie."

Then she went back to her typing and I left, thoroughly shaken. I think at this point I had better mention that Dan Fish was the agent Ronald Colman had gone to when he was trying to break into pictures. Ronnie had taken *his* pictures in. Across one of them Dan Fish had written "Nice voice. Short. Splay-footed. Can't act." I've seen it.

I finally ended up with Frank Zeitlin, who condescended to take me on as a client. He was the *nebbish* brother of Alf Zeitlin, a very lofty agent indeed, of the firm of Parnell and Zeitlin, who were in the rarefied atmosphere of being known as impresarios. I got into the routine of dropping in to Zeitlin's office every morning about eleven to be sure he didn't forget me. But I rarely saw him, so I would chat with the other hopeful ones sitting there whose sole ambition, apparently, was to be called for crowd work. Most depressing. In the afternoons I would drop in to a movie, or go to the tea dances held at the Savoy Hotel.

One morning, after about a month of this, I dropped in to Zeitlin's office as usual and was immediately pounced on by his receptionist. Mr. Zeitlin had been trying to get me all morning, and I should go in right away. Zeitlin was standing in front of the window when I entered. He turned and looked at me as if I were some strange sort of insect and finally asked, "Is it true that you are some kind of a marksman?"

"Yes," I replied. "You know that, it's on my sheet."

He snorted, "Oh, balls. Who the hell ever believes all that crap you people put down. But if you really are, go down to B.I.P. studios right away and see a man named Allen, he's been calling for you all morning. He's in the casting office and don't forget to tell him I sent you."

I shot out of there like a thief, took a cab to the station, and was at Elstree within an hour. Allen was waiting for me on Stage Two, which had been transformed into what looked like a huge conference room, about sixty feet long and thirty wide. Five or six men were standing at one end. Allen began to explain the reason for the rather hurried call. They had just started shooting a picture called *The Informer*. (This was the original one, not the one made by John Ford a few years later.) The director was a German named Dr. Arthur Robison, and a stickler for realism. He had engaged a German sharpshooter to do the trick shooting, of which there apparently was quite a lot. The sharpshooter had arrived at Victoria Station the night before. Just before stepping off the curb, he had taken a look to the left to be sure there was no traffic coming, then he'd stepped off—and was immediately hit by a bus approaching from the right. He had forgotten this was England. I think that's one reason the Germans lost the war.

Allen had remembered what Estelle had told him about me, so here I was. He took me down to meet the rest of the group, an actor named Moore Marriott; Joe Grossman, the studio manager, who seemed to have a bad case of Saint Vitus's dance; the cameraman, who was named René Guissart; Walter Mycroft, a writer; and Dr. Arthur Robison. He must have been six and a half feet tall and wore a long black alpaca coat and pince-nez with a wide black ribbon. The reason I'm listing all these people is that they are witnesses to what happened. Robison asked if I was a professional marksman, and little me, remembering my three and a half years in the cavalry, said, "Yes, sir." He turned to Grossman and said, "Very well, give him the rifle and let me see what he can do." It was a Belgian Browning .22 caliber automatic, a beautiful thing, and held twelve L.R. cartridges. Robison went to the end of the room and drew a chalk circle around an English half-crown, a little larger than a half-dollar.

"Fire at that," he said, "as rapidly as possible."

"Where from?" I asked.

"The other end of the room." I asked permission to take one practice shot, explaining that all firearms behaved differently and that I had never handled this weapon before.

He said, "Very well."

I paced the length of the room which, as I thought, was sixty feet. It didn't mean anything but I thought it might impress them. I took careful aim and squeezed off the first shot, and then went down to see where the bullet went. The direction was perfect but the shot was about an inch high, so I went back, made a mental correction and let fly with the other eleven. When the smoke cleared we all went down to see what had happened.

Now I have an affidavit, signed by every single one of them, to prove this. All eleven shots had made a hole you could have covered with a quarter. It had taken no more than ten seconds. I couldn't have done it again. Nobody could. I got the job. The pay was to be twenty pounds a week for eight weeks, starting the next day.

chapter vii

At this time almost 80 percent of the pictures shown in England were American and were full talking pictures. England, however, kept insisting these talkies were just a fad, they wouldn't last. So with true British cunning, they went on making silent films. Halfway through the production of *The Informer* they decided to make a gesture toward modernism and do the last half with dialogue. That is when the fun started. Here they were, making a purely Irish story with a German director; the leading man was a Swede named Lars Hansen; the leading lady was a Hungarian named Lya de Putti; the whore was being played by a French girl who was born in Mexico City, named Mona Goya; and the informer was played by an Anglo-Dutchman named Karl Harbord. The cameraman was French and the assistant director was Scottish. (His name was Walter MacEwen, and he later became chief story editor for Warner Brothers in Hollywood.) And the sharpshooter was a Welsh farmer. This wasn't Irish stew—it was bouillabaisse mixed with goulash.

They finally decided to dub everyone's voice after the picture was finished—with the exception of that of the young French girl, Mona Goya, who spoke English fairly well. They figured if her French accent was overlaid with a touch of Welsh it would be acceptable. They were *so* right. I was just the fellow to do this and was very glad to coach her in my spare time. For a gal with a broken nose she was the most exciting and attractive creature I had ever come in contact with. Absolutely fascinating. Of medium height, very thin and blond, with blue eyes that were rather Asiatic. But it was her nose that was so beguiling. From the point where it started just at the bridge it took a sharp turn to the left and only slightly thickened. But it seemed right. One couldn't imagine her without it. She said she had got it by falling into a toilet in the dark, but it looked to me as if her nose had been shaped by a short left hook. Later, after witnessing some of her tantrums, I was sure of it.

One day, when the picture was about half finished, I happened to be perched on top of a rostrum loading the Browning. I was preparing for a scene where I was to fake the effect of machine-gun shots crossing a twenty-foot window. I heard someone call, "Reggie, can you come down for a minute? We would like to talk to you." It was Allen again, standing there with two men.

"Sorry, Mr. Allen, I can't right this minute, they're about ready to go. Thay're going to break for lunch. Can you wait five minutes?"

"All right, we'll wait."

Just then the cameras started to roll and I got the signal. There'd be no second take—it would have taken half a day just to replace the glass after I got through with it—so I let go. All that noise and smashing glass, it was a joy. I cleaned out the barrel with a pull-through and climbed down, walked over to Allen and the two other men, and said, "Yes, sir."

Allen gestured to the two men and said, "Reggie, this is Mr. Ed Newman, who is producing a picture on the next stage, and this is Mr. Castleton Knight, who is directing it. They've run into a bit of trouble this morning. Their leading man broke his leg driving to work, so I've persuaded them to let you try for the part. It's a big chance for you and I'm sure you can do it. But they have to test you and you'll have to do it in your lunch hour. Do you want to try?"

I was stunned to say the least, and a touch of panic set in. I stammered to the three of them, "Of course I'll try. But I must tell you that I've had no experience whatsoever, although I've been doing a lot of watching. Where do I go?"

"We'll be set up on the next stage in fifteen minutes," Newman said. "Meet us there."

Castleton Knight never said a word, he just watched me, then they both left.

Allen grabbed my arm and excitedly whispered, "Now don't worry about this test. It's nothing. Just be yourself. If you're no good it's not the end of the world. Anyway, I've got a hunch. Now calm down and get in there." And he left me. I looked around and the stage was empty. They had all gone to lunch and I was alone in the world.

I began to wonder what a test was. I'd heard of the term, but it couldn't mean that I'd have to pee in a bottle? If every actor had to do that to get a leading part, half the town would be out of work. Hell, no. It had to be some sort of photographic test, find out whether you walked properly, that sort of thing. Well, I wasn't going to find out standing in this empty stage, I'd better get in there.

I was told to take off my tie, mess up my hair, smear some dirt on my face, and stand at the back of an old kitchen chair while they fiddled with some lights. After a few minutes of this the director said, "Now, I want you to come in through that door, walk up to the chair, and start swearing."

"Just swear?"

"That's right, just swear."

I thought for a minute. "But who do I swear at?"

The director grinned and said, "Well, you can swear at me if you like. It's been done before."

In the past three and a half years I had acquired quite a vocabulary. I thought what the hell, I've got nothing to lose. So I came in through the door, walked to the chair, and let him have it. By the time I got through, the director was laughing and the crew were looking shocked. I was told to go back to my own set; they would be in touch with me before I finished that night.

The outcome was I got the part, and it seemed that all hell let loose. First, Robison, the director, wouldn't let me go because he'd lose his sharpshooter. They straightened that out by persuading him to hold all shooting scenes until my lunch hour on the new picture. Then the publicity department got going. To read some of the releases you would think they had dragged me off a horse in the middle of Whitehall. They put out the damnedest collection of bilge you could imagine. Some of it still follows me to this day. I felt nothing but shame. I didn't want to go anywhere or be seen by anyone. Certainly not by the boys in B Troop. The trouble was I had replaced one of England's most promising film stars, Cyril McLaglen, the brother of wonderful Victor, who, incidently, had also been a member of the Household Cavalry in the First World War. There were five brothers, and believe it or not, their father was a bishop. Their lives were living proof that heredity is a myth, with the possible exception of Andrew, Victor's son, a gentle giant of much intelligence but a lousy golfer. But I'm straying again. I've got to get back to the harrowing hegira of me.

The question of my name came up in the next few weeks. It was obvious, they said, that I couldn't be billed as Reginald Truscott-Jones, because people would laugh. Did I have any suggestions? When I said no, I hadn't thought about it, they started with a list that went back to William the Conqueror. One son-of-a-bitch even suggested Percival Lacy—it was so odd people might believe it. He damn near lost his teeth with that one. I was tired, and the bloom was going, and I wanted to be back with Luisa, I wanted to catch shrimp with my hands again, I wanted to swim in the warm watered pools of the mill lands,

I wanted—! That was it! That was the name I wanted! Mill Land! I wanted always to remember those simple days, the ones that were clean and chaste, because I had a feeling I would never see them again. I explained it, and I was adamant. The bastard who'd suggested Percival Lacy said you couldn't have a name with three Ls in it. "Well, for Christ's sake, take one out!" I also insisted that I keep the initial R, because I had a dressing case with that initial on it, which had been given to me by my mother in one of her lush periods. So they decided on Raymond, and I agreed anything was better than Reginald. I've really known only three Reginalds I've liked: one was Reginald Owen, one was Reginald Gardiner, and the other changed his name to Patric. A couple of others changed it to Rex. Why, I'll never know.

The picture was called *The Flying Scotsman,* and it was the story of the famous express that ran from London to Edinburgh. I played the roughneck fireman. Moore Marriott played the driver, who loathed me because he thought I was trying to seduce his daughter. A very profound story. Anyway, I went through eight weeks of embarrassment. I knew nothing about acting or theatrics of any kind, and I am inclined to hide my emotions, especially in front of strangers. But the director, Castleton Knight, was a very kind and understanding man, and he pulled me through it. Besides, I was being paid a fat twenty-five pounds a week, which in those days was a lot of money.

I must have done all right, because two weeks later I was told I was to be signed for a six-month contract. No options. Just six months. I still don't understand it. I was to be paid twenty pounds a week for twenty-four weeks, and my next picture was to be a thing called *The Lady from the Sea,* the lady to be played by Mona Goya and my father to be played by Moore Marriott. It was a story of the Lifeboat Service: we were members of the Deal lifeboat, fishermen in our spare time.

I don't think it was ever released. I know I never

saw it. But we had four weeks on location at Deal, and Mona and I had a roaring time. But God! she had a temper. Many's the time I felt like putting her nose on the other side but my innate delicacy always came to the fore. Also, she was capable of slipping a knife between my ribs.

This epic brought my true talent to the surface, which turned out to be the size of a sardine. But I was not to learn this until long after the film was finished, when I began to notice that people were not quite so friendly.

On my idle days I would walk around the stages watching other pictures and other actors work. On the stage they were shooting a picture called *Blackmail*, the first all-talking film to be made in England. It starred Anny Ondra, who is now Mrs. Max Schmeling, and Donald Calthrop, the erratic one. As I was watching the stunning Anny Ondra, hardly daring to blink my eyes in case I missed any move she might make, I was approached by an egg-shaped individual with a pontifical manner, who bowed with a slow seventeenth-century grace and said, "I am the director of this phantasmagoria and my name is Alfred Hitchcock." He pronounced it as if it were two words—*Hitch Cock*. He still does. We shook hands, and he wished me luck. Then he said, "Now if you will excuse me, I must get back to the animals." He stared at me, tossed his non-existent hair out of his eyes, and padded away.

I left the stage with one thought, "I'm out of my depth. I've got to get out of this business, because if they're not mad, I must be."

It was at this time that Mlle. Goya and I came to the inevitable parting of the ways. She did it rather sweetly, I thought. One of the gay spots in those days was called Skindles on the Thames at Maidenhead, about twenty miles southwest of London. It was the setting for strange, very chic mésalliances. One could have an excellent lunch in the garden at the edge of the river. I remember Mona and I had just finished our lunch with the exception of dessert which, due to my passion for ice cream, consisted of Cherries Jubilee (Which, for the benefit of those clods in the kitchen at Bel-Air, is made with vanilla ice cream doused with hot black cherries simmered in Kirsch and cointreau). It had just been served when I looked up and saw my youngest sister, Olivia, walking through the tables toward the exit. I jumped up and hurried over to her, and we greeted each other with delighted amazement and a smacking great kiss. Apparently she had just become engaged, and her young man had preceded her to repurchase his car from the parking attendant. She was a very happy, vibrant, out-going girl, and—this was the kiss of death—very pretty. I suppose at that time she was about nineteen years old. I congratulated her, gave her my phone number, and suggested we get together the next day. Then with another kiss and a pat on the cheek she left, and I returned to my table. When I sat down I got a dish of hot Cherries Jubilee right in the nose. Mlle. Goya stood, picked up her bag and gloves, and left. At speed.

That was not the last of dear Mona. In 1961, some thirty years later, my wife Mal and I were vacationing in Europe. It was springtime, and spring in France has the same characteristics as its inhabitants. It is unpredictable, volatile, and capricious. But the spring of 1961 was perfection. The days were warm and the evenings soft and still. My wife and I were driving south from Paris through western France toward Bordeaux where we intended to spend the night before going to Spain and then the Mediterranean. As we were approaching Bordeaux I asked my wife to open the *Guide Michelin* to the page which had the plan of the city and to tell me which way to turn once we had crossed the Garonne, because I was unfamiliar with the town. After about twenty minutes of left and right instructions from my life's companion, we found ourselves back on the wrong

side of the river again. I was just about ready to
blow my cork when Mal quietly got out of the car
and walked around to the driver's side and said, "Move
over." I did, and we got to our hotel in five minutes.
Now, one of the reasons for our staying the night
in Bordeaux was that there is, or was, a famous
restaurant there called Chapon Fin, and we wanted
to try it. After a shower and a change of clothing, we
went downstairs and found out from the concierge
that the restaurant was only a ten-minute walk from
the hotel—only *we* took a taxi and got there in three.
The dinner was fabulous. After two and a half hours
we decided to call it quits and walk back to the hotel
for coffee and dessert up in our room.

On our stroll back we happened to pass a theater
where a musical revue was playing. I glanced casually
at the playbill to see if anyone of note was in the
company. And then I saw it! In BIG letters "La Grande
Comédienne de Paris, MONA GOYA." I stood there
while my elegant and beautiful wife looked at me
and said I reminded her of someone giving birth to
a chair. I told her it was nothing, just a sudden attack
of heartburn after the enormous dinner. We continued
on to the hotel and up to our room, where I announced
that I just couldn't go to bed after such a dinner
without walking a little more, to settle my stomach.
Mal said she would order herself some dessert and
coffee and hoped I wouldn't be gone too long. With
an expression of sad suffering I let myself out of
the room and back down the street, where I immediately hot-footed it back to the theater.

I strolled casually into the lobby and asked to see
the manager. After a few minutes a jovial little man
approached and asked my business. I told him that
I was a very close friend of Mlle. Goya but hadn't
seen her for many years because of my absence in
America. Could he arrange for me to talk to her for
a few minutes and, if possible, to surprise her? He
was cooperation itself. He suggested that I go to her

dressing room and wait for her. She would be off stage in about five minutes. He explained the situation to Mlle. Goya's maid and advised me to sit on a chair behind the door facing her dressing table. Within five or six minutes I heard the tremendous clatter of the company coming off stage and racing up the stairs to their various dressing rooms, hurrying to clean up and get out of the theater.

The door slammed open and in charged a buxom and riotous-looking madam muttering and snarling about an orchestra leader who was a clown and someone else whose mother must have been a Siamese ape. Suddenly she looked in the mirror and stopped. An expression of amazed and cheerful delight came on her face. She whirled around, made a beeline for me and grabbed me to her (by now) ample bosom. She kissed me on the nose, both cheeks, chin, and ear. But not on the mouth. She had always had a touch of delicacy. Besides, there was someone else in the room. She turned to her maid and in an idiomatic stream said I had been the love of her life, that we had been like Dante and Beatrice, Pelleas and Melisande, Tristan and Isolde all rolled into one. We talked for about ten minutes more, than I figured I ought to get back to the hotel and my wife. She was fascinated by the sound of my wife and would just love to meet her. I told her that we were leaving early in the morning but if she would give me her Paris address we would look her up when we passed through on our way home. Then I beetled back to the hotel, forgetting, unfortunately, to wipe the theatrical makeup off my cheeks and chin.

When I walked into the room Mal was daintily eating a dish of dessert. She looked up with a smile that instantly became edged with frost, then sweetly asked what it was that I had on my chin. I looked in the mirror, saw the lipstick and makeup, and hastily turned to explain. Then I got it. Right on the nose. That's right, Cherries Jubilee. Gospel.

chapter viii

"It's no use, Norah. I've just got to learn something about acting *somehow*. I can't expect to get by forever on just appearance. I've got to give myself a chance at this profession before I get the reputation of being a terrible actor. If I find after six months that I just don't have the talent for it I can quit. I will still only be twenty-three."

We were sitting in Bobby Page's club this particular evening, and Norah Howard was rehearsing for *Bittersweet*, Noel Coward's big hit that was due to open in a couple of weeks.

She said, "Why don't you talk to Bobby Page? I hear he's finally going to get his feet wet by putting up some money to send out a touring company of that thing that's playing at the Garrick. At best it'll be second rate, and probably playing twice nightly, but it would be great experience. You can't lose by asking." And that's what I did. And this is what happened.

I landed the part of the juvenile lead in this drama called *The Woman in Room 13*. It was an American play written by Sam Shipman and Max Marcin. We were to rehearse for three weeks and then open in Southport up in Lancashire. At the end of the first week I not only knew my own lines but everyone else's in the play. Hey, I thought, maybe, maybeeee!

The company left for Southport on a Sunday morning by train, but I decided to drive up in my car. As we left the rehearsal hall on Saturday, Tommy Shannon, a middle-aged American who was playing the character lead, told me to be sure to leave early so that I would have time to find myself some digs. Apparently, very few actors stayed in hotels. Too expensive. And I could well believe it. Here I was playing the second lead, and my wages were the equivalent of twenty-five dollars a week. Luckily I found an inexpensive place to stay.

T. A. Shannon was good to me. He steered me past some pitfalls, but he could do nothing about the pratfalls I was to make that first week. Actually, the first perforance, which was at 6:30 P.M., didn't go too badly. Aside from being terribly nervous and sweating profusely, I got through it without too much trouble. It was during the second performance that I made my big smash. During the hour wait between shows Tommy and I repaired to the little actor's bar usually located in the wings of most provincial theaters in England. Tommy had a beer and I had a gin and peppermint. He began by saying, "Now, you've got this first performance under your belt, so you'd better calm down for the second house, because this is the one the critics will review. Actually there'll only be two, so come over to my digs in the morning and we'll read the notices. Now just collect yourself and cool off."

After a few little criticisms he went to his dressing room to freshen up and get ready for the second performance, while I pondered and had a second drink. I was brought back to reality by the sight of the "orchestra" going into the pit to play some dirge while the house was filling up. The "orchestra" consisted of three dropsical beldames in gray lace—violin, piano, and bass. They couldn't be seen by the audience because the pit was covered over with palm fronds. But by God, you could still hear them.

Everything progressed satisfactorily until the middle of the second act, when my "wife," on an exit, kicked up the carpet into an obvious hump down near the footlights. On my next entrance, which was almost immediately, the stage manager told me to work downstage and kick it back. And that is just what I did, only I caught my shoe in the footlights, and over I went. Down through the palm fronds, onto the piano, and into the bass fiddle, scattering the three harpies like a fox in a chicken coop. At this, the earthy provincial audience began to roar and didn't stop laughing until I had crawled back up on the stage. I had the presence of mind to fake a slight limp, which got their sympathy and quieted down the guffawing. During the intermission before the last act I thought I'd better have another gin and peppermint to quiet my nerves and to see if I had torn off any buttons or broken anything. Everything seemed to be in order, with the exception of my teeth, which hurt a little. A few years earlier, while taking part in an army boxing exhibition, I had happened to come up against a Coldstreamer who did most of his hitting with his head. The bout ended with two of my upper right teeth in his skull. When it seemed that I might become an actor, I had a bridge made, and being an English bridge, it consisted of a hard substance, resembling rubber, called gutta-percha. It felt like a Spanish bit in my mouth. So I had another gin and pep to ease the pain.

The last act went quite well until the final scene, which was a confrontation involving my unfaithful wife, myself, and Tommy Shannon. It took place across a large oak table, which had on it a big copper bowl that was supposed to be filled with flowers. As I said before, though, this was a second-rate company, so the bowl was empty. When I came to my deathless final line it happened. The line was addressed to my wife, and it went, "You have defiled our home!"

As I hit the *D* in *defiled,* out popped the bridge and went clanging into the copper bowl, and the house exploded. With great élan, I reached into the bowl, wiped the bridge off, jammed it back into my mouth, and went on with my final line. But nobody heard it and Tommy Shannon sat in the chair and had hysterics. Then the curtain came down. Fade out.

Fade in. Right after breakfast the next morning I popped over to Tommy Shannon's digs to read the notices. One of them I shall never forget. Here is the last paragraph:

> *Of Mr. Shannon's performance I can only say that he showed his usual solid competence. The role of the wife was played by Miss Molly Shannon (no relation) who shows a definite talent. Miss Nancy Eshelby as the tart is to be commended. There was also an extraordinary performance by a young actor named Raymond Milland. Extraordinary.*
>
> J.R.B.

I will not draw veil over the rest of my stay with that delightful company. I gave them a harrowing time and was handed my notice at the end of the second week. The reason they gave was that I was too tall and that I was accident prone. I had to play three more weeks until my replacement got up in his part. It turned out he was a roaring fairy, but devout. Most deflating. Strangely, when I left there were more than a few tears. Ah, these theatricals, so emotional. But at least I had trod the boards and had played in five towns (the last was a split week), and I had made friends. I thought I came out ahead.

At that time in London there was a very respected drama coach named Kate Rorke, to whom professional actors went when they needed special coaching in a part, usually Shakespearean. She would also take one or two promising beginners. It was, however, harder to get an appointment to see her

than it was to get a job. After a week of arduous
wangling she finally consented to see me. Miss Rorke
lived in a huge early Victorian house in Bayswater,
and promptly at three o'clock on the appointed day
I rang the bell. I was admitted by a thin, bilious-looking
maid, who told me to take a seat on an oaken bench
in the hall and then disappeared. Seated on the other
end of the bench was a most attractive girl, about
twenty-one or -two. I introduced myself and said
I was nervous. She said she was Miss Zepha Treble,
that she was one of Mr. Cochran's Young Ladies,
and that she also was nervous but that she was determined not to go on being just a show-girl. C. B.
Cochran at that time was the Flo Ziegfeld of London,
and it was he who had arranged her audition. She had
one of those tortured upper-class Kensington accents
which, if she was going anywhere, had to be fixed.

After about fifteen minutes we were taken by the
maid into what appeared to be a ballroom. There
were chairs and couches around the walls on which
were seated four or five prosperous-looking individuals, obviously in the profession. All alone in
the center of the room stood a small, dumpy little
woman with her hair done up in a bun and a fierce
expression on her face. My God, I thought, a miniature
Twydle! She carefully looked us up and down and
then told the others to go out and have a cigarette
or something and be back in fifteen minutes. Then
she came over to me and I saw that she must have
a wooden leg.

She stared up at me and said, "Young man, I'll
take you first. Tell me what you've done."

I mumbled about my two films and my five weeks
on the road.

"Very well. I want you to read something for me,
and for God's sake speak up! Now here is a play
script and the part you will read in Gloucester. I
will take the other parts. In case you don't recognize
it, it's Shakespeare."

Now Shakespeare is not my idea of entertainment.

As children in school we found it incomprehensible, but we had to wade through it and the scars still remain. The play I now had in my hand was *Richard III*. It's the one where Gloucester speaks of "this sun of York." I got through the page somehow, and Miss Rorke looked at me very intently. As if I had two heads.

She drew a little away from me and said, "You give me the cues and *I* will do Gloucester. And pay attention."

Then, without a script, she started, and a transfiguration took place. This short, round little woman, with a wooden leg and at least seventy years old, became Gloucester before my eyes! The body was suddenly deformed, the face twisted and malevolent, and the voice that of a crow. It was eerie, and I was quite speechless and forgot to give her the cues. It didn't mean anything to her, she played all the parts and went through to the end of the page.

"Now, Mr. Miller, try to give an approximation of the way I played it."

Well, it was quite hopeless. I had been blinded. I managed to get through to the end of the page and stood there awaiting her reaction.

She stared at the floor for several seconds. Then, without looking up she said, "Young man, what were you doing before you decided to grace our profession?"

I muttered that I had been in the cavalry.

Another pause, and, "Hm. You had better get mounted again. Good afternoon."

I reported to Norah backstage at *Bittersweet*. Stew Ross was with her, and they asked me what had happened.

"She didn't like me," I said. "Perhaps I'd better give up the whole idea."

Norah came at me like a tiger. "Oh," she said. "Oh ho! Now *there's* a brilliant idea! Absolutely bloody *mah*velous! Why, you silly young twat, d'you know how many interviews I went on before I got my first job? Eleven! And do you know how long the play lasted? Two nights! And it was seven months before I got my next job. And right now I'm in the biggest smash in London and will probably run for two years. *That's* what this business is all about. Give up my arse!"

As she stopped for breath, Stewart chimed in, "She's right, you know, cocky. You can starve for quite a spell in this racket, but if you *do* get lucky it makes up for everything. It's the world's biggest con game, but if opportunity *does* come knocking, you'd better be ready for it, so my advice is to stay in there, keep watching, and keep learning. As I said before, you've got the build for it. And who knows? You may have the talent."

I left them then and walked home, deep in despondency. It wasn't that I wanted so much to become an actor. I just wanted to become something, or somebody. Christ, I was twenty-three years old! Time was getting short, I had to get going! So I went to bed.

Strangely enough, I got up the next morning feeling quite cheerful, as if I had crossed the Rubicon, or perhaps escaped something. A modern-day method actor could probably have given me a complete diagnostic interpretation of my feeling of gaiety, delving into rejections and the bursting of chains. And he'd have ended up with a bust in the nose. After a breakfast at Lyon's Corner House I toddled off to my dancing class, which, and I think I forgot to mention it, was at Max Rivers' School of the Dance, in Regent Street. It was a school run by and for professionals. Someone had suggested that I should take up a little soft-shoe, seeing that I was pretty good on my feet, and it would only help. At the time I was trying to perfect a routine fitted to a piece called "Lucky Me, Lovable You," The place was a warren of little rooms called "studios" and my pianist was a woman called Lena, with myopic eyes, flat feet, and terrible B.O. But she loved me. I had been having a little trouble with this soft-shoe routine, but on this particular morning it all came together beautifully and I was enjoying it.

Suddenly, Lena had stopped playing and was looking at the door and saying, "Yes?"

I turned, and there was a man standing there, a big man with a dark overcoat, black homburg, and horn-rimmed glasses. I said, "I'm sorry, but this is a private session. The room will be free in fifteen minutes. Thank you."

And he quietly left. Five minutes later Max Rivers came tearing in, babbling, "Goddamit, d'you know who you just tossed out of here? Charlot! André Charlot of Charlot's Revue, you asshole! He's putting together his new show and he's opening the brand-new Cambridge Theatre with it. He came to take a look at you at my suggestion and *you* threw him out! But, luckily for you, he's got a sense of humor. You're to be at the Hippodrome Theatre tomorrow morning at nine o'clock for an audition. He thinks you might be right for the leading juvenile. Why I'll never know! Take your music and your shoes!" And with that, he stormed out.

I showed up at the Hippodrome at nine the next morning. By ten o'clock I had sung my one chorus of "Lucky Me, Lovable You," and done my soft-shoe routine. I was called down into the auditorium, where I met this kind and gentle man, André Charlot, who, to people of my generation, was just about tops as a producer of musical revues. He told me that he was casting a new show at a new theater, that the star was to be Beatrice Lillie, and that he thought I might fit in very nicely. Could I arrange to be at his office at three o'clock that afternoon? I could indeed. He was a Frenchman, and his manners were impeccable. I came out of his offices that afternoon with an unsigned contract in my hand that called for fifteen pounds a week and an option for two more shows, the second at twenty pounds a week and the third at thirty pounds a week. The leading soubrette with whom I would be teamed was to be Constance Carpenter. Rehearsals were to start in two weeks. I practically ran all the way to "His Majesty's" to catch Norah at the end of her matinee, but I was too late. She'd already left. That was all right. I would go around at the evening performance.

I was never to do those shows. As a matter of fact, it was thirty-five years before I set foot on the stage again. Bear with me, and I'll try to tell you what happened.

I caught up with Norah at lunch the next day. Feeling very flush and on top of the world, I invited both her and Stewart to the Carlton Hotel for a champagne celebration brunch. It turned out to be more than just that, because they had decided that morning it was time they got married—people were beginning to talk. Those were the days when respectability still stalked the earth. Before lunch was over we were joined by Noel Coward and a young English actor named Louis Hayward. They brought not only added gaiety but also two more bottles of the bubbly. People at neighboring tables seemed to be enjoying our party as much as we were, especially a group about two tables removed, who looked to be a family, the man quite impressive, the mother amused and tolerant. What I took to be their children, a boy and a girl, seemed to be in their teens.

Just as I, with great flair, was asking for the bill, the man got up and approached our table. He addressed Noel Coward, saying, "My name is Robert Rubin and I want to thank you, Mr. Coward, for *Bittersweet*. My family and I saw it last night and we thoroughly enjoyed it. And you, Miss Howard, were a delight." After a few more remarks he turned to me and said, "You *are* Mr. Milland, are you not?"

When I said I was, he told me that he was in the film business and that the morning before he had happened to see a film in which I had appeared, called *The Flying Scotsman*. He wondered if I would be good enough to call him between four and five that afternoon at the MGM offices in Great Tower Street. I said I would, and then he left. The others hadn't paid much attention to our little conversation, so when the party broke up I went home to do a little wondering. And some wishful thinking.

It was a struggle, but I waited until four-thirty before making the call to MGM. When I did I was put through to a Mr. Sam Eckman, who asked if I could drop in by five o'clock, or would I rather wait until morning? I said I would be there at five. When I got there, I was shown into Mr. Eckman's office, and Robert Rubin was with him. They were extremely polite, not at all what I had expected. They asked me to sit down and tell them about myself. Not just my theatrical experience but my life in general.

They listened very attentively. When I had finished they looked at each other and Eckman nodded, whereupon Mr. Rubin said, "How would you like to go to Hollywood? Just to put your mind at rest, I'll tell you that I'm J. Robert Rubin. I am vice-president and general counsel of Metro-Goldwyn-Mayer. Mr. Eckman is the director of all British activities for our company, so you may be assured that this is a bona fide offer. The contract will be an optional one, the first period to be nine months at one hundred seventy-five dollars per week. The succeeding options, if they are taken up, will have graduated increases. We will provide first-class transportation there and back and reasonable traveling expenses. What do you think?"

It was quite a while before I answered, because my mind was full of pictures. Strangely enough, I wasn't thinking of Hollywood. I was seeing New Mexico and Arizona and the Utah of Zane Grey and the far Pacific. I was brought back to Great Tower Street by Mr. Rubin's saying, "Look, why don't you think it over this evening, talk to your friends, and then come back tomorrow morning about eleven and give us your decision? The contracts will be ready by then,"

I said, "This is awfully quick and sudden, Mr. Rubin. If you really don't mind, I *would* like to think about it. I'll come in the morning."

They both smiled and got up, shook hands and I *think* I walked out of there. I was in such a daze as I walked home it's a wonder I wasn't killed several times. When I came to, I was standing outside the Empire Theatre in Leicester Square, the MGM showcase. I don't remember the name of the picture, only that Charles Bickford and Kay Johnson were playing in it. I went in and sat through it twice. I devoured every tree, every street, every set, and every face. I kept marveling at the prospect that I could be seeing these very places and people in a matter of weeks. Could this be happening to Reggie? This incredible day? Suddenly I was very tired and saw that it was almost midnight, and I wanted to go home and dream and be alone.

When I awakened it was almost ten in the morning and by the time I had sorted out my brains, had breakfast, and got dressed I had no time to call anyone, so I set off for Great Tower Street and got there exactly at eleven. When I was shown in, there were three men in the room, Rubin, Eckman, and man so blond he was almost an albino. He was immaculately dressed and rather pedantic. His name was Robert Lisman. As I found out later, he was a story and talent scout who worked for MGM on a commission basis. The contracts were ready, but they looked like play scripts, so I turned to Mr. Rubin and said that it would take me too long to read them and that I wasn't sure I could understand them if I did. Would he be kind enough to tell me the gist of them in as few words as possible and that I would take his word for it and sign them. This he did, with the proviso that I must be ready to leave within two weeks. Very satisfied, smiles, and admonitions to work hard and there was no telling how far I could go.

And then it hit me! I said, "Wait a minute, there's something I forgot to mention. In all this excitement it went completely out of my mind!" From all three of them, "What?"

So I told them of my arrangement with Charlot. I was to begin rehearsing for his new revue in two weeks, and worse still, my contract carried an option for his next two shows. They looked at each other and started walking about the room and kept glancing at me as if I were a moron.

"Did you sign a contract?" Lisman asked.

"No," I said, "but I promised."

"That's all right," Lisman said, "because I think I can fix that this afternoon. You jump in a cab and get over to the American embassy and get your visa forms and meet me at the Savoy Grill at one-thirty."

I was sitting in the cocktail lounge studying the visa application when he came in. He came right to the point by saying, "We're going upstairs to talk to someone who has a great deal of pull with André Charlot. You just listen to me do that talking. All you do is look sad." And up we went. We were ushered into one of the river suites by a floor waiter. There was no one in the sitting room, but a table was being removed that had held somebody's breakfast. Lisman shouted, "Anita?" and a voice croaked, "In the bedroom!" He motioned me to follow him, and we went in. There was a large bed facing us and in the middle of it was a tiny little woman who looked like a gnome. She had short cropped hair that looked ragged and alert black eyes with very dark shadows under them. She looked ill. She had a bottle of some black liquid in her hand, and on the nightstand stood almost a dozen more. Ah, I thought, a dope fiend of some kind.

Lisman introduced me and said, "And this is Anita Loos, who is going to help us." Miss Loos was a successful author, known for her play, *Gentlemen Prefer Blondes*.

She looked at me very clinically and said, "How are you? Have a Coke."

I shook my head. "No, thank you, Miss Loos." I wasn't going to touch that stuff!

Then Lisman launched into my problem. He was very good. When he had finished she said, "Gimme the phone." She asked for a number and when it answered she said, "Is he there? This is Anita Loos." While she waited she drank another half-bottle of the black stuff, then, "André, listen—."

On the seventeenth of August, 1930, the *Majestic* sailed from Southampton, and I was on it. André Charlot had been, as always, gentlemanly and understanding. In return for my paying twenty-five pounds to the Actors Orphanage, he agreed to release me from any obligation I had with him. For this I can only thank that strange little gamine, Anita Loos. I was never to see her again.

The voyage was everything I was told it would be. I was fascinated by two things, the hot saltwater shower in my bathroom, and the shoes and feet of the American women on board. The shoes were so beautifully designed they made a woman's feet and ankles seem absolute perfection. But perhaps it was the other way around. Anyway, they and the weather made the voyage just about perfect. Robert Lisman was also on board, on his way back to Hollywood, but I didn't see much of him because he never came out of his cabin. The only things that did come out were bedpans and nurses. He was so susceptible to seasickness he started to throw up on the boat train. He finally surfaced the day we docked. He looked whiter than ever.

I was met in New York by an MGM publicity man and one lone photographer, a very laconic individual who proceeded to take half a dozen pictures and then drifted away. He seemed very bored. The publicity man said, "I'll get you through immigration and customs and bring you to your hotel. You take the rest of the day to unwind and I'll pick you up in the morning at ten o'clock. Here's my card and if there's anything you need just call me."

It was lunch time when he left me at the Plaza Hotel, in a large and singularly unattractive bedroom, with instructions to just sign for anything I needed. It was August and terribly hot, so I took a shower and put on my thinnest suit. I went down to the dining room, ordered a seafood salad and a tall whiskey and soda. The waiter said he could get me the salad but the whiskey was out. I asked him why. He replied, "I don't know where you've been, sir, but this is the United States and we have a thing here called Prohibition." Then I remembered. This was the country of that monumental stupidity, the Great Experiment, the idea that was almost to wreck America. It really did exist and wasn't simply something one read about.

I had arranged to go dancing that evening with a delightful creature named Florence Watkins who came from Winona, Minnesota, the sound of which fascinated me. She and her friend, a girl named Acosta, were the star attractions on board the *Majestic*. They picked me up at nine that evening and took me to the Central Park Casino, where we danced to "Joe Reichman, His Piano and His Orchestra." They had brought a bottle of Scotch in a paper bag, so we ordered ginger ale and ice and that's what we drank. I couldn't get rid of the feeling that we were like kids hiding out in a woodshed. I mean, this country couldn't be serious about Prohibition. But it was. Thank God for the ginger ale, because the Scotch was lousy. By the time they dropped me back at my hotel I was feeling definitely under the weather and I made straight for the bathroom. It was almost dawn before I left it.

The next day I discovered a compensation. Chocolate malted milk! So thick you almost had to eat it with a spoon. Truly a libation of the gods, not only were malted milks a new taste thrill for me, but that day they saved my goddam life, because when I got out of bed that morning, I looked and felt like a frayed shoelace. It was almost a year before I touched alcohol again.

MGM kept me in New York for five days, and during that time I saw two shows and a dress rehearsal. One was George White's *Scandals,* in which I was fortunate enough to see three of the funniest performers of this or any other time, Jack Benny, Phil Baker, and Patsy Kelly. The other was a rather dull play, but with a wonderful actress, Laura Hope Crews. The third one was a dress rehearsal of *The Warrior's Husband.* The leads were played by Franchot Tone and Katharine Hepburn. I don't know how it came about but I found myself the guest, along with two others, of one of the Shuberts, the one who was small and dark and had thin black hair. I thought the play was very amusing, but apparently it wasn't meant to be, because at one point when I laughed a little too loudly (we were standing at the back of the theater), Shubert glared up at me and said, "Ah, what the hell do you know!" Then he stalked out.

Another thing one had to do in those days was to spend an evening in Harlem. The night I went there was spent at the Cotton Club. I think Noble Sissle's band was playing there. I thought it exciting but tawdry. The dancing, though, was marvelous. I was out of my league. Also at our table that night was a man named Robert Benchley, who was feeling no pain whatsoever. He became very concerned about my health because I wasn't drinking. I finally had to tell him that I was afraid to drink, that my family were all alcoholics and I thought it best not to start, in case I also had the affliction. He looked at me with such utter concern it was comical. He ended up by inviting me to lunch the next day, saying that I would be a good example for some of his unfortunate friends and that he would pick me up at twelve-thirty. The lunch was at the Algonquin Hotel, and we sat at

a large table with about eight other people, two of
whom were women. Benchley introduced me as a
rising young Welsh revivalist, a statement which produced looks of absolute loathing. I caught the names
of only two others at the table. A big man named
Herbert Bayard Swope, who seemed a complete extro-
vert, and a man who struck me as being professionally
lugubrious, who was introduced simply as F.P.A.
They all promptly ignored me, so I just sat and listened. They were all trying to impress each other with
quips that they hoped would be quoted elsewhere.
They seemed to be waiting for one or the other to stop
talking so they could be heard. I found out a year
later that I had been sitting at the famous Algonquin
"round table." I hadn't found it too entertaining.
But of course I was a callow youth in those days.
I later became quite friendly with F.P.A. and Swope.
And with Benchley I became very friendly.

That afternoon I boarded the *Twentieth Century*
for my journey to California, and frankly, I wasn't
sorry to leave New York. To me, New York was
not an attractive city and it is even less so now. With
the exception of the Plaza Hotel and a few other
buildings, since torn down, I thought it angular and
dingy, with the dinginess of squalor, not age. Admit-
tedly, it was just after the big stock market crash and
the Depression was setting in, but I've paid hundreds
of visits since and the city hasn't improved. Quite
the opposite.

I hadn't expected anything from Chicago, and I
wasn't disappointed. To New Yorkers, anything
beyond Jersey City is the West, but I had no way
of telling, because the *Twentieth Century* thundered
through the night and Chicago seemed a suburb of
New York. That night I caught the *Chief* for Los
Angeles. The next morning I began to get a little
worried. Where were the lands that Clarence E.
Mulford had promised me? The lonely plains and
quiet rivers of James Fenimore Cooper? Later that
day I began to feel easier. The country began subtly

to change. Great vistas started appearing, tawny deserts. Far in the distance one could sense mountains, and suddenly there was Gallup, New Mexico. And Albuquerque and my first real Indians in all their regalia, sitting on the bricks of the railway station. I bought a silver and turquoise brooch from one of them to send to Aunt Luisa. My America really did exist. Then came the cacti and the Joshua tree, the deserts and orange groves of California and, before I was ready for it, Los Angeles.

It was a bright and sunny Saturday morning and already very hot. As I stepped off the train I was approached by an exquisitely dressed young man who inquired, "Are you Mr. Milland?" I nodded and he introduced himself. "My name is Jerrold Asher and I'm in the publicity department of MGM. I'm supposed to look after you and see you settled in your hotel. We've got a room for you at the Ambassador for a week, but after that I'm afraid you'll be on your own. Ever been in America before? No? Well, don't worry about it. I'm always at the end of a phone and I'll be glad to help any way I can."

With that, we collected my luggage and climbed into a huge limousine and drove off. And we drove and we drove. Christ, I thought, if this was Europe I'd be in another country by now. We finally arrived at the Ambassador, which, for those days, was an amazing place. Huge gardens, swimming pool, restaurants, and of course, the famous Coconut Grove. Asher turned out to be a delightful character who seemed to enjoy a pose of bitter disillusion. He knew everyone, it seemed. But when his ashes were put away thirty-eight years later only my wife and his brother-in-law were there.

Before he left he told me that Robert Lisman, the MGM talent scout, who had arrived the day before, would be picking me up at six o'clock that evening together with a Mr. and Mrs. Rohde, who were writers. We would have dinner at the Brown Derby and then go on to a premiere at the Pantages Theatre. He,

Asher, would pick me up on Monday morning to take me to the studio and help me find an apartment. When he left I went downstairs to the coffee shop and had a chocolate malted milk. It was even thicker than the ones in New York.

I don't remember what I ate at the Brown Derby that night. I hardly looked at my plate because I was too busy watching and listening to the parade going on around me. I saw people whom I had never really believed existed. There was Tom Mix, dressed Crawford, the gross-looking, shambling Wallace in white leather, and much shorter than I expected. There was the flashing, beautifully dressed Joan Beery, the breathlessly lovely Corinne Griffith, and a rather common-looking girl with platinum hair and a surly expression, which was just about all she wore, who turned out to be Jean Harlow. And then my evening was made, for, with a joyful smile and rollicking walk, in came Victor McLaglen. If there is any reader still with me, let me tell you something. *There* was a *man*.

I asked Lisman, "Do these people eat here all the time?"

"Hell, no," he said. "This is just because of the premiere tonight. It's a Garbo picture, otherwise it would be mostly tourists and gawkers."

The film turned out to be *Romance* with Garbo and a new leading man named Gavin Gordon. I'm afraid the show at the Brown Derby was better.

After the theater we drove slowly down Hollywood Boulevard, where they pointed out gossipy landmarks. With the exception of Grauman's Chinese Theater I wasn't too impressed. I don't know what I expected, but I felt vaguely disappointed. Then they drove me out Sunset Boulevard along the bridle path and stopped somewhere near Hillcrest to look at the lights. There, spread out before me, were the lights of Beverly Hills, West Hollywood, and in the near distance, Los Angeles. I said, "This is magnificent!"

"And just think," Lisman snarled, "that it all belongs to Ramon Novarro!"

"What do you mean?" I asked.

"I mean," he said, "that Novarro is the reigning romantic star at the moment, so tonight it belongs to him."

The following day, Sunday, I spent by myself. I swam and had lunch at the side of the pool. Later I took a walk, but I never seemed to get anywhere and it was terribly hot, so I went back to the hotel coffee shop and ordered something called a root beer float. Delicious.

It was 7:30 P.M. and I was just thinking about dinner, when the phone rang. It was Asher, the MGM publicity man, calling to see it there was anything I needed. I asked if he had any suggestions about a place to eat that might be interesting. His reply was that I was sitting right on top of the most interesting spot in town that night. Sunday Night at the Grove happened once a month, and the place would be lousy with celebrities all fighting for a chance to get up and do a little entertaining. It was impromptu of course, and all of them just a tiny bit shy and just the slightest bit reluctant. But just *try* and get the bastards off!

I thought for a minute and then said, "Look here, why don't you join me, I'll call down and get a table for two and you can sort of clue me in?"

"Not a bad idea," Asher said. "It's about time I got rid of a little bile. But don't you call for a table because you'll never get it. I'll call. I know the maître d'. I'll be there in twenty minutes."

He was as good as his word and we found ourselves seated at a minute table at the top of the stairs on a balcony facing the orchestra. I've been told the room has been completely remodeled within the last few years. I've not been there recently, so for the all-hair and no-bra group I would like to describe it as I first saw it. For a room devoted to good food and good music, it was huge. I imagine it seated about four hundred. In the center was a large dance floor with the bandstand on the left as one entered. Scattered among the tables were tall coco palms with monkeys hanging from them in all sorts of attitudes, some of them with lighted eyes that blinked. The rear wall was a huge panorama of a tropical island with an impossible silver moon suspended there. The tables were individually lighted, and the waiters dressed in tuxedos, the orchestra was Gus Arnheim's, whose vocal group was the three Rhythm Boys—Bing Crosby, Harry Barris, and Al Rinker. It was quite a room. On this night it was packed, and on the floor level black tie was de rigueur.

Asher was in splendid form. He pointed out all the greats and near-greats with a little aside for each. For example I asked him about a beautiful girl who was doing a bit of table-hopping and a lot of leaning over.

"Ah," he said, "Little Miss Round Heels. She's an up-and-coming actress and has been for years. The reason she leans so much is because of those goddam holy medals she's got around her neck, every one blessed by the pope, and to be sure that her tits get the proper exposure. I understand they were especially blessed by a cardinal in Havana."

Another time I asked him about a famous film star whose success I didn't quite understand and who seemed to be having quite an argument at the head of the stairs. "Well," said Asher, "he didn't want to come tonight. He'd rather be in Long Beach."

"Why Long Beach?"

Asher's eyes were now glittering like freshly opened oysters. "Because that's where all the sailors are, and I hear he practically *owns* a destroyer down there." That one almost got by me, but I finally caught on. And that's the way it went until the entertainment started.

I won't attempt to describe the whole evening, because I didn't know most of the performers and a lot of it was dreary. But there were three high spots for me, the first being when Grace Moore sang "Mimi," standing at her table to the accompaniment of the orchestra's xylophonist. Incredibly beautiful. Another was when W. C. Fields was tenderly escorted up onto the stage and demanded three cigar boxes, which he proceeded to juggle brilliantly, except that the middle one would occasionally drop to the floor. He would pick it up with the other two and go on with increasing rage, until he reduced them all to matchwood. Then the threw the debris into the piano and stalked off, demanding to see the madame of this house of joy. Quite hilarious.

The third and most moving happening of the night was the final one. I thought it was an odd choice until I remembered this was Sunday. One of the Rhythm Boys, the blond and lackadaisical one named Bing Crosby, stepped to the microphone and in a surprisingly fine baritone started Gounod's "Ave Maria." Immediately there was a hush; not even a plate moved. It is not a long piece and is usually reprised. When he came to the reprise I heard a soprano softly drift in from a table near the stage. Toward the end both voices came in full, and when they finished the hush remained. I looked at Asher, but he didn't know I was there. He was rapt, transported. Then the roar started, chairs were pushed back and people stood and the applause was deafening. It was so emotional, and to me, strangely reassuring. As we were saying good night I asked Asher if he knew who the soprano was. He looked at me with his veneer back in place and said, "Coco the bird girl!" I found out later it was Lily Pons.

The following week I spent meeting people and exploring the studio, which, with the exception of the palatial executive suites, I thought rather tacky and broken down. There were one or two new stages built of stucco, but the rest were all wood and rather swaybacked. The more creative the department, the more broken down the accommodations. The writers' annex looked like a flophouse in Pago Pago, and to make matters worse, the whole complex was painted the color of a dead mouse. But everybody seemed to be happy, everybody smiled—that is, everybody except Benny Thau, who at that time was the casting director and later became vice-president. He never smiled, and hasn't to this day.

I accomplished a lot that first week. I bought a car on time, a secondhand Nash coupe. I also found an apartment and experienced my first earthquake. I had gone to a real estate office in a small frame house just off Santa Monica Boulevard. I turned the knob, but the door seemed stuck, so I shook it and by God the whole building shook, windows rattled, and I heard something crash inside. My word, I thought, they certainly build things cheaply out here. Then I looked at my car parked at the curb and it was doing a shimmy. Suddenly the front door of the house popped open and out rushed a man and two women who seemed scared to death. One of the women squealed "Earthquake!" and I began to feel sick. Then everything stopped. People who had run out of the other houses stood looking up and down the street for a few minutes and then my real estate man said, "I guess that's all." And everybody went back inside.

I stood there for quite a while hardly realizing what had happened, wishing that it had lasted just a little longer. Then I went back into the office and approached the woman who had squealed. She looked up from her desk and very sweetly inquired, "May I help you?" Not a word about what had happened, nothing. I felt like Alice in Wonderland. Anyhow, that's how I got my first apartment in a court on Hayworth just below Sunset called The Inglaterra. Living room, bedroom, bath, and kitchen completely furnished, telephone, and weekly maid service all for forty dollars a month. Oh, the phone was four and a half dollars a month extra. Ah, those olden, golden days!

The first time I stood in front of a camera in Holly-

wood happened the following week. It was a test for
Cecil B. De Mille, who was preparing *The Squaw
Man.* It was also a first for the man who directed
my test, a young set designer for De Mille named
Mitchell Leisen. I don't know which one of us was
the more nervous, but I think Leisen had the edge.
He seemed to tremble a lot. I soon calmed down
when I got a look at myself in a full-length mirror
on the set. They had dressed me in a sort of khaki
bush jacket with brown corduroy pants stuck into
knee-length laced-up boots, and on my head a hat
straight out of *Girl of the Golden West.* What with
all the makeup and eye shadow I could have passed
for Jeanette MacDonald if they hadn't stuck a Jerry
Colonna moustache on me. I looked absolutely
ludicrous. But I was the only one who thought so
apparently, because they went right on with the test.
I understand they ran that thing for weeks just so
other people's rushes would look good, but it didn't
bother me too much. I figured I was just along for
the ride anyway.

Two weeks later something occurred that left a
mental scar I've never quite lost. I had been assigned
to play a very small part, a bit, actually, in a picture
called *Son of India* starring Ramon Novarro and
Madge Evans. The part was that of a young subaltern
in the British army in India. Suave, smooth, and
murderous with women. The set was a huge ballroom
in an Indian maharaja's palace, with an orchestra
and about two hundred guests, half of them in uniform
and the rest in evening clothes. They were beautiful,
for in those days the extras had pride. Most of them
dressed better than the stars, and it was always possible
to be noticed and picked out of the crowd and given
a special bit. A lot of stars started that way. But
those days are gone now. You've got to belong to
the right union.

The scene called for me to dance with Madge Evans
and then escort her to the bar, where I was to continue
my obvious efforts at seduction, a role much better

suited to someone like Ivan Lebedeff or Cesar Romero than to me. I was terribly nervous and self-conscious, mainly because I did not know a soul on the set and the two hundred extras were watching me like ferrets. You see, I was a stranger and I represented competition. We walked through the moves for the camera, and then the director, who was perched high on a high boom, called for a full dress rehearsal complete with orchestra. I did my best but apparently it wasn't good enough, for the director called another run-through. I got Madge Evans to the bar all right and had started my lascivious campaign when the director screamed, "Halt, halt! Everybody stop!" He seemed quite maniacal and in the hush that followed, he began his tirade. In a voice loaded with ridicule and venom, he wanted to know where I had ever got the idea that I was an actor. What clown in the casting office had been responsible for foisting on him such a cretinous imbecile? Why didn't I go back to whatever country I had come from and whatever job I had had and not waste the time of directors such as he?

He paused in the shocked silence that followed, while I prayed that the tears of humiliation wouldn't fall or even show, a quiet firm female voice said to the great director, "You incredible bastard. How dare you speak to *any* human being the way you spoke to this young man? Until you are ready to apologize before all these people for what you have just said to this boy, you will find me in my dressing room." And she walked from the sound stage. A split second later there was a round of applause from everyone on the set, technicians included. In the midst of it I ran.

Her name was Marjorie Rambeau, a great artist and a fine woman. I've loved her ever since. Oh, yes, the director was a Frenchman named Jacques Feyder.

All that day I sat in my apartment desperately fighting a desire to go back to the studio and murder the son-of-a-bitch, and then, thankfully, nostalgia

came and I longed for home. Except for a waiter
or two and a few people at the studio, I didn't know
a soul. The phone rang six or seven times that day,
but I didn't answer it until almost seven o'clock. When
I did it was Asher. Did I mind if he came over?
Not at all.

He came at seven-thirty and brought a young woman
named Marcella Knapp. She was Benny Thau's assistant in the casting office, and she had the most gentle
and beautiful eyes. They talked to me for two hours,
telling me that this incident was not going to hurt
me at the studio. They said this particular director
had done such things before, so why not stay home
the rest of the week and come in Monday morning
and have a little chat with Mr. Thau. He's very understanding and I would be a lot calmer. Okay? I
said okay. Then Marcella suggested that I go home
with her and Jerry Asher and have dinner with Momma. I would like Momma.

Like her? I fell madly in love with her! She was
a short, fat, gray little woman who wore her hair
with an old-fashioned bun on top. She was gentle,
shy, and could hardly speak a word of English, although she had been in the United States over thirty
years. But goddam, she was a cook! It was my first
home-cooked meal since I left England. I'll never
forget it. It started out with ice-cold borscht with
shredded beets and sour cream, something I had
never tasted before. Great. This was followed by
stuffed cabbage with hot gravy and little new po-
tatoes, and then came the nonpareil, hot deep-dish
apple pie with short crust lightly powdered with sugar
and a big dollop of slightly sour whipped cream.
Ahhhh. *Okay,* Feyder, you have just been re-
prieved. I went home and slept like a baby.

I awakened about six the next morning with
nostalgia still riding me, so I put on some boots and
breeches and drove down to the Riviera Stables out
Sunset toward the beach. I had been there once before,
and it was quite a layout. Two polo fields with grand-

stands, a huge jumping ring with all the regulation obstacles, a bit manège used mainly for dressage and schooling, and another one for teaching. There was also trail riding in the hills nearby and stabling for about two hundred head, a lot of them privately owned and the rest rental hacks. The whole place was run by an Australian named Snowy Baker, who had served in the British army during the First World War. Fifth Dragoon Guards, I think. I had met him on my previous visit to the place and all he wanted to do was reminisce, the outcome being that he would be more than glad to have me come down at any time and help exercise the good stuff, that he was a little short of qualified people. I spent about three hours there that morning and worked two horses. One was a nice little half-bred Barb that showed a lot of promise at dressage but was being ruined by polo. The other was a big, rangy thoroughbred gelding who could jump over a house but was completely mad. He later killed an actor named Monroe Owsley.

I went back two more times before the week was out and on one occasion I met a most attractive girl who was taking lessons from an Australian instructor. You know, it's a strange thing when a foreigner first comes to the States. He is struck by the fact that some Americans speak more attractively than others. To a foreigner, they all speak exactly the same language. American. But some are pleasanter to listen to. And this gal was pleasant indeed. All aspects of her. She also had a wicked sense of humor. We went out dancing on Saturday night and went swimming on Sunday at Malibu. There was only one thing wrong with her. She lived in Glendale. I defy any stranger to find his way back from Glendale to Hayworth and Fountain at one o'clock in the morning, and I was no exception. I got lost every time. I'll call her Bernadette Conklin, which is not her real name, because I met her fourteen years later in very sad circumstances which I will bring up later. I asked her why she took riding lessons at Riviera when there were good stables at Flintridge no more than three or four miles from where she lived. Because, she said, the lessons were being paid for by a homosexual dentist in Pasadena, for whose problem she had apparently done wonders, and Riviera was far enough away so that there would be no complications. As I mentioned before, she had outstanding qualities. After all, Glendale isn't the end of the world, but it's pretty close.

Toward the end of that week I went in for my little "chat" with Benny Thau, at the time MGM's casting director, and this, roughly, is how it went.

THAU: "Now listen, sonny, the first thing you've got to do is to learn to speak like an American. You've got to try and lose this limey accent, because as long as you've got it you're going to be limited. And that'll be too bad, because physically you've got everything going for you."

ME: "But Mr. Thau, I don't understand. What about Herbert Marshall and Ronald Colman and Clive Brook? They are stars, big ones. One of the reasons for their success is their English 'accent' as you call it."

THAU: (A *patient sigh*) "Clive Brook, Herbert Marshall, and Ronald Colman were stars when they came here. Parts are written to fit *them*. In your case you're going to have to fit any part that comes along and you're not going to get anywhere being a johnny-one-note. Now my advice is that you attend the drama school we've got right here on the lot. The coach is one of the best in the country."

ME: "I can't do that, Mr. Thau, I'm sorry."

THAU: "Why not?"

ME: "Because when I was taken in to meet him when I first got here, he sort of sidled up to me and kept feeling my arm. I had a hard time to keep from letting him feel my fist. So rather than get into that sort of trouble, perhaps the best thing would be to send me back home."

There was a peculiar contractual distinction in the studios in those days. If you were earning a hundred dollars a week or less, you were a "stock" player and therefore could be called upon to do all kinds of publicity gimmicks, go to all the openings, whether they were of outhouses, department stores, or gas stations, and you had to attend drama school. Over a hundred dollars a week and you were a "contract" player and were more or less immune to that sort of thing. So Thau didn't press it. Besides, if I were to go to drama school and get groped every once in a while, it was going to be for a lot more than $175 a week. I am what you might call fervidly heterosexual. Instead, Thau asked me if I had made any friends since I had been here, someone with whom I could spend a lot of time and who would be willing to pick holes in my English "accent," someone with humor.

I thought for a moment and then, "Yes! But there's one thing—she's a girl."

"Well, what the hell is wrong with that?" Thau said. "Is she a girl girl, or is she somebody it's fun to have around?"

So I told him about Bernadette Conklin.

When I had finished he thought for a moment. Then he said, "I'll tell you what I'll do. We'll pay her fifty dollars a week for a month to spend every day with you. At the end of that time you'll come in here and you can pick a scene from one of our scripts, rehearse it with one of our stock girls, and do it on executive night at the drama school. Okay? Oh, when you get through with her, slip me her phone number." He didn't exactly leer, but I could tell he was interested.

For a month Bernadette and I had a ball. We also did a lot of speech therapy, so much so that at the end of four weeks I thought her a little wearing. But now for the denouement.

I had picked a scene from a picture called *Passion Flower*, soon to be made with Kay Francis and Robert

Montgomery. To work with me they had assigned the cutest, prettiest little Dresden doll I had ever seen. Her name was Mary Carlisle and she was about as big as a bar of soap but as strong as a horse. I would imagine she was insurmountable. But luckily she had a great sense of humor. We rehearsed only one day before having to appear in the "bird cage" as it was called.

At the end of the rehearsal she said to me, "I thought you were English."

"I am," I said, "but in this scene I'm supposed to be an American. Don't you think I sound like one?"

"Oh," she said, "you do, you do. Yes, indeedy."

Now this "bird cage" where these little playlets and vignettes were performed for the executives, and/ or their assistants had been converted from an unused projection room. The stage was glassed in, so that you couldn't see or hear the audience but they could you—but me, with my eyesight, I could see them. Whenever they wanted to talk to the performers they hit a button on the sound console and it became two-way. When it came time for Mary and me to do our little scene, which was only three pages long, some-body obviously had left the key open, because all the way through it I kept hearing giggles and chuckles and at the end roars of laughter. One bastard was actually lying on the floor. I couldn't understand it. It wasn't supposed to be a funny scene. It turned out that Miss Bernadette Conklin came from a place called Pineapple, Alabama, and I had acquired the damnedest Southern accent ever heard north of the Panama Canal. Curtain.

Two weeks later I was given my first legitimate part. It was in a picture called *Bachelor Father,* and it starred Marion Davies and the Englishman, C. Aubrey Smith. It was the story of an old reprobate who had fathered three children in his youth without bothering to get churched. One in America (Marion Davies), one in England (myself), and one in Spain

(Nina Quartero). Now in his dotage he found himself saddled with them. The movie was directed by an elephantine gentleman named Robert Leonard, who immediately restored my faith in American directors. He was well-mannered and patient and very much respected. The film was produced by Cosmopolitan Pictures (owned by W. R. Hearst) and released through MGM. Before the actual shooting began it was decided that we should all go up to "the ranch" to rehearse for two weeks. This meant San Simeon, the Camelot of California. Just the four members of the cast and Mr. Leonard. But that didn't mean we had the place to ourselves, far from it. Because when we got on our palatial private train for the two-hundred-odd-mile trip, there were at least twenty other guests. From all over the world apparently, very regal indeed.

Now I don't intend to go into a long, descriptive panegyric about San Simeon, because that has been done before by people much better qualified than I, and in some cases by people *not* as qualified. But there are a few things worth mentioning. For instance, the only time I ever saw paper napkins and bottles of ketchup and other condiments scattered down the length of the dining table was at breakfast, which was run rather like breakfast in an English country house, guests dragging in at different times. Lunch was quite formal, and dinner was served with all the panoply of Saint Petersburg. As a matter of fact, I think the dinner service once belonged to a Czar. I was invited again about three months later, the only difference being that the dinner service had once belonged to Napoleon. Black tie was obligatory, and drinking was not allowed until the meal was over. After that, though, any toddy your heart desired.

There were about twenty-five guests all told, and a very mixed bag they were. I got to know only about six or seven. One of the nicest was a man named Ed Hatrick, who was one of Hearst's excutives, very droll and slightly world-weary. His descriptive rundown on the other guests was funny, penetrating but never cruel. His daughter Gloria is now married to Jimmy Stewart. He also warned me about three of the other guests, two well-disguised faggots and a woman in her thirties known as the Burlingame Barracuda. I stuck pretty close to Ed. Our rehearsals took place in Hearst's private theater, but they never lasted more than an hour each morning, so there was plenty of time for swiming, tennis, or riding. Most of my time was spent at the stables attempting to master the restrictive Western saddle and trying not to castrate myself in the process. The ranch had between thirty and forty head but nothing very good, mostly range ponies and quarter horse types with mouths like iron. I'd go out with the head wrangler, whose name I think was Morgan, who told me that there were over two hundred thousand acres in the spread.

One night at dinner, toward the end of our stay, Mr. Hearst announced that we were all going on a picnic the next morning, to a spot ten miles from the castle. Those who wished to ride could ride, and for the rest there would be cars. It would be a real Western barbecue, he said. Those who chose to go on horseback would leave at ten A.M. and the others traveling by car would leave at eleven. Ah, I thought, finally a taste of the real West! It was a beautiful morning, and at ten I was ready at the foot of the steps. Morgan was there with a couple of wranglers and a string of saddle horses. Then I looked to the right and got a bit of a shock. There were five limousines parked in line. Two Lincolns, a Cunningham, a Pierce-Arrow, and a bloody great big Belgian Minerva. All glittering. I looked at Morgan popeyed. He said, "Better get mounted." There were five others who had chosen to ride: the two masquerading mackerels, the Bay Area dame, Ed Hatrick, and a bubbly character named Kane.

Only one thing untoward happened on that lovely ride. The wranglers were riding one and leading two, and a jack-rabbit jumped up under the nose of one of the led horses. He spooked, broke a rein, and took off with me right after him. He and I had a lovely time; I got him in about a mile and an eighth. Twenty minutes later we topped a rise and there below us, in a stand of live oak with a stream running throught it, was a shallow dell and the damnedest setup you could possibly imagine. There were six low Japanese-style tables decked with white linen and crystal, three stainless-steel grills each about two feet by seven, a bar nine feet long with bottles and bowls of ice, three chefs and four waiters all dressed in white, caviar from the Black Sea, lobsters from Morro Bay, and on the grills boned squab, ducklings stuffed with tangerines, and a baked salmon that must have weighed forty-nine pounds. Sitting at the head of it all, looking like the Sultan of Zamboanga, was W. R. I got through the meal with only one thought in my mind; Clarence E. Mulford, you stepped on your cock *again*.

Later that afternoon the ride home almost made up for it. The two fugitives from Fire Island and the Lily of Laguna decided to return by limousine, so Hatrick, Kane, the wranglers, and I quietly ambled home, riding one and leading two. Halfway back, the mountains faded, and I was back in Surrey riding morning exercise with Gillam beside me and Dunbar whistling "Cock o' the North" and B 63 just waiting to take off. Suddenly I felt very lonely, and nostalgia came again, only this time it was more insistent. Pedants have said it is a childish emotion that should have no place in a mature mind. If this is so, then I am a child still. It is always with me and will be until I die.

There is not much more I want to say about San Simeon, except perhaps to point up a few peculiarities that other diarists seemed to have missed. For instance: On the night Mr. Hearst announced the barbecue we were told that if we needed riding clothes the housekeeper would outfit us completely. We were taken down to a room that looked like a combination of Berman's and Western Costume. Everything was there, and in all sizes up to and including costumes for the entire cast of *Aida*. And all of it immaculate. Mind-boggling.

Another thing: I never slept in Richelieu's bed. According to all reports, that must have been the most overworked bed ever made, although I was lodged in a most beautiful guesthouse, called, I think, "Casa del Sol," a mixture of Byzantine, Moorish, and Spanish, but everything of museum quality. But the bed *was* French by the feel of it, because in the center was a slight depression. It must have been either Madame de Montespan's or the Du Barry's.

Throughout the castle grounds and far into the distances of the ranch were telephones, usually in the trees so that one was never out of touch, all necessary to the Hearst operation. However, each call made by a guest had to be paid for. Except mine. This is how that came about. I had talked to Mr. Hearst perhaps three times. On the last occasion I had told him that when I was a youngster I had raided his orchard at his castle in Wales many times. He gave me a sharp, intent look with his frosty gray eyes, and then he chuckled, althought I don't think he was a man of much humor. In a sort of stage whisper he said, "Just for that, feel free to use the telephone at any time. There'll be no charge." He was a strange and forbidding man, about six feet three and quite heavy. I imagine that if Oscar Wilde had been able to beat the rap and had lived to be the age of Hearst they would have looked like twins.

Over the years my feeling for Marion Davies approached adulation. She was a little scatterbrained and had a slight stutter, was mischievous and was kindness itself. She was also a very courageous and very generous woman. I always adored her. Following *Bachelor Father* I made another picture with her called *Polly of the Circus,* in which her leading man was Clark Gable. But I'll tell you about that later. First, I've got to get married.

chapter ix

"How about driving out to Pasadena with me Sunday morning? I know a family out there who have a tennis court, a swimming pool, two daughters, and a good cook. I think you'll enjoy it." The speaker was Rex Ross, a young premed student from New England who had taken a year's sabbatical for a look at Hollywood. I had met Ross through Jerry Asher a week before, a tall young fellow about the same age as myself, very good-looking, who spoke very slowly and had a rather shy, diffident manner. We were waiting around on the set of *Bachelor Father*. The scene was a birthday celebration and we were both dressed in tails, lords of the earth.

"That's very kind of you," I replied. "Yes, I'd like to very much. But you had better warn them that I'm an actor, foreign, and I don't play tennis."

"Oh, hell," he said, "that won't matter. You can't be any worse than I am. Besides, they're nice people and they'll be glad to have you."

It was decided that he would pick me up on Sunday morning at ten o'clock, but we would use my car. After all, he was still a premed student from Clambroth, Rhode Island, doing occasional dress-extra work, while I was a contract artiste! Rex was one of the first friends I made in Hollywood and he has remained so. Today he is one of the most respected surgeons in California and lives just down the road from me.

We arrived at the MacLeod house in Pasadena about 10:45 A.M. It was a large, stone, Provençal-style house just off Colorado Boulevard with a courtyard in front and a tennis court and pool down to the right. There were voices there, so that's where we headed. We came upon umbrellas, tables, and about six or seven summery-looking people, all very chic and all of them with that aura of ease and blatant camaraderie that I found very unsettling. The hostess, Mrs. McLeod, was a woman around fifty or fifty-five years of age. From head to foot she was gray: hair, eyes, and her rather long diaphanous dress. She was very thin and I had a feeling that all was draped on a frame of stainless steel. There was a Miss Celeste Durand, who had short, reddish hair and a slightly masculine manner and who was holding the biggest Scotch and soda I had ever seen before lunch. There was a very pleasant and warm-looking woman of about thirty whose name seemed to be just "Woody." Next came a lean and flashing dark man in his midtwenties who apparently was English, because he called me "chum." His name was Grant. I found out later his first name was Cary, a very cheerful type. And then I met the daughters. The first one was Robin, who was called Bob, a rattled and sulfurous-looking girl with very dark hair with coppery glints in it and features that were pure Byzantine. She smoked a cigarette as if someone was going to take it away from her. She just stared at me and said, "Hi." Than I met her sister Janet, who was quite the opposite. Dark blond hair, blue eyes, and fair skin, a very young-looking girl, who was in fact a year older than her sister. It was hard to imagine two more dissimilar people. Yet they had one thing in common. They were both six feet tall.

Janet turned out to be beautifully mannered and

considerate, a lovely greyhound of a girl, whereas Bob was the unpredictable Doberman. I was in the process of asking Janet if I could have an orange juice when Bob suddenly barked, "How about some tennis?"

"No," I said. "I don't think I'd better."

"Why not?" she asked. "You're dressed for it."

I replied that I had never played tennis and that I would only spoil their game.

"Hell," she said, "that doesn't mean a thing around here. Give him a racket, somebody, and let's get going."

This was my introduction to the gentlemanly and polite game of tennis. It turned out to be a battle for my life. My partner, thank God, was Janet, and we were opposed by her sister and this chap named Grant. Janet was good, but I played as if I thought the game was polo. Every time the ball went to Bob she slammed it right at my head. Hell, the way I had to duck and weave I might as well have been back in the ring in some distant armory. Finally the set was over and I quit, to the sound of Bob's asthmatic roars of laughter, and Rex took my place. I sat and talked to Mrs. MacLeod, who had a talent for unobstrusive cross-examination which was masterly. Within fifteen minutes she had my entire life laid bare. Then she very kindly invited me and Rex to the house for dinner the following Wednesday. She had a good Scottish cook and she thought a home-cooked meal might be a change, and she was right. The last one I had had was cooked by Cecil Knapp months before.

It was through this family and especially Janet, that I met most of the friends I have today. And it was through her that I met my wife Mal. I made a deal with Janet that if she would teach me to play tennis, I would teach her to ride. This led to our going dancing a lot, at George Olson's, Frank Sebastian's Cotton Club, the Coconut Grove, and lots of private homes, as well as to my first and only speakeasy

in California, where I became violently ill. It was
a dreadful little shack, a bungalow somewhere south
of Santa Monica Boulevard. There were about eight
or ten people scattered around the living-dining room
area, all very quiet and surreptitious. I had the feeling
that I must have wandered into an opium den
somewhere in Limehouse. Quite joyless. I seated
myself at the end of a foundered couch, next to an
extraordinary-looking girl. Round face, red hair,
heavy pouting lips, and a black eye. And when I
say a black eye I mean a shiner. She was dressed
all in white and was feeling no pain at all. I had
met my first real Hollywood star. She was Clara Bow.
She scrutinized me for a moment or two and then
said, "Hi, don't drink the Scotch, it will kill you.
Take the gin. It might not." Then she turned back
to the fellow next to her. I kept staring at her, completely mesmerized, until I felt a sharp jab in my back
and it was Janet wanting to know what she should
order.

I said, "Gin, don't take the Scitch, I mean Scotch."
And she went to the kitchen, where you bought the
drinks. I couldn't understand why the place hadn't
been raided; you could smell the stuff a block away.

Janet finally came back with two small glasses
of gin with ice in them. I tasted mine and gagged.
I looked at her with tears in my eyes and asked if
there might be some ginger ale around. She suggested
I try the kitchen and bring some back. I did and
it was the best brew in the house. So we diluted the
gin and stood leaning on a big Sparton radio and
sipped. Boy! Were we living! I asked her who was
the fellow with Clara Bow. She said he was a well-
known leading man named James Hall, and would
I go back to the bar and get two more drinks.

It was about fifteen minutes later, when the ice
was beginning to rattle, that Miss Bow, was was beginning to get bellicose, suddenly banged Mr. Hall right
smack in the beezer and charged out of the front
door. Hall got up and made to go after her, but the

bouncer or proprietor or whatever he was stuck out his foot. Mr. Hall dove head first into the Sparton radio, and our drinks went flying. It seemed they wanted him to pay the check before leaving. Then the barman said we should have two fresh ones on the house. It was in the middle of these two drinks that I suddenly began to feel very, very floaty. I knew I had to make a choice; either throw up or die. So I bolted for the door with Janet after me. I just made it, and when I got through I still wanted to die. I asked Janet if she would drive me back to my car, which we had left at a restaurant where we'd had an early dinner. She insisted that I should not drive home, and I insisted that I should and that I would meet her at Flintridge Riding Academy at seven thirty Sunday morning as arranged. Somehow I got home and, after throwing up again, went to sleep.

I was awakened the next morning by what sounded like cannon fire. I looked at my watch and saw that it was 8:15 A.M. I felt like death. Slowly it dawned on me that there was someone at the door. Somehow I got myself into a dressing gown and wove an interesting path through the living room and opened up. There were two policemen standing there, a young one and one with gray hair. They looked at me and then at each other and then back at me, the young one with the beginnings of a grin and the older one with what I thought was a touch of sympathy. No wonder, I must have looked like the wages of sin. The older one asked if my name was Milland and did I own a Nash coupe.

I said, "Yes, why?"

"Where do you usually keep it?"

"In the garage at the side of the court. It there something wrong, officer?"

He looked at his partner and then back at me. "If you'll get some clothes on and take a little walk with us," he said, "we'll soon find out."

I stuck my head in the sink, ran some cold water over it, dried myself, and got into a shirt and slacks,

and we set off. We walked down Hayworth almost
to Santa Monica Boulevard and turned into a private
driveway and all the way back to a wooden garage.
As we got there a woman about fifty years old came
boiling out of the kitchen door and started in on me.
And what a wonderful performance it was. Obviously,
what had happened was that I had found my street
all right and for no discernible reason had picked
on this driveway and driven all the way back to the
garage, which was one of those long structures that
hold two cars. I then shoved my Nash in back of
the car already there, locked up, and walked all the
way home. That was my first and only visit to a speakeasy. As a matter of fact, it was many months before
I took another drink. Very chastening.

It was a warm, dry afternoon in December when
the lightning struck. I had gone to a late brunch and
bridge party in Beverly Hills. The house was huge,
part of a compound of four and all owned by a crusty
little millionaire named J. J. Murdock. The story
was that he'd had a tunnel built under all four of
them, the other three being occupied by his executives
and their families, and that he had had listening devices
installed. Sounded like Nightmare Park. Fascinating.
I had tagged along with Janet and a girl named Martha
Sleeper, who happened to be Murdock's niece. There
seemed to be thirty or forty people there, most of
them young and attractive, and I was enjoying myself.
At one point in the afternoon I got myself roped
into a bridge foursome. It was supposed to be auction
bridge but with all the chatter and gossip at the table
it was more like Snakes and Ladders.

Soon my partner concentrated enough to steal a
bid and I was dummy. I felt a touch on my shoulder,
and it was Janet with another girl in tow, to whom
I was introduced. I never heard her name because
my world suddenly stood still and I felt completely
lost. The room was empty and there was just her,
tall, with dark hair with some silver in it and eyes

that were truly sapphire. Her expression was gently humorous while I mumbled some garbled inanities. I was still doing it even after they moved on. I dropped into my seat with a thud, looking and feeling very odd. The fellow on my right, Johnny Truyens, asked if I felt all right. Could he get me something? I said no, it was just that I had forgotten something and I had to get to a phone right away. And with that I left the room.

I walked out to the pool, and even though it was December there were three or four people swimming in it. They paid no attention to me, so I sat down on a stone bench and watched for a while. I didn't see them for long, though. I kept seeing this girl. But the funny thing was, I couldn't recall her face exactly, just her eyes and her smile. I was bemused and felt the tiniest touch of panic. Up until now I had never felt any really deep emotion; no one had ever touched me inside. I had been self-sufficient or, more correctly, self-centered and solitary. Suddenly I had met someone I wanted terribly to impress and I didn't even know her name. I had to get hold of Janet and, without arousing her suspicions, find out who she was and all about her.

I set about my plan with all the deviousness of someone trying to sell a farm, with the result that at the end of the following week, after our early-morning session at Flintridge, Janet announced that she was taking me to breakfast in a house in Hollywood.

"What sort of a house?" I asked.

"Oh, stop worrying," she replied. "It's a house, for God's sake, with a family who like to have a lot of people for breakfast on Sunday mornings. And you can park you car at your own apartment, because they only live a block from where you live.

And where I lived in Hollywood in those days was a most intriguing area. It was an area made up of big old California houses of stucco and wood, Victorian monstrosities straight out of Ronald Searle, trashy little Mexican apartment courts, and the most beautiful apartment houses ever designed. Places like La Ronda, Andalusia, the Garden of Allah, none of which could be built now. Because elegance and taste and artistry seem to have died. People today are forced to live in the obscene chicken coops that have taken their place. But in those days Carole Lombard lived there, and Ernest Torrence, Allan Dwan and Gloria Swanson. And often in the still, early hours of the morning one could see tortured and pallid writers slowly plodding under the trees sweating out scenes of *Black Oxen* or *Greed*. Charon! Charon! What time's the next ferry?

The house that Janet took me to was in the middle of all this, big and white and of no architectural pedigree, set back from the street by about fifty feet of lawn. At the back was a huge garden with fig trees, avocados, citrus trees, and flowers. There was also a sort of Mexican summerhouse and a large swimming pool. Scattered throughout were four or five tables with folding chairs and about twenty people. There was a long table to one side which held hot plates and dishes of sausages, eggs, and hotcakes from which people were serving themselves. And coming toward us was *the girl!* She took us around and introduced us to everyone, but the only name I remembered was hers. It was Mal, and this was her home. I met her family, which consisted of her sister, her older brother, Herbert, and his wife, her mother and her father. The minute I met her father I knew I was in trouble. Welsh charm was not going to help me here. To begin with, he was big and powerful, with a head that belonged on Mount Rushmore. When I was introduced to him he bent his head as if he didn't quite catch the name, and when I repeated it he stared at me and said, "You're English, I think."

"Yes, sir."

Actually, he made it sound like an accusation. With an offhand invitation to help myself to some food, he moved away. The rest of the family were a delight. Later I was to learn that the house was always like this, always filled with people. It took me a long time to figure out who were relatives and who were friends. It all seemed to revolve around this wonderful girl and her mother. Before I left that morning I asked if I could call her and perhaps drop around some evening, since I lived only a block away. She supposed that would be all right; I could always get her number from Janet.

Now I don't propose to go into the long and troubled story of my courtship. I only want to say that I had been kissed by the angels and that there must have been something good in me to have been able to recognize the good in her. I didn't know it then, but I know it now.

It took almost two weeks to get her to agree to go to the movies with me. Her reluctance had something to do with the fact that Janet was her good friend and also because she was attending USC. So Friday night was the only night available. On Wednesday I started to worry about the Nash. This was no car to be taking a princess to the movies. I had to get something more plush and, thinking of her father, something more conservative.

As my option had been taken up, I was feeling very Turkish, so I hied me down to the Kelley Kar Company on South Figueroa to look over their stock. Like an idiot I wore my best light gray suit with the double-breasted vest, and that was all the salesmen needed to see. They had me in the closing room so fast I thought I'd been caught in a washing machine. That's the room with no handles on the inside of the doors. Once you're in there's no way out until you've signed the papers. In my case Dear Ole Kelley himself handled the deal, and I found myself the owner of a brand-new chocolate-brown Chrysler Straight Eight sedan—or at least 30 percent of it. I took delivery on Friday morning and drove straight home. I put this extravagance in the garage and spent the day polishing it. That car was going to be glittering when I picked Mal up. Eight o'clock on the dot. I rang her doorbell. It was answered by the Filipino houseboy, who said. "They be out putty soon."

They? I wandered back out to my car at the curb and checked it for dust. I turned as I heard the front door open. But it wasn't her. It was her brother Herbert and a friend of his, a little birdlike chap named Eddie Rubin, a very comical and easy type who asked, "New car?"

"Yes," I said. "Just got it this morning. D'you like it?"

"Sure, but somehow you don't look like a sedan type to me."

I was about to tell him that that was the idea when I heard the front door again. I spun around and there she was, and the arrow socked home, never to be pulled out. It's still in there, deeper than ever.

Somehow I drove quite sensibly to Grauman's Chinese, parked the car, and was at the box-office window before I realized that there were four of us, because apparently Herbert and his friend had no intention of allowing this flower to be alone with such an obviously decadent foreigner. Anybody who wore a double-breasted vest was not to be trusted. Not at first anyway. They were thoughtful enough to let me buy the tickets, and when we got to our seats, Rubin went in first, then the vision, then her brother, and me on the aisle. And that, more or less, was the way our courtship went. Eight months later we were married at the Riverside Mission Inn. There were two hundred and fifty guests and three rehearsals. At what I thought was the last rehearsal, when we got to the part where the groom is supposed to kiss the bride, I didn't, whereupon my lovely bride hissed, "Kiss me. Kiss me!"

I said, "No, let's wait for the real thing."

She whispered, "This *is* the real thing!"

I almost fainted, and then kissed her. Right in the eye. I don't remember much about the long drive back in what must have been the longest cavalcade of cars ever seen along Foothill Boulevard. The reception was held in the garden of her home, and from all the attention that was paid to me, you would think I was an unfriendly draft from under a bathroom door. And then there was the frustrating attempt to get away on our honeymoon, the maddeningly juvenile efforts of a lot of the guests to keep us apart for as long as they could. Finally I got together with a friend of mine, a young actor named Duke Wayne, who had been one of the ushers. We conspired that he would get my wife to an awful dump called Barney's Beanery and I would sneak off, get my car which I had hidden down the street, and meet them there. He did, and that's how we got away to spend our honeymoon in Carmel.

During that eight-month campaign I appeared in three pictures. Two on loan to Warner Brothers, and one at MGM. But the only one worth any comment was a picture called *The Man Who Played God*. I played a very small part in it, and the film itself was easily forgettable. But it gave me the opportunity to watch a true professional at work, a man completely dedicated to his trade, a man of immaculate good manners. He was George Arliss, and at that time probably in his sixties. He was a small man, thin, with bony features and a slight cast in one eye. He appeared on the set promptly at ten minutes to nine every morning knowing every word and nuance he would be using that day; promptly at five o'clock, when his valet would appear, he would look at his watch, even it he wasn't wearing one, and murmur, "Dear me, five o'clock. Good night, everyone, and thank you." Then he would leave. It didn't matter whether we were in the middle of a scene or just rehearsing. When that valet appeared he left. But in the hours in between he was a whispering articulate dynamo. The part of his protégée, a young girl, was played by Bette Davis, in those days a very pretty and pleasant creature, but just the tiniest bit earnest, you know the sort of thing, given to sitting at people's feet in rapt attention. No sign of her later arrogance and imperiousness.

I suppose I must have been adequate in the small part I had been given, because Warner Brothers borrowed me again four months later for a slightly better part in a film staring Jimmy Cagney and Joan Blondell. I think it was called *Blonde Crazy* or perhaps *Larceny Lane*. I don't remember. One thing I *do* remember, though, was Cagney's lousy piano playing. It was occasioned by a three-page scene we had together, all dialogue, which was supposed to take about three minutes to play. The way Cagney and I went through it, the scene was over in twenty-six seconds. You see, in those days Cagney spoke even faster than I did. With a look of utter disgust, the director, Roy Del Ruth, decided to call it a day.

"You two remind me of a couple of goddam woodpeckers," he rumbled. "Now tonight, get together somewhere and go over it so that tomorrow we can understand it. Right now I'm catching one word in four. Good night!"

I think it was Cagney's second leading role, and the studio had great hopes for him. Before driving home we arranged to meet at his apartment, which was on the second floor of a court much the same as mine, but at the bottom of Holloway Drive, about four blocks from my place. "Don't bother to eat," Cagney said. "I'll have my wife fix us some hamburgers—she's pretty good—and then we'll get at it."

The apartment was standard for the area, with a rather large living room, a dining area, one bedroom and a bath and a kitchen. There was an upright piano at one end of the living room, and the rest of the furniture was Barker Brothers Mexican. His wife, most attractive and calm, went into the kitchen to prepare the dinner, and Jimmy and I went to work on the scene. In half an hour we had slowed it down to what we thought was a *very* pedestrian pace, and then hamburgers were announced. Now I had always considered myself one of the fastest eaters in the world, but on this particular evening I came in a bad second. From the first bite to the last I don't think Cagney took a breath. By the time I had finished he was seated at the beat-up piano looking through some music.

"Hey," he said, "know anything about music?" And before I could reply he said that he was taking piano lessons by mail. "Listen to this."

I think it was a piece called "Love for Sale," but by the time he got through, it could have been anything by John Philip Sousa. That was Cagney. Several years later I asked him if he had ever finished his mail-order course of piano lessons. "Nah," he replied, "the goddam neighbors got a court order and I had to send the piano back."

We got to know each other quite well over the years. He and his brother Bill could have been twins except for temperament—Bill being ebullient and gregarious where Jimmy was something of a loner. Our friendship was based upon our mutual love of boats. We never talked about the theatrical world, just boats. We knew the faults and shortcomings of every boat from San Francisco to San Diego together with the faults and perversions of their owners. At one time Jimmy owned a small and lovely old Gloucester schooner called the *Martha* and I was the proud owner of a Sparkman and Stephens yawl called the *Santana*. We both kept them in slips at the same landing with one boat between us, and that was the *Sirocco* owned by Errol Flynn. Time and again Jimmy would plan trips to Catalina Island or perhaps even Mexico, but each time he set foot on board he turned a pale Nile green. I don't think he ever made it out of the harbor. He would much prefer to watch the Errol Flynn Follies on the *Sirocco* every night. That was always a good show until the gendarmes arrived.

I remember one time when Errol was being sued for the deflowering of a tall, ravishing showgirl who had been one of a group invited down to the *Sirocco* for the weekend. According to her complaint Errol

Flying Scotsman, made in England in 1929.
The first time I ever acted for money and I
played the role of the fireman, top right.

Up to now my acting experiences had been in a
very light vein. *Payment Deferred*, 1932, with
Charles Laughton and Maureen O'Sullivan was
my first exposure to drama. You can tell by the
puzzlement on my face. *MGM*

Opposite, above   My first picture in America
was made at MGM in 1931. It was called
Bachelor Father. The girl on the left is Nina
Quartero, the one in the middle is Marion Davies,
and I'm the girl on the right. *MGM*

Below   My second picture at MGM, *Polly of the
Circus,* and here I am with Clark Gable. *MGM*

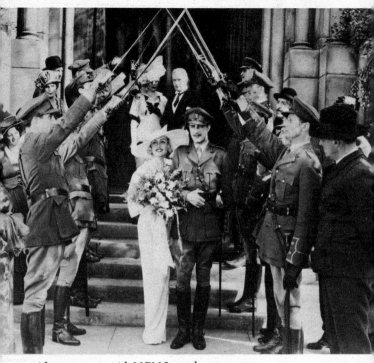

After two years with MGM I struck out, went to
England for a year and then returned to
Hollywood, where I was picked up by
Paramount. This was my first role at Paramount
where I played an army officer and fiancé of
Carole Lombard in *Bolero*. The leading part was
played by George Raft. *Paramount.*

Opposite, above My first honest-to-God leading
role in America was with Dorothy Lamour in
Her Jungle Love, which appeared in 1938.
Paramount

Below *The Gilded Lily*, Paramount, 1935, with
Claudette Colbert. The first of several pictures I
was lucky enough to make with her. *Paramount*

As a result of a misspent life, I was given the role
of the father in *Love Story* with Ali McGraw in 1971.
Copyright © 1970. Paramount Pictures Corporation.
All rights reserved.

Opposite, above   Forever and a Day, 1941,
acted in by every actor in Hollywood with British
origins for British war relief. *RKO*

Below   1946. The Lost Weekend. Life Photo
by Ralph Crane

Alter and Ego. With Charles Jackson, author of
The Lost Weekend. Paramount

Receiving the *Look* Magazine Award from
Ingrid Bergman on the Bob Hope Show.
Standing next to Ingrid Bergman is L. B. Mayer
and behind him is Billy Wilder. *Paramount*

The night of nights for
me was in 1946. And this
is why.

The very first command performance when the
lights went on again after the Second World
War. Being presented to King George VI and the
Royal Family. *London News Agency*

At the age of three, first exposure. *Paramount*

At camp, the legendary Troop "B" of the Royal House Guards at Pirbright in 1927. From bottom left: Dunbar, Casey, Gilham. Second row right, me. Behind me, Wheeler.

Opposite In full regalia of the Household Cavalry. *Paramount*

Advance base, Solomon Islands, 1943.

With my wife, Mal, 1946, on the *Queen Elizabeth. Keystone*

Opposite Jumping a fence in an obstacle course, at that time my one professional accomplishment.

Mal and me in Berlin, 1946.

Location-hunting for *Lisbon*. So what am I doing here in the Roman Forum?

Paris, 1961. With my wife, my son, Daniel, and my daughter, Victoria.

On the occasion of being presented with an award by the French government. Shaking hands with Georges Bidault, Premier of France.

In Schiaparelli's establishment with my wife and
Mrs. Frank Farley on the right. "This perfume
can't cost this much!"

had enticed her down to his cabin below decks to view the moon through one of the portholes, and while she was doing this—and to her great surprise—he upped and did it. Now all I can say it, the portholes of the *Sirocco* were about seven inches in diameter and only two feet above the waterline, and if this Aphrodite *had* been looking through the porthole as alleged, she would have been staring eyeball to eyeball at me. Or Cagney, Or Ward Bond. Or any one of a half dozen other voyeurs. This was no penny arcade, *this* was a window on the world. No doubt about it, Flynn was quite a boyo. He must have had the most overworked prostate gland in the universe. What a way to go.

About two weeks before I got married a small incident occurred which almost nipped my career in the bud. I had been cast in another picture with Marion Davies called *Polly of the Circus* and as I mentioned earlier her leading man was Clark Gable. At that time Gable was just making his mark as something new on the Hollywood horizon, a leading man who did not conform to the pattern, big, tough, and with a calculated disrespect for women. You know the old adage treat a lady like a whore, and a whore like a lady? Well, for him it worked. He hit the screen like a wagonload of catnip. I don't remember what sort of character he played in the movie, but I had been cast as a young gym instructor in a boys' club. He was supposed to visit the club and put on a boxing exhibition for the benefit of the boys and I was the goat. It was just a thirty-second scene and quite well rehearsed. One of my instructions was not to hit him in the face. He was big and very strong and outweighed me by about thirty pounds. But he was just a little bit slow, and he wore a partial bridge in the upper left side of his mouth. About halfway through the scene he stuck a straight left in my ear and I countered with one of my own, purely reflexive, done without thinking—and out popped the bridge, only to fall right under my foot. That finished the scene and also the

Tru-Bites. The picture was delayed two days and I might as well have had leprosy. From that day on Gable never really trusted me, although we met two or three times a month at different parties over the next thirty years. We also belonged to the same golf club and played in foursomes together dozens of times, but he would never take me as a partner, there was always that touch of suspicion. I was one of the foursome in the last game of golf he ever played. It was while he was making what turned out to be his last film, *The Misfits,* the one he did with Marilyn Monroe. They were shooting it in Nevada and were having a little trouble with her. At one point she decided to take a week off, so he came home for a couple of days to get in a few rounds of golf and try to unwind. He seemed very depressed and despondent with the way the film was going, and felt he was working too hard doing stunts and unnecessary work to fill in the wasted time. He flew back to Nevada that afternoon and that was the last we saw of him. He never lived to see his son.

chapter x

The events that led up to the first and only separation between my wife and me were caused mainly but not solely by my father-in-law's dislike of me. Even after we were married he had the irritating habit of not quite remembering my name, and whenever we were invited over there for dinner, he would be overly polite, as if I were a visitor he had just met. This drove me into towering rages which I tried not to take out on Mal, but I'm afraid I distressed her terribly. They were a very tightly knit family and my father-in-law always succeeded in making me feel like an interloper who just wasn't good enough. In such circumstances one very rarely is.

Early in the new year of 1932 I was assigned to do a picture called *Payment Deferred,* which starred Charles Laughton, newly arrived from England. In it I played a young relative of his from Australia, one with a little money. Laughton was supposed to be a shop clerk very much in debt who, when he saw the roll I was carrying, decided to do away with me by poisoning and then bury me in the garden. I stayed with him for a week, the attraction being his young daughter, who was very pretty, played by

Maureen O'Sullivan. I had seen Laughton in a play in London just before I left. It was called *On the Spot* and in it he played a Chicago gangster with dyed black hair, a velvet moustache, and long beaded eyelashes. This, combined with Laughton's fat, sloppy physique and his tendency to flounce, made the whole operation somewhat bizarre to say the least. I was puzzled when the play and Laughton's performance were acclaimed by the West End cognoscenti.

Naturally, Laughton was signed up by Hollywood, and now, three years later, I found myself playing in a picture with him. The director was Hungarian, Lothar Mendes, a man of great charm and a lot of humor and patience. He needed all of it, because he had to contend not only with my lack of talent and inexperience but also with Laughton's outrageous grotesqueries. In the scene where he got the idea of poisoning me Laughton was supposed to walk the length of the little parlor right up into the lens for a huge closeup so that the audience might read in his face the birth of the idea and his decision to go through with it. First his eyes rolled and then they went right up into his head till only the whites showed. Next his upper lip began to twitch and quiver and then, by God, he started to slobber. This went on for over a minute until I really believed he was having an epileptic fit. Suddenly he turned it off, reached into the glass case for the cordial, mixed the lethal concoction, and came back and presented it to me as if it were a piece of the true Cross. At that point Mendes, the director, called, "Cut," and proceeded to give the cameraman the next set up. In the wait that followed I sidled up to Mr. Mendes and asked his indulgence. Would he give me his opinion of the scene we had just witnessed? Did he consider it fine acting, because if it were than I would have to change my thinking and start all over.

"No," he said. "It's not good acting. It's self-indulgence, theatrical masturbation. But don't sell Laughton short. He'll do this sort of thing many times throughout the picture. Thank God, though, I'm a good editor so there will be little if any of it left in the final cut and he'll come out smelling like a rose. But don't *you* start feeling superior, because you'll be doing it yourself if you last that long. It's an occupational disease with most actors."

Two weeks after the picture was finished MGM dropped my option and I was out of a job. Normally, I wouldn't have cared a hoot. I was twenty-five years old and the world was wide open, just a great big candy store, and I would have gone on my wide-eyed way. But things were different now. I was a married man and I had responsibilities, and the future had suddenly intruded. For the first time in my life I felt the cold touch of worry. I had absolutely no belief in my talents as an actor and was there without the buckler of dedication and confidence that is so necessary in the theatrical profession. In the five months that followed I got only one job, and that was in an experimental film that was never released, but I made seven hundred and fifty dollars, which was pure manna. It was also five months of constant denigration by my father-in-law. It broke my heart to see my wife change from the gay and gentle willow wand I had married to a bewildered, sad, and unhappy child. Mal was just twenty-one and quite unable to divide her love and loyalties. I spent five months watching this and trying to keep my temper and frustrations from boiling over. Finally things came to a head and it was decided that I would go back to England and start all over again, that the cachet of two years in Hollywood might open a few doors. Also, my depression was being made worse by increasing nostalgia and, to be quite truthful, my desire to hide. If by any chance I *should* get lucky, then my wife would join me.

The question of financing my voyage back to England was automatically solved by the terms of my contract with MGM. They had to pay for my first-class transportation back to London, together with my traveling expenses. After digging around several travel agencies I cottoned to a young apprentice in one of them named Dan Scariano, and between us we evolved a way to get back for one-third of the first-class fare. We cashed in the MGM tickets and I set out on a train called the *Sunset Limited* for Houston, Texas, sitting up in a chair the whole way. From Houston I took a streetcar to Galveston on the Gulf of Mexico, and it must have been the fastest streetcar in the world, because it did the sixty miles in seventy minutes. I had a second-class ticket on a boat called the *Mohawk* of the Clyde-Mallory Line sailing that evening for Miami and New York. It was terribly hot and after checking my baggage on the boat, I went ashore and bought some swimming shorts. To a European, the Gulf of Mexico is the most exotic-sounding place and to be able to say that one had swum in it sounded very romantic indeed. It turned out to be a disaster. I was so badly stung by jellyfish that I spent the next two days in my bunk anointed and bandaged by the ship's doctor and well cared for by a fellow passanger who shared my cabin. By the time we docked in Miami I was able to get up and go ashore, but I didn't see much of Miami, because they were busy boarding it up in expectation of a hurricane. We pulled out that evening, but we couldn't outrun the hurricane, it caught up with us just north of Cape Hatteras.

By the time we got to New York we looked like a hospital ship. We were twelve hours late, and I had barely enough time to get my stuff across the pier to a White Star-Cunarder called the *Laconia,* on which I was ticketed. She was an eight-day boat to Liverpool, and, it being late in the year, was not fully booked. Even though I had only a second-class ticket, I had a cabin to myself. It was a pleasant voyage and on it I met a man who was to remain a good and lasting friend. His name was Arthur Baker and he was to become one of the most respected publishers in England. During the eight-day run to

Liverpool he gently extracted most of my miserere and my lack of immediate plans. The day before we landed he told me that he had a brother named Vere Baker who was a partner in a successful theatrical agency called Connie's Agency, in Regent Street. He suggested that I go in to see him as soon as possible and said that he would call ahead to say I would be coming in. Arhur became a wonderful friend, but it's a callous thing to say, I don't know today whether he'd alive or dead.

When I got to London I took a room in a small hotel called Oddenino's, right smack in the middle of Piccadilly Circus, for the equivalent of six dollars a night bed and breakfast. I stayed there for three days while I searched for something more permanent and possibly less expensive! And I found it—as a paying guest in a pension in Earl's Court, an establishment that could only have been devised by Albrecht Dürer.

Before moving in I spent a week in Wales with Luisa and seeing my father. It was not a very pleasant visit. I found my father more of a recluse, and Luisa seemed to have aged a lot in five years. But it was a backwater I needed. I did no riding, mainly because Bello had died the year before from a heart attack and I felt an idiot sense of loyalty. I walked and thought a lot, mostly along the banks of the Usk, watching the salmon swirl and hearing something I hadn't heard in my two years in America. The sound of church bells on a Sunday morning, so simple, so innocent. As long as I can remember that sound I will always be enraged by the obscene spectacles of the Reverend Ike, and Kathryn Kuhlman "(In Person)."

I didn't see my mother on this visit because she had remarried, this time to an art dealer in Cardiff. I didn't feel up to her bogus affections of respectability and her denigration of all things bucolic. So I returned to London and Earl's Court. God Help me.

Two days after my return to London I made an appointment to talk to the two partners of Connie's Agency—Miss Connie, and Vere Baker. After a very proper ten-minute wait I was shown into Baker's office first. He turned out to be totally unlike his brother Arthur, rather short and military with a fiercely up-brushed guardee moustache, a handkerchief tucked in his sleeve, and a West End manner, very chic indeed. I spent about ten minutes with him, during which he told me that his brother would be calling to invite me for the weekend to his place at Chessington, in Surrey. He took me to see Miss Connie, his partner. The moment I walked into her office I knew I had seen her before. Then I remembered, she had been the secretary-receptionist at the Dan Fish Agency two or three years before, and she remembered me. This time she had a hat on, a big black beaver affair with the brim turned up on one side rather like an Australian army hat. From that time on I don't think anyone ever saw her without it. It was her trademark.

They were both extremely nice. After a half hour's talk, it was agreed that they would act as my agents for one year. Then we went down to have a drink in the Café Royal, which was practically next door.

Arthur Baker's place turned out to be a sort of dower-house on his family's estate about twenty miles outside London, where he lived with his wife and two young children. Across the road from it was a large riding establishment, with stabling for about thirty or forty head. It was used mainly by members of the Mid-Surrey Drag Hunt, who boarded their horses there, most of which were pretty good stock. They also operated a riding school with a manège, and a field with about a dozen varied obstacles. The weekend I was there happened to be a sort of opening day, rather like the opening of the yachting season. As a matter of fact, with the amount of beer and port consumed that weekend they could have *floated* a good-sized yacht. Easy.

I *did* meet a most spectacular creature who turned

out to be a lifesaver. She was tall, with jet black hair and very light gray eyes. She was the epitome of chic, and, consequently, her manner was quite imperious. Her name was Doris Zinkeisen. She was a famous painter and theatrical designer, equally at ease whether hunting with the Pytchley or the Quorn or in some crapulous theatrical warehouse. She was married to the managing director of Johnny Walker whiskey and had two small children, both girls. At this time, however, I think the marriage had grown a little strained.

Her sister Anna was also a painter and equally acclaimed, but quite opposite in appearance. She was blond and blue-eyed and very calm. Her husband was Guy Heseltine, a director of Shell Oil, one of the few men I ever knew who wore a monocle because he needed it. They've remained my friends ever since. Except Guy; he's gone now.

My reason for telling you all this is that indirectly these people were the cause of my coming a cropper that damn near finished me physically. Doris had bought a new hunter, a big beast about six years old, seventeen hands, and with a mind of his own. For the time being, until she sent him up to Lincolnshire, she kept him at Chessington. Toward the end of October, I was spending a weekend at the Bakers' and Doris came down to work this beast over on a Sunday morning. She was putting him at some triple bars, but she was too gentle with him and he kept refusing. So I asked her, very diffidently, remembering her volcanic capabilities, if she would mind my trying him. With a stare of pure ice that seemed to last for five minutes she finally dismounted and I got aboard in a hurry, not even stopping to adjust the stirrups. The last thing I remember saying was "You've got to let him know who's in charge." As I walked him away from her I heard a long-drawn-out "Really?"

I shoved him up to his bit and gave him a few good belts to get his attention. I manhandled him around the perimeter, walked him up to the triple

bar, and let him look at it, then I hauled him around
and put him at it. He went over like a bird and came
around on the other rein as docile as you please.
I put him at it again, only this time I could feel him
bunch up. He took off a stride too soon and hit the
top bar, which got me on the inside of my left thigh
as I was leaving him. And that's all I remember until
I woke up in Arthur Barker's best bedroom with
three worried faces staring down at me. Doris, Arthur,
and a man who turned out to be a local doctor. And
a blinding headache coupled with a horrible pain
in my thigh.

I spent a week in the local hospital and three weeks
in bed at my digs in Earl's Court with a slight concussion and the muscles and sinews in my left leg pretty
badly torn from knee to groin. I woke up on Christmas
morning to the knowledge that I was flat broke. At
least I could walk.

Mentally I was at a very low ebb, and if it hadn't
been for Doris' kindness and concern, I think I might
have gone out of the window on more than one occasion. She not only phoned every day, but several
times sent her car to take me out for a drive. Eighteen
Lexham Gardens, Earl's Court, S.W. Let me tell you
about it.

During the later years of Victoria's reign it was
a rather fashionable and elegant residential area, but
by the time I forced to live there it had deteriorated
into the shabby gentility of ladies of quality in reduced circumstances taking in "paying guests." The
particular house in which I found myself immured
had eleven other guests. All women and only one
of them under sixty—she was fifty-five and afflicted
with acute flatulence. The house was run by the Misses
Gibbs, three fading spinsters who had been brought
up in Inja. But we inmates saw only two. The third
one was kept locked up in an attic on the fourth floor,
not mad, mind you, just eccentric. I paid the equivalent of eighteen dollars a week, for room and board.
My quarters consisted of a converted boxroom on

the third floor with a single bed, a washstand, a small chest of drawers, a chair, and a length of bedraggled cretonne, nailed to the wall, under which I hung my clothes. The bathroom was on the floor below. Three meals a day were served. At lunch and dinner it was de rigueur for everyone to be seated at the huge mahogany dining table and be served at the same time by a catarrhal slattern named Brenda, who was the parlor maid. The meals consisted of a *thin* soup, a fish course, a nameless entree, dessert, and then cheese. Better cheese could be found in a rattrap.

Breakfast, however, was something else. That meal you could eat alone, provided that it was not later than eight-thirty. The fact that I ate breakfast alone for the three months I endured there would not surprise you if you could see the meal. There was an urn of tea on the sideboard which was pure tannic acid and a large tureen of what appeared to be suppurating cat food. It was a concoction called kedgeree, very popular in Inja, and as far as I could make out was made up of all the abandoned kippers in the neighborhood cunningly seasoned with chopped-up rubber Wellingtons. The whole thing was immersed in a gray bubbling paste. When people tell me I'll surely go to hell when I die, I just laugh at them. I've already been there. It's in Earl's Court.

There we sat, all twelve of us, living lives of quiet desperation. There was one telephone in the house, downstairs in the front hall, and whenever I got a call, which was rare, every one of the old ladies would come out onto the landing in front of her room and listen, and then would rustle back when I had finished. One day just after lunch I received a telephone call from Doris, who wanted to know if I felt like going with her to an odd sort of musicale the next afternoon. Needless to say, every crone in the house knew it and began speculating on what sort of an assignation it would really turn out to be, since Doris, who had once visited me there when I was ill and bedridden, had the sinful quality of being both beautiful and affluent.

The next day Doris, in pure Zinkeisen style, picked me up in her Hispano-Suiza landau, the kind of car in which the chauffeur sits out in front in the wind and rain. As I got in and we pulled away from the curb, I could feel my back being skewered by eleven pairs of whispering eyes. We got out at a recital hall in Bond Street, where we were to hear a new experiment in music. The Victor Recording Company had just succeeded in taking the voice of Caruso off an old recording and re-recording it with new orchestration. It was an aria from the opera *Lucia di Lammermoor,* which in the original is counterpointed by a soprano, As we took our seats I looked around at the other guests, of which there were perhaps two hundred. With one or two exceptions they were quite mature, even elderly, but all of them were obviously there with more purpose than I. After a few explanatory words from the man who had arranged the afternoon, the music started. The first record they played was just the voice of the castrato Caffarelli in something from *Norma.* Then they played a recording of only the orchestration, which was followed by an explanation of how it was done.

The next item was the recording of Caruso together with the modern orchestration on one disk. I was too young to have heard Caruso sing and had never quite believed all the things said about him. The past is full of superlatives, according to one's parents. And who is to prove them right? But on this afternoon they were vindicated. I will not attempt to describe his voice and musicianship, it has been done many times before by professionals. But as I sat there I was entranced. Suddenly, I heard someone quietly crying. I stole a look to my left, and there, two seats away, was a tiny lady who appeared to be in her sixties, sitting with her head up and her eyes closed, her face wet with tears. At that moment the voice of Caruso stopped and the orchestra gently slid into the soprano's part of the duet. As I bent down to wipe a tear of my own, the hall was suddenly electrified by a woman's lovely coloratura, singing from the audience, the part the recorded orchestra was playing. It was the little woman two seats away. Then back came Caruso's voice—and there we had it, the duet sung by a giant long dead and a little old lady in a recital hall. In the ecstatic hush that followed I heard something in wonder whisper her name. It was Luisa Tetrazzini.

Early in 1933 Connie finally came up with a couple of movie jobs. By the time I finished both pictures I felt very flush indeed, with over two hundred and fifty pounds in the bank. But England was beginning to pall and I was longing to see my wife. I missed the sunshine and the sea, the fresh orange juice and the decent laundries, all the things Americans take for granted. I began planning the quickest and most economical way to return.

Then Roosevelt closed the banks and everybody panicked. I went down to American Express in the Haymarket to see if there was any mail from my wife the following day, and the place was absolute bedlam, with the ubiquitous American tourists milling around in complete bewilderment, some of them even crying, quite unmanned, and dollars selling on the sidewalk twenty to the pound. I mean, this just *can't* be happening to the land of Lincoln! To Peoria and Chicago, to Denver and Council Bluffs, not to mention Taft, California. I tell you, Roosevelt was not popular that day, and I could only think of the Wailing Wall. I stood on the side of the curb watching them and my eye was taken by a young fellow with reddish hair, leaning on a bicycle that had a large hiking kit strapped on the back. He was staring down at the pavement with a look more sorrowful than apprehensive and I had a feeling I had seen him somewhere.

I stepped over to him and said, "Hello. Haven't I met you before?"

He looked up at me for a few moments and then he said, "Yes, I think so. Yes, of course. It was at the MGM studios sometime last year. I had just graduated from Stanford and was down there for a look around. You live here?"

"Yes," I said, "for the time being. Looks as if you're all in a jam for a while."

"Seems that way," he replied. "But I'm afraid my problem is a little more urgent than most. An emergency. A family one." He said his name was Delmer Daves and that he had been on a cycling tour of Europe. When he got to London, the day before, he had found a cable at the American Express, telling him that his father was seriously ill and to return home as quickly as possible. He had plenty of money, or what used to be money two days before. However, he couldn't buy a ticket home until the dollar situation had resolved itself, and he couldn't wait.

Now, to anyone who had lived in America it was inconceivable that the fiscal situation could be anything but just temporary. Within a couple of weeks things would surely be back to normal. I did some hasty mental mathematics and figured that I could sell him about fifty pounds, which was the amount he said it would take to get him back home. We went immediately to my bank, which was at Oxford and Berners streets, where I cashed a check for fifty pounds and got from him a check for five hundred dollars. I made a few token remonstrances about it being too much, but I only spent about five seconds on that. After all, he said, he would have had to pay at least 50 percent more on the street. With great earnestness I agreed, and away he went. He made it all right, because he now lives in a mansion just down the road from me, has an enviable reputation as a writer-director, and the red hair has turned to white.

Three weeks later I cashed his check for a little

over eighty pounds, which meant that I had made a profit of a thousand miles nearer to my wife. Over the next week I did a lot of soul-searching and made the decision to go back to California. For three days I shopped around for the most inexpensive way to do it and came up with the following: a second-class ticket on the *Europa* sailing from Southampton for New York, a second-class ticket on a Panama-Pacific boat through the Panama Canal to Los Angeles. It was actually cheaper than taking the train from New York, when one considered porters, taxis, and meals. Besides, I'd get to see Havana and Panama.

chapter xi

Early in August, after one more picture I set out for California once again, only this time I had purpose, and there were overtones of the young Lochinvar, of Pizarro conquering Peru, and the slightest touch of trepidation. I stuck to my original travel plan and bought a second-class ticket on the *Europa* and a second-class ticket on the *Pennsylvania* through the Panama Canal to Los Angeles. But it was a queer crossing to New York: there were only thirty-five passengers in second class and barely thirty in first. When you consider that the *Europa* was the newest and most modern of the Atlantic greyhounds, designed to carry a thousand passengers, you can understand why it was an odd sort of crossing. To begin with, the time was the depth of the great American Depression, to which I hadn't given the slightest thought. But that wasn't the only reason. It was because Hitler had just come into real power and his saber rattling and police-state repressions were beginning to worry the world. What we were experiencing on the *Europa* was an unspoken boycott of all things German, she being a North-German-Lloyd vessel. We had the run of the boat and the most marvelous food I'd ever eaten, but still, it was an odd crossing.

We docked at 11 A.M. and by five o'clock the

same afternoon I was headed back down the bay on the *Pennsylvania*. It was very hot, but Havana three days later was hotter. Not just because of the weather, but also because they were having a minor insurrection put on by the students of the university and the city was swarming with trigger-happy militia. I bolted into Sloppy Joe's Bar, where half the passenger list seemed to be gathered, and we stayed there until sailing time, which was at midnight. Three days later, Panama and the Canal. And what a wonderful achievement it is, even more wonderful when you consider how primitive the area was, the heat and the exotic diseases that had to be endured, the technological equipment available at the turn of the century which, by present-day standards, would be thought archaic. I think of it as the eighth wonder of the world, or more properly, the second, the Pyramids always being first.

I rented a car with two middle-aged married couples, and we backtracked all the way to Colón on the Atlantic. It was only forty miles but it seemed like eighty, there was so much to see. We came back filled with thoughts of Goethals and de Lesseps and Walter Reed, only to be met by the licentious chucklings of the other passengers, who had apparently spent the day in the cathouses of the Coconut Grove area, the red-light capital of Central America. I made some mental notes and we sailed at midnight. The run north took seven days and was quite uneventful except for one wondrous night when the sea was like glass and I saw the moon reflected in it without a path. Just the full moon looking like a twenty-dollar gold piece. I've never seen it like that since, but there's still time.

When at last we docked at San Pedro I made arrangements to pick up my trunk as soon as I could find living quarters that would be more or less permanent. Then I hopped the bus to Hollywood with the L.A. *Times* under my arm and started perusing the apartment ads. After much deciphering I found what I thought was something suitable. "Furn. bach. All uts. Wkl. md.s. El. $25. Orange Grove Apts. Suns. & Fairfax." The location was perfect, so I went to see it, and it wasn't too bad. It was on the top floor of a five-story building now called the "San Ramon" on the south side of Sunset and fifty yards from Fairfax. It consisted of a sitting room, small bathroom, and tiny dressing room, and a folding Murphy bed that came out of the wall. I took it on the spot, arranged to have the phone hooked up, and then set off to find some sort of car. I found one, a Model A Ford coupe that had once belonged to Buster Crabbe. A real rattler, but it was only fifty dollars down and fifteen dollars a month. At that time, in the Depression, they were glad to sell anything. Then I drove back to the apartment and sat down and counted my money. I had a hundred and sixty dollars left. So I pulled down the bed and went to sleep.

I got up early the next morning and walked the two and a half blocks to the Laurel Drugstore, at the corner of Sunset and Laurel, which was run by a very decent chap named Joe Halff and frequented by most of the unemployed actors who didn't patronize Schwab's across the street. At that time Schwab's had not had the benefit of Sidney Skolsky's gossipy blatherings, although John Carradine had been known to grace Schwab's with his presence when Joe Halff periodically cut off his credit. Fifteen cents in those days bought you a huge slice of apple pie and coffee. Refills were free, and I think that is as good a breakfast as any. The farinaceous requirements of the body are taken care of by the crust and for fruit you've got the apples. Besides, it tastes good.

After breakfast I shut myself up in the phone booth and started calling around trying to find an agent. It's a strange thing about Hollywood, it's sometimes easier to get a job than to get an agent, very uppity they are. After three days of trying I finally found a couple who condescended to handle me. Their names were Bernard and Meiklejohn. The only trouble was their office was located in the Orpheum Theatre Build-

ing, way down in Los Angeles. I had known Meiklejohn
before but I had never met Bernard. He turned out
to be a very quiet and likable fellow and strangely
enough, quite shy, a quality which, when found in
an agent, is absolutely hilarious. I became slightly
apprehensive, however, when I looked at the photographs scattered around the walls of their office. "Rae
Samuels, the Blue Streak of Vaudeville." There was
one of "Routledge and Taylor," also a group shot
of a bunch of seals wearing beanies, acrobats, jugglers,
and a gorgeous shot of an aging Shakespearean thespian made up as Shylock. His name was Keane. I
think he stuck on the extra *e* so that people wouldn't
confuse him with the original.

Needless to say the weeks went by and nothing
happened. In the meantime I saw Mal once or twice
a week, and we talked on the phone every day. We
also agreed not to set up housekeeping again until
I had three thousand dollars in the bank and an honest
job. But the way the Depression kept hanging on
it was going to be a long haul.

Time kept slipping by until one morning I awakened
to find myself flat broke again, so I trudged up to
the drugstore and had a little chat with Joe Halff,
the outcome being that he would let me have one
full meal a day "on the cuff." It could be either lunch
or dinner but not both. I managed to pick up eight
or ten dollars a week in the back room of the cleaning
establishment that was just two doors away. It was
a well-camouflaged horse parlor, which in those days
was very illicit. It had a half dozen phones installed,
two of which were direct lines to Eastern racetracks
and were attended by two very wide women who
called the races as they came over the lines from
some central clearinghouse. The room usually had
eight or nine horse players, who lounged around with
racing forms and intricate betting systems. On a very
busy Saturday one of the women didn't show up and
"Schlemmy" the boss asked me if I would help out
by calling a few of the races. I must have done a

creditable job because he kept me on until four o'clock, when the lines closed down. He slipped me five dollars and made me official relief caller.

As my car had been repossessed a couple of weeks earlier, it became extremely difficult for me to run around trying to find an "honest" job of some kind. I did make the effort, though, even to taking the bus down to the main offices of the Shell Oil Company in downtown Los Angeles. I thought that if I threw around the name of Guy Heseltine, Doris Zinkeisen's brother-in-law and a director of the company, something might surface and by God, something did. One Friday morning I got a phone call from a Mr. Beynon, asking me if I could drop by the Shell offices before ten o'clock that morning for an interview. *Could I?* I put on my best blue suit, hopped on a bus, and was there on the dot. Fifteen minutes later I was hired on a trial basis as assistant manager of a Shell station at Sunset and Clark, salary $27.50 a week, to report at seven A.M. Monday morning. As I waited for the bus to take me back to Hollywood, roseate dreams of myself as a future captain of industry began to float through my mind. Trouble-shooting trips to Arabia, concession intrigues in Venezuela, going to the mat with Sir Basil Zaharoff and Gulbenkian. Oh, yes, things were looking up. Then the bus came and I hopped on, only to find that I had one dime in my pocket, which meant that I would have to get off at Van Ness and Melrose and walk the other three miles home. But I wouldn't have cared if it had been thirty.

Four blocks beyond where I got off stood the gates of Paramount Pictures, the best studio in town. As I came abreast of the Log Cabin Coffee Shop, a hundred feet from the gate, the casting director, Joe Egli, walked toward me, stopped, and crooked his finger. "Just a minute," he said. "You're just the guy I'm looking for." Over the past three or four months I had come into contact with Egli several times in my futile search for a job, and he had always been decent.

Feeling very large, I said, "Yes, Joe. What can I do for you?"

He replied that they had run into a problem that morning on a picture called *Bolero* with an English actor who had just been stabbed by his boyfriend the night before. Egli thought I would be an ideal replacement, so would I come on the set and meet the director. What could I lose? So in I went.

The casting director took me to Stage Five and told me to wait just inside the door while he went over and talked to the director, who was sitting in a chair looking very morose. After a few minutes of conversation that I couldn't hear the director, who was Wesley Ruggles, turned and cased me from head to foot. Beckoning me, he asked, "Can you play an Englishman?"

"Yes, sir," I replied, "I am English." As I said it I could feel Aunt Luisa writhe.

Ruggles looked at me for a few seconds more, said, "Okay, Joe. I'll take a chance," and with a very defeated demeanor, turned away.

Back to the casting office went Egli and I. When we got there Joe turned to me and said, "How much? There's a two-week guarantee and the budget says three hundred a week and that's it, so don't get any ideas."

"Weeell," I said, "I've never worked for Paramount before, so just this once I won't argue. When do I start?"

He said, "Monday morning. Here's the script and the scene numbers for Monday. It calls for white tie and tails, which I know you have. Then go up to makeup and have Wally Westmore fit you with a moustache before you leave. Your call will be nine A.M., and good luck."

I shot up to the makeup department, where Wally fitted me with a fierce military moustache, because I was to portray a British army officer, fiancé to Carole Lombard, who was playing a dancer. As soon as the moustache was finished I asked if I could use the phone to call my agent. Sure. I got Meiklejohn and told him that I had landed a fat part at Paramount and that I had no way of getting home. Could he come and pick me up, because I didn't have a dime.

"Hell," he said, "I can't pick you up. They repossessed my car two days ago. What sort of a deal did you make?"

"Two-week guarantee, three hundred a week starting Monday," I said.

"Goddammit," said Meiklejohn, "you should have demanded three fifty."

I hung up and decided to call Joe Halff. I just couldn't let anybody know I was flat. When I got him I told him the wonderful news and explained my predicament. He didn't waste a second.

"I'll have the wife look after the store and I'll pick you up at the De Mille gate in half an hour. Wait for me."

That night the Halffs put on a little celebration dinner for the regulars and I can still taste it. It was hasenpfeffer and delicious. One guy volunteered to drive me to the studio every morning, I think it was John Carroll, only his name at that time was Julian La Faye. Then John Carradine wanted to know if my wardrobe was all in order, if there was any little thing of his I would like to borrow.

"There is one thing," I said. "I don't have any dress gloves and I may need them on Monday."

"Don't give it another thought, dear boy," said Carradine. "I have them in all colors." And that's the way it went: no envy, no petty jealousies, one of the shirtless ones had got a job.

Outside of a very daring experiment, at least for those days on the Hollywood screen, a mighty explosion between George Raft and the producer, and my irritating self-consciousness, the picture went along quite smoothly. The daring experiment was the first nude dancer to be seen by the general public in a Hollywood film. Today, the scene would be laughed off the screen. It was Sally Rand and her famous fan dance, and everybody on the lot piled into Stage Five to watch it, including some characters who made it over the wall from RKO. I was sitting at a ringside table and never felt a twinge. Perhaps it was because my table companion was Carole Lombard, a smashing girl, a true original and a hell of an actress. When she was annoyed, her language was that of a stevedore. She loved practical jokes and could tell a bawdy story with the best of them. In any company, her taste was impeccable. A far cry from today's crop of beaded beatniks. They're so nauseatingly *natural,* so bloody earnest, so dull. Ah, well.

The other thing, the blowup, happened ten days before I was due to finish and was responsible for my getting an extra week's salary. Nothing to do with me, but it caused a switch in the schedule which delayed my finish just enough to get me an extra three hundred dollars. My call was for eleven A.M., and just as I got on the set a hell of an argument started between the producer, Barney Glaser, and George Raft. I have known George for forty years and I have always found him to be a kind man, a taciturn sentimentalist, and a true romantic, though he has spent a lifetime hiding it. At one point in the script there was a scene where he was supposed to stand over his mother's grave and swear on her body that he would or would not do something, I've forgotten exactly what it was. George's mother was still alive and he idolized her. He refused point-blank to utter such an oath, even though it *was* in a picture, and no goddam producer was going to make him. This argument had been going on all morning and finally Glaser blew his stack and said that Raft was going to play that scene even if it meant staying on the set all day and all night. At that, George hauled off and hit him right in the nose. Glaser hit the deck, and Raft headed for the door, and we were excused for the day. Hitting a producer in those days was like biting the left hand of God. Needless to say, the eventual peacemaker was Carole. The director, Wesley Ruggles, just looked amused. It was one of the few times I ever saw him smile. We finished the picture on the morning of Christmas Eve, 1933, and Carole threw a party for the cast in her dressing room at midday. When I got there one of the first things I saw was Glaser and Raft with their arms around each other and tears in their eyes, swearing eternal friendship. I thought they were stoned until I remembered that Raft didn't drink and never had, and right then I saw through his shell.

There's one thing I forgot to mention. On the day I got the part I called up Mr. Beynon of Shell Oil and told him that I had broken my ankle getting off the bus and would he hold the job at the Shell station for a month. He said he would. I figured that if I flopped in the picture I'd still have something to fall back on. No use burning one's bridges. But I needn't have worried, I remained at Paramount for twenty-one years.

By the time I had paid my agent and my debts, I had four hundred and forty dollars left and a lot of caution. My debt to Joe Halff can never be repaid. I am ashamed to say that I haven't seen him in twenty years, although I am aware that he lives somewhere in Palm Springs. I rarely go to the place, because to me it's like visiting one of those horrifying Leisure Worlds, filled with people who smoke cigars and wear plastic belts and perforated shoes. But if I'm to look him up, I'd better hurry. He's about seven years older than I am.

A week after I had finished *Bolero* I had to go back to the studio for a day of retakes because in one sequence William Frawley, who played Raft's agent, could be seen in the bedroom slippers he always wore between scenes. He said his mother had given them to him twenty years before, and you could well believe it. They were pretty scruffy. Quite a character, Frawley. He had been a well-known Broadway actor when MGM brought him out to California to play in a picture to be produced by Harry Rapf. Upon his arrival he was immediately ushered into Rapf's offices, where several of the studio executives were gathered discussing the imminent production, which was to be quite a big project. He was seated facing all six of them, and then Rapf started.

"Mr. Frawley, you're new out here. We'd like to know something of your background, what experience you've had. Also give us a rundown on the parts you've played."

The rather sparse hair on Frawley's neck began to rise like a grouse's ruff, but he calmed himself and began reeling off his credits, which were considerable.

When he had finished there was a silence and then one of the executives, I think it was Eddie Mannix, said, "We were figuring on somebody with more hair."

At that, Frawley's cork went, and he stood up and roared with quite some choler, "If it's hair you want, hire a fucking lion!" And then stalked out in high dudgeon. I don't think he ever did work for MGM.

As I was leaving the set that day, having finished my stint in the retakes, I bumped into Barney Glaser, who said, "Hey, you read lines pretty good! Look, I'm starting a new picture in two weeks with Crosby and Lombard called *We're Not Dressing*. There's a part in it that'll be right up your alley. A Russian pimp. You wanna do it? Take about five weeks."

I told him I felt very flattered and thanked him profusely, whereupon he told me to get my ass over to the casting office and see Joe Egli, which I did. I ended up with a five-week guarantee at the same three hundred dollars a week. I saw no point in trying to squeeze a little more; they might think I was a little grasping. Besides, I was still eating at Joe Halff's drugstore, and the sight of so many out-of-work actors made me feel very grateful. The film took seven weeks and had the damnedest cast ever assembled outside of *Dinner at Eight*, Bing Crosby, Carole Lombard,

Ethel Merman, Burns and Allen, Leon Erroll, Bob Burns, a six-foot bear who could roller-skate, and Jimmy Dorsey's band.

Three things happened on that picture which will bear mentioning, and the first shall be the least. We were on location at Catalina Island for two weeks and the entire company was staying at the Saint Catherine Hotel. For some reason, possibly virginal, Merman had her mother with her. After dinner, and because it was out of season, the only activity left to us was bridge, the usual foursome being Merman, Leon Errol, myself, and a hyperthyroid hairdresser named Nellie. It was like trying to swim in an empty pool. We played for a twentieth of a cent a point, real swingers. At the end of two weeks Merman owed me six dollars and twenty cents, and when I somewhat diffidently mentioned it she told me to see her mother, a hopeless prospect. One might have been more expectant of mercy from Madame La Farge. It's been forty years now, Merman, but I'll never forget! You hear me, Ethel? Six dollars and twenty cents!

The second incident was a tragic one. A great deal of the picture was supposed to take place on an ocean liner. There were several scenes in which the passengers got their exercise walking around the promenade deck, while the bear went around on roller skates. Each night the trainer would ask the assistant director to be sure that no women for whom it was the wrong time of the month would appear on the set the following day. Appearently one of the dress-extra girls lied. I suppose she did not want to lose a day's work. When we got on the set the next morning the bear was acting a little salty and the trainer was very nervous. Sure enough, about eleven o'clock, when the bear was doing his skating stint around the deck, he made a grab for the girl and the trainer made a grab for him and everybody ran screaming. It was almost five minutes before the trainer could be separated from the bear through the efforts of his two helpers and their wonderful Alsatian. By that time the poor man was a mess and had to be rushed to the hospital. Ten days later he died. There was no more work for that day, and I made a mental note never to work with wild animals. Haw! Little did I suspect.

It was a week before the picture finished, and I happened to be doing a scene with George Burns and Gracie Allen. Suddenly the script went right out the window and the scene became an ad-lib shambles, much better than the original. When it was over, the director, Norman Taurog, a delightful man, said to me, "I think this studio should put you under contract. I'm going to call the front office and tell them so. That okay with you? Even if nothing comes of it, my call won't do any harm."

And he went right to the wall phone and did it. Three minutes later he came back and told me I was to go to the front office and see the chief production executive, at that time a man named Al Kaufman. I tried to thank him but I'm afraid I was quite tongue-tied.

"Ah," he said, "maybe nothing will come of it. But if something does, do your best. I'll be watching you." Then he waddled away and I suddenly wanted to go somewhere and cry. There's so much kindness.

At four o'clock I was through for the day and without removing my makeup, I beetled down to the main executive offices and presented myself to the secretary of Mr. Albert Kaufman. After a twenty-minute wait I was shown into his office. I saw a smallish man with the mournful charm of a coonhound. I was nervous and he could see it. "Sit down, son, sorry to have kept you waiting but I'm having a little trouble with this Polish canary we've got, Kiepura. Y'ever met him? No matter, you haven't missed a thing. Like a drink? No? Well, I never do myself until six o'clock, but it must be almost that in Phoenix so I think I'll mix one. You just sit there and tell me about yourself. By the way, you're not Czech, are you?"

"No, sir, Welsh."

"Well," he said, "that's not too bad. I used to

manage a Welsh singer once—Madame Clara Novello Davies. Not a bad broad, good singer, but she had kind of a flighty son. Come to think of it, he looked a little like you. But don't let me stop you. Go right ahead."

All this in a deep and soporific bass, which was very calming. I wondered whether he knew that the flighty son of his long-ago client had now become one of Britain's biggest stars, the darling of the gods in the upper balconies, Ivor Novello? Probably not.

I was very frank with my little saga and when I finished he slowly made himself another drink and stared out the window. Then he said, "Tell you what I'll do. We'll sign you to a seven-year contract with options. The first two will be six months each, the other six will be one year each. Starting salary for the first period will be one hundred seventy-five a week, with appropriate raises with every option picked up."

"But Mr. Kaufman, I'm already getting three hundred dollars a week for the picture I'm doing now!"

He eyed me for a few moments with an air of gentle suffering and then said, "That's just a one shot, my boy. It may be six months before you get another. This way the money comes in every week. But I'll tell you what I'll do. For the first two periods I'll make them a straight twenty-four weeks each, no layoffs. Okay?"

You bet your ass it was okay! Most contracts in those days were for forty weeks out of fifty-two. After he told me that the contract would be ready for signing in the legal department on Friday, we shook hands and I left. I couldn't wait to get to a phone.

It took me ten days to convince Mal that a contract with Paramount was a hell of a lot more attractive than three thousand dollars in the bank and an "honest" job, that I had the world in my hand, anything was possible. So what if Paramount *was* selling for 2¼. The whole country was in the depths of a depression

and had only one place to go, up! Goddammit, sweetheart, as a nation it's barely a hundred and sixty
years old! Why, the house I was born in was old
before this continent was even thought to exist. It's
just been the victim of its own exuberance. Please,
honey?

Afer a few hours of this she sighed and said, "All
right, but call that Beynon and tell him the truth."
What a performance! I was proud of myself and
deliriously happy. One week later we were ensconced
in a little duplex in an apartment building called "Les
Maisonnettes" on Fountain, three blocks from her
family home. It was run by a dropsical Jewish woman
named Mrs. Karp. We furnished the whole place out
of Barker Brothers' basement for four hundred dollars.
And then everything slowed down to a crawl. Unless
you were a very high-priced contract player you were
ignored, sort of relegated to a grab bag of reserves,
to be used only in case of an emergency, practically
forgotten. You still had to get out and make a name
for yourself before they'd notice you, even though
they were paying you every week. It was a very con-
stricting situation, the fact that you were tied to one
studio. I did one or two inconsequential things in a
couple of forgettable pictures before my restlessness
began to become a problem.

My makeup is such that I have to be busy. I must
always have a project of some sort going. During
my last year in the army I had taken flying instruction
at a semimilitary club sponsored in part by the Brigade
of Guards, and for a nominal fee I learned to fly.
When I think now of the equipment then in use, I
shudder. I soloed in one of the first Gypsy Moths
ever built. It looked as if it had been pasted together
from discarded stamp albums, powered with a Brough-
Superior motorcycle engine stuck on the nose. Top
speed a bare forty knots. But oh, the sense of peace
when you were up there, the lonely sky!

One morning, without consciously thinking of it,
I found myself out at Mines Field, now Los Angeles

International Airport, and within an hour I had signed up for enough hours to get my private license. The plane I used was a Kinner Fleet, a two-place open biplane with a top speed of a hundred m.p.h. and a ceiling of about ten thousand feet. In helmet, goggles, and a scarf made from white parachute silk, I'd head out over the Pacific until I got to peak altitude, cut back the engine to idling, and do a series of 1,080 spirals and just dream. Ah, Snoopy, I'm with you every morning. Then after a few mild aerobatics I'd head back to the field very content. But because of the gang in the coffee shop who watched every landing, hoping for at least a ground loop, I never made a normal run-of-the-mill landing. No, sir, not this kid. I chose to come in losing height rapidly in one long side-slip, so that when I touched down my speed was less than thirty miles an hour. Then I'd turn and taxi up to the apron and stroll into the coffee shop just the tiniest bit bored. One thing amateur flyers have in common with skiers and fishermen and yachtsmen is their love of gab. No fish is ever caught easily, no cruise is ever made without some horrendous hazard, and no flight is ever made without some lousy maintenance man's having forgotten *some*thing. The bunch at Mines Field were no different. Matter of fact, I think a lot of them kept on flying just to be able to get back in the canteen and talk about it.

Only one thing would stop the gab instantly and that was the sound of an engine missing. When that happened everybody made a dash for the apron and avidly watched the approaching ruptured duck. Junior Birdmen. One day it was my turn to bring a little joy into their lives. I had been out over the sea lollygagging around not watching the clock, when I saw the fog bank silently creeping in from Catalina. I quickly turned for the field. As I came over the beach at El Segundo I got the first cough, and when I came into the pattern I got five or six more. Before I could get to the point for my final turn the engine quit and

I was faced with a dead engine and very little room to run. Nothing for it but to do a little fancy side-slipping, my one proficiency, and land like a gooney bird. I did. I must have looked like a female hurdler because my under-carriage collapsed and spread from left to right and I sat there like a tired whore. Out came the fire engine and the gang from the coffee shop. At least nine guys helped me out of the cockpit and damn near broke my arm doing it. I kept yelling, "I'm okay! I'm okay!" But it was no use, they wouldn't be denied. With just the slightest touch of imagination one could see Buddy Rogers and Richard Arlen pulling the young replacement from a burning Sopwith. *So* much concern! But what the hell! So long as they were happy.

I got home about five-thirty to be greeted by an excited yell from upstairs. "Darling," Mal said, "there was a phone call a half hour ago from the studio. You're to call a Mr. Hackensack at Universal Studios because Paramount has loaned you out to them for a wonderful part that has to start right away. I called you at the airfield, but you had already left—go on, call, call, call!"

By this time she was shaking me and pointing to the telephone, her mouth half open, breathing quickly, and her eyes, God, I can't describe them. Normally, my wife is a tall, elegant woman, quietly humorous and absolutely stunning to look at. But at this moment she was a seven-year-old child on Christmas morning. I held her tight.

After a while I called Universal and asked to speak to Mr. Hackensack. The operator came back and said, "Hackensack? Nobody here by that name. What department?"

I explained the situation and said that I thought he must be a producer.

"Ah," she said, "you must mean Joe Pasternak. Just a moment."

And indeed, that's who it turned out to be. He asked if I could get out there right away; he would wait for me. It was six-thirty by the time I got out there. I was shown immediately into his office. Two men were in there and they both inspected me without saying a word. Then the little one asked me to sit down and introduced himself as Pasternak, Joseph. The other one, taller and younger, was the director, Henry Koster. After a few more moments of inspection they broke into an animated conversation in a language so odd that it could only be Hungarian. Then with great charm they proceeded to explain that they had engaged an actor two weeks earlier in New York and he hadn't been seen or heard from since. Just disappeared. Someone at Paramount had suggested me as a suitable replacement. They gave me a rundown of the script and described the part I would play in it.

Have you ever heard two Hungarians describing a play and acting it out? No? Then you've really missed something. Pasternak doing Alice Brady had me almost strangling, and the spectacle of Koster playing Charles Winninger was the most hilarious thing I'd ever seen. But the topper came when Pasternak and Koster together played a scene between Mischa Auer and Deanna Durbin having a music lesson, all done with their atrocious Hungarian accents, which had me absolutely on the floor. Compared to them the Gabor sisters are Vassar graduates. Then they turned to me and said, "You like it, huh?"

I gasped, "Yes, yes. When do I start?"

"Tomorrow morning," replied Koster. "First thing, in smoking jacket. You have one?"

"Yes," I said. "But tell me one thing. What is the name of the actor I'm replacing?"

And in unison they told me. "Louis Hayward, an Englishman." I left.

At that time, Universal was in pretty bad shape financially, as were a few others, and they were trying desperately to prune their payroll. The picture Pasternak was making was sort of a catchall for a bunch of their players whose contracts were coming to an end—Alice Brady, Charley Winninger, Mischa Auer, Deanna Durbin, even Pasternak himself. The studio's intention was to get one more picture out of them before they left the lot. I think Universal's troubles stemmed mainly from nepotism, with which it was riddled. Sometimes, walking around the lot, I found it easy to imagine myself in Mittel Europa; English seemed to be a foreign tongue. So much brown-nosed incompetence. But that's the way "Uncle Carl Laemmle" was, a kindly man.

On our little picture everything went swimmingly, except that the hours were appalling. It was a time before the Screen Actors Guild was even thought of, and to shoot until two or three in the morning was not unusual. I remember one time we were working in the old *Phantom of the Opera* set, where Deanna, at that time about fourteen years old, was supposed to be making her debut for charity. She had finished her aria and had been sent home at midnight. Then the cameras were set up on the stage to film a series of reaction shots of the audience. At three A.M. the cameraman conked out. We were dismissed and told to be ready on the set at nine A.M. next morning to carry on from where we'd left off. I climbed down from the box where I had been resplendently seated for almost eighteen hours in white tie and tails, and without stopping to change, got in my car and drove home. The next morning I was fifteen minutes late getting to the set, and I honestly believe it was the only time I have been late in the forty-three years I've been in this profession. When I got to the stage I sneaked up the back stairs, eased into the box without anyone's seeing me, and took my seat. The audience of dress extras were all in place quietly whispering, the cameras all on stage and ready, and the director and his assistants walking up and down looking at their watches. Suddenly, the first assistant director, I think his name was Art Black, looked up and saw me sitting in the box all very innocent. He turned to the director and said, "There the bastard is now!"

"Where?" asked Koster.

"Up in the box" said Black.

Then Koster, "Ray, darling, where were you? We have been waiting."

"Well, Mr. Koster," I replied, "it was almost four o'clock by the time I got home this morning. I was so tired I didn't stop to change my clothes, and consequently when I got to my house I found I had no key. So in order to get in I had to knock up my wife."

At that the three hundred extras exploded and kept on cackling for several minutes. I demanded to know what was so funny, since what I had said was the truth. Art Black promised that if I was real good he would tell me at lunch time. The faint professional resentment that all extras seem to feel toward members of the speaking cast quite disappeared and from then on I was accepted.

(Note to young Britons coming to the United States for the first time: Watch the colloquialisms, they tend to have an entirely different meaning, usually salacious.)

Ordinarily it takes three to six months after completion before a picture hits the screen, but *Three Smart Girls,* which this one was called, had its first showing within sixty days because of Universal's need of ready cash. The reviews were ecstatic and the picture turned out to be a blockbuster. Universal was back in the chips. The cast members' options were picked up, Pasternak and Koster were the golden boys of Lankershim Boulevard, and a little of the glow even fell upon me. But during the sixty-day hiatus I had done two inconsequential parts for Paramount, who assigned me to help in a series of tests designed to find a new girl to play in a comtemplated picture called *The Jungle Princess.* In all, they tested about a dozen girls and I appeared with every one. Not much of me I admit, mainly the back of my head and an occasional eye and tip of my nose. Finally they picked up a smashing young girl, whose figure lent itself beautifully to a sarong and who had long brown hair that hung below her waist. She was a singer with Herbie Kay's dance band and quite unknown in Hollywood, and I thought easily the best of the bunch tested. She also had a good sense of humor and all the courage in the world, which, by God, she was going to need.

Now, the question arose, where were they going to find a suitable leading man? We'll make some tests they said.

Then the girl they had just picked upped and said, "But what about the actor who played in the test with me? I thought he *was* the leading man. I can't think of anyone who would be better."

They looked at her as if she had some foul disease; this broad was going to be a troublemaker with these revolutionary ideas. Let's call the casting director, Joe Egli, they said, and see what he can come up with. But Egli's opinion was the same as the girl's, God love her. Her name was Dorothy Lamour, known in her circle at the time as "The Dreamer of Songs," and a simpler, nicer individual doesn't exist. When the reviews of *Three Smart Girls* came out, the part was mine, the first in a series of three pictures in the same genre. The stories were supposed to be different, but they were not, just the names were changed to protect the innocent, because all three had the same cast. In support of myself and Dorothy there were always Akim Tamiroff, Lynne Overman, Jiggs—the stinking, oversexed, three-hundred-pound gorilla who was the bane of my existence—and a five-hundred-pound Bengal tiger named Limau who I'm sure was a homosexual because he just loved me. His breath was terrible.

Another odd thing about these pictures was the fact that the heavies were always Englishmen, wise in the ways of slave trading and the robbing of temples, and typical of the "Traveller's Club" or the "Carlton." When they came upon me in the jungle, they berated me for "letting down the SIDE."

The first picture, *Jungle Princess,* was made for

about $300,000, and I think has so far grossed close to $15,000,000. It is still playing in outlandish places forty years later, and after relating one humorous incident I think I'll leave it. The director of the picture was a man of no small talent, who made it out of Germany one step ahead of the Brownshirts. He was short, round, gray, myopic, and given to towering, apoplectic rages at the slightest excuse. His name was Wilhelm Thiele, and he had the whole crew scared to death, including me, which was quite understandable considering that this was my first chance as a leading man in America.

In the story I was supposed to be a young aviator who crashed in the jungle. I was discovered by this young child of nature who was nursing me back to health. She lived all alone in a cave above a jungle pool, her only companion being this five-hundred-pound Bengal tiger. The scene in process was where I was supposed to be teaching her English while lying on a rock above the pool wearing some tattered shorts. We were doing that tired bit where I say, "Me Chris. You Ulah."

She would reply, "Kees?"

I'd say, "No, Chris."

And again she would say, "Kees?" Then I would demonstrate the difference between Chris and kiss.

When I kissed her she sat back on her haunches as if she had just tasted her first banana split. Then a look of absolute joy came on her face and she leaped on top of me wanting more. With that I was supposed to struggle free and dive into the pool with her after me. She would emerge and we would embrace with the water just up to her breastworks. An idyllic scene, wouldn't you say?

On the morning we were to shoot this little vignette we had scattered clouds, which caused some delay, sunlight being necessary for the entire scene. Everything was set. I was lying on the rock, Dorothy kneeling beside me, the cameraman watching the clouds through a smoked glass, and Attila the Hun pacing

up and down building up a nice head of steam,
ready to explode. Everybody was triggered to go as
soon as the sun broke through, and then I felt the
first twinge. I had to go to the bathroom. Oh, God,
I thought, not now! not now!! It was at least fifty
yards to the nearest cover, and if I went and the
sun came out that Pomeranian pimp would slaughter
me. No, I had to stick it out somehow! I whispered
Welsh prayers. I sent a little plea to Luisa. I crossed
and uncrossed my legs. But slowly and inexorably
the pressure built and panic came. Then someone
shouted, "Here it comes! Get ready! Roll 'em!" By
this time I was *in extremis*. How I got through the
dialogue I'll never know. But by the time Dorothy
started manhandling me I knew I had to go. So I
went, head first into the pool with Dorothy after me.
As I came to my feet the dear girl surfaced in front
of me and as she put her arms around my neck and
started kissing me, the cold water of the pool did
its work and I let go. Ah, the sheer sensuous bliss
of it, never have I had a more wonderful pee! And
all the time I was doing it, Dorothy and I were necking
like teen-agers in a hayloft.

Then I became aware of Thiele's voice shouting,
"Come out, come out and dry yourself off. That vos
vunderful. Vunderful. It had a simple extase."

I went over to the rock and started drying myself
and feeling quite odd, when Akim Tamiroff shambled
over. He didn't happen to be working that day, but
being a dedicated actor, couldn't think of anyplace
else to go that might be as interesting. He noticed
my preoccupation and asked what was bothering me,
so I told him what had happened. The laugh started
in his toes and swelled to a roar. Slapping me on
the back, he said he thought it was the most wonderful
joke, why was I looking so depressed? "Because I
liked it. That's why!" I said. "It's the sort of thing
that leads to perversion!" And with that, he collapsed
and I walked away.

Over the next eighteen months I did two more

of these jungle epics, interspersed with two other pictures, *Small Miracle* with Richard Barthelmess and another loan-out to Universal for *Next Time We Love*, with Jimmy Stewart and Margaret Sullavan. My contract had been rewritten and my salary more than tripled, but I was tired. Tired and more than a little homesick, with a nostalgia that has never left me. Immature? Possibly. But I think that psychologically and emotionally I was not cut out to be an actor. It has always been a fight for me to appear at ease, to be polished and uncomplicated in a role, like the image poor George Sanders tried to create, everything with a touch of contempt. But George, inside, was a snake pit of nerves and disillusion. And always for me there's been that niggling feeling that I was being an emotional prostitute. I've outgrown it, become almost prideful. But in those days, theatrically speaking, I was undoubtedly something of a prig, definitely an opportunist for whom the profession was but a means to an end. The frustrating thing was that I didn't have an end in view.

chapter xii

One morning in the fall of 1936 we awakened to find the rain pouring down, and if there's one place more depressing than Southern California in the rain, I don't want to know about it. After I'd stared out of the window for fifteen minutes, the idea suddenly hit me. "Darling, let's take a trip!"

"Where can we go in weather like this?" Mal asked.

"Europe!" I said. "If I don't get out of this place for a few weeks I'll go out of my mind."

After the initial shock her eyes began to brighten and then sobered as common sense took over. "Darling, how can we possibly afford it? What would it cost? I know you're tired and feeling a little homesick, but we've got to be practical."

I had the bit in my teeth though. "Get some paper and a pencil and let's figure it out." We discovered we had $5,200 in the bank, no debts, and my next year's option had been taken up three days earlier. The only problem was getting the time off from the studio. After an hour's work with the pencil I figured the trip would cost us a little over $3,000 for five weeks without having to skimp. (Costs in those days were less than one-third of what they are today.) Hotel rooms and food were ludicrously cheap and we would still have $2,000 in the bank when we came home. Then my wife began to tremble. "You hurry over to the studio right away and get the time off somehow. I've got to call Lily MacMurray. Go!"

I said, "What are you calling Lily for?"

"Well, you don't think I'm going to Europe in these rags, do you? While you are at the studio, Lily and I are hotfooting it down to Magnin's and Bullock's Wilshire."

Then and there I lowered the nest egg to be left in the bank from $2,000 to $1,000; I had never seen her so excited, so wonderful. After that, my session with the studio heads was a walkover. *What* a performance! They even gave me use of a company car while we were in London and Paris! MacMurray was working on Stage Six, so I slipped over to tell him what my wife and I were going to do. Fred and I had been signed by Paramount at about the same time. He had been playing a saxophone in a show in New York, where his darling Lily had been a model. They were our closest friends, and we hung onto each other like four Christians in the Colosseum.

I told Fred what Mal and I were going to do and then casually mentioned that Lily had gone with my wife down to Bullock's and Magnin's to do some shopping. He turned white; Fred has always been what one might call a leetle careful. Having ruined his day, I beetled to Scariano's travel agency and spent an hour checking trains and boat departures, then on to the bank and finally home, where I pored over cabin plans far into the night.

Five days later we left on the *Chief* for New York. After two days there we sailed on the *Manhattan,* at that time a new American liner built to compete with the Europeans on the North Atlantic run. She was under thirty thousand tons but beautifully done, with service almost as good as on the British boats. But the passenger list was a little on the dreary side, it being November. Sober-sided denizens from small, fashionable New England towns, who wouldn't be found dead on the *Ile de France* or the other glamour boats. A few rudely polite English couples and a flock of young American business types in their cordovan brogues, all of whom seemed to walk like apes, though their conversation was polysyllabic indeed.

There were also, thank God, a couple of dozen other people who seemed to be intent on having a quiet good time. But the belle of the boat was my wonderful girl. Mal has a miraculous talent for making friends, something which is sadly lacking in my make-up, and within two days I found myself included in all sorts of groups. At night, when everybody gathered for dancing in the bar-restaurant, three or four tables would be pushed together and we would be in the middle of a group of a dozen or more. And they all danced with their arms going up and down like pump handles, diving and swooping over the moving and tilting dance floor, which had been lightly sprinkled with water by the stewards to prevent accidents. This wasn't for me, so I told everyone I had just been operated on for a broken ankle and I didn't want to take any chances. For some reason all the men who wanted to dance with my wife thought they'd better buy me a drink, and at one time I counted five daiquiris lined up in front of me.

Meanwhile, the desiccated drabs left with me at the table were condescendingly plying me with questions about Hollywood. Why do they have to be so tastelessly rude, so patronizing to people from California? Good God, Westerners earned their money from hard work and hazardous pioneering, not slave trading and opium running, where much of this "old money" on the Eastern seaboard was made. And why, for Christ's sake, do some of these dried-up beldames get themselves up as if they were still attending Miss Cudlipp's Academy? The dull, funereal bobbed hair and those silly barrettes! They look like scullery maids. All those goddam garnets and rose-cut diamonds and high school nicknames like Poochy and Twinkie being dropped in overloud voices. Oh, God,

please, Mal, get tired and let's go to bed! Ah, the
heartburn caused by daiquiris! On our last night at
sea, long after midnight, I took Mal on deck and
walked her toward the bow. When we got to the end
of the promenade I told her to stare ahead into the
darkness a little left of the bow and watch. In a few
moments there was a flash and then a second one;
she gave a convulsive grab of my arm and gasped,
"What is it? What is it? Is it Europe?"

I said, "Well, not really, it's Ireland, and that flash
is the lighthouse on the Old Head of Kinsale, and this
is your first glimpse of the Old World."

She just stood there trembling, breathing in short
shuddering gasps. "How wonderful! How wonderful! I just can't believe it!"

I finally got her to move by telling her that we
would be stopping at Queenstown, as it was called
then, in less than two hours. We would be at anchor
there for more than an hour in order to disembark
some passengers onto the tenders and to let a few
dozen Irish peddlers come on board to sell shawls,
laces, and blackthorn walking sticks. With that, she
shot down to the stateroom. When I got there she
was madly changing into a tweed suit and scram-
bling around trying to find the right shoes. I told her
there was no need to hurry, that it would be at least
an hour before we came in sight of the town. She
stopped for a second and said, "Listen, darling, this
stuff may be very old hat to you. But this is my first
trip to Europe and I don't intend to miss a damn
thing. We've only got two and half weeks here, so
you lie down for a while. I'll be up on deck." And
she bolted. I slowly took off my jacket, opened a
bottle of gift champagne, sat in a chair, smoked a
cigarette, and smiled for a while.

I must have dozed off, because I was suddenly
aware that the boat had stopped, sundry bells were
ringing, voices were calling and the big gangway was
being lowered with a rattle. I looked through the
porthole and sure enough, there was the big Queens-

town tender tied alongside. I decided to go up on deck and try to keep a checkrein on my wife, who would look like money from home to those Irish hucksters. Those biddies with their overdone brogues could sell you anything. I got there just in time; she was already surrounded by three of them. She was feverishly examing a huge lace tablecloth.

Mal looked up as I approached, and her eyes were enchanting, all sparkle and excitement. "Darling, just look at this. Isn't it beautiful? And all hand done. Better than anything you could get at home. We need one so badly. It's only forty dollars. Why, it's practically a gift. I can't wait to get it home and show Lily. Can I buy it, sweetheart?"

What could I say? Except that she could probably get the same thing in London for less money.

She looked at me aghast. "Why, you unromantic clod! Doesn't it mean anything to you that this is my very first sight of Europe? That it's five o'clock on a dark Irish morning? That this cloth will remind us of this moment for the rest of our lives? Besides, look at the lace!" Sadly I reached in my pocket and paid the woman. The heart had gone out of me.

The bustle and foreignness of customs and immigration when we landed in England, the boat train with its childlike whistling and the E. Phillips Oppenheim atmosphere of our arrival at Paddington Station in all its dinginess, our drive to the Savoy Hotel fascinated and enthralled her. I had cabled my old agent, Connie, to meet us in the Grill for supper on our arrival. There was a message waiting for me saying that she was across the street attending the first night of *Tovarich* and would meet us when it was over. Now, as far as I'm concerned the Savoy Hotel is famous for only two things. The Grill and the beds. Oh, those wonderful warm and caressing beds, made only for the Savoy, so comforting that sleep in them was almost sinful. The little gilt clock in the mantel said eight-thirty. As neither of us had had any sleep for thirty-six hours I suggested that we rest for a couple of hours and leave a call for eleven P.M. We could go down to the Grill when the theaters let out. Within thirty seconds we were asleep. Promptly at eleven the telephone awakened us and we somehow staggered around getting dressed and made our way down to the Grill.

Connie was already there, seated at a table in the center of the room with two other men, Paul England, one of her associates, and the other I think was young Freddy Brisson, who at that time was learning the intricacies and infighting of the theatrical profession while working in her office. Judging by his position today, he must have been an apt pupil. After the introductions had been made, we started looking around the room, which was rapidly filling, and I began pointing out the famous ones to Mal. The Prime Minister, Stanley Baldwin, was there with a group, looking just like a farmer. At another table Winston Churchill was holding court in high good humor. The old Aga Khan was there with a large party that included Douglas Fairbanks, Sir., who, I was surprised to notice, was a very short man. He was so deeply tanned that he looked darker than the Aga. It seemed that every notability in Europe was there, both the famous and the notorious, with us right in the middle.

Around one-thirty the place started to empty, so we said good night to Connie and the others with me promising to drop by the office at five the next day. It was one of those balmy evenings that one often gets in London during November, so I suggested to Mal that we take a little walk before going to bed. The night was clear and the moon almost full as we strolled down the Strand toward Trafalgar Square. I showed her Nelson on his lonely column, the church of Saint Martin-in-the-Fields, and then we went down to Whitehall and the spot where B 63 and I had waited for so many boring hours. It seemed as if it must have been someone else, so long ago, so distant, and yet, I thought, it had been only a little more than six years. We crossed Whitehall at the Cenotaph and continued on toward the river keeping to the left side until just before the corner that opened up the lovely vista of the Houses of Parliament. I asked her to stop and close her eyes and not open them until I told her to. I then walked her the few steps to the corner, tipped her head up and said, "Now open them." And there, high in the sky with his face lighted, was Big Ben, saying it was two o'clock in the morning. She stood there quite still for fully a minute, and then she slowly turned her face into my shoulder and whispered, "Honey, even if we had to go back home tomorrow, tonight would have been worth it." She didn't say another word all the way back to the hotel, but as we were waiting for the elevator she said, "Don't answer any long-distance phone calls for at least a week!"

The seven days we spent in England were practically perfect, we even had a London fog the day before we left for Paris, a real pea-souper where they had to light oil fires in the main thoroughfares to guide traffic. Nothing for it but that I had to take her walking along the Embankment and this when it was pitch-dark at three o'clock in the afternoon. There was even a London bobby who loomed up and advised us to go home. It wasn't very safe, especially for foreigners. I bridled a little, but said nothing and turned back to Savoy Hill. My wife was ecstatic as she said, "They never did catch Jack the Ripper, did they?" Pure Roger Corman.

We left for Paris the next day on a huge Imperial Airways triplane—English: they even had a writing room on board, also three male stewards in full regimentals. The rest of the passengers were all loaded down with lap robes and jewel cases and pet dogs and loud overaccented voices. One could almost imagine it was the sailing of the *Leviathan* for New York. Why do the English always seem to appropriate whatever transportation they are using as if it were their own private property and all the other passengers intruders, obviously there because of some stupid mistake in the booking office? On the other hand there are some who travel like church mice.

Paris was wonderful. Mild, gray, and with all its intriguing smells and places. We stayed at the Hotel Gallia on the Rue Pierre Charon, just off the Champs Élysées: a huge sitting room, a bedroom almost as big, with those gorgeous brass beds, and a bathroom you could stable five horses in. And we had a valet and a chambermaid who were jewels. The cost? Five dollars a day! But that was Paris in the thirties. An excellent dinner at Lucas-Carton would rarely cost more than five dolars. Today, a large Scotch and soda can cost that! In those days all visitors to Paris felt like millionaires. They could afford to.

It was in Paris that I got my first taste of what it was like to be in the public eye. The French are very film-conscious and *Three Smart Girls* was a big success there. *Jungle Princess* had just opened and they loved it. I don't know how the magazines found me, but they did. Very intense and dedicated people they seemed to be, insisting there was something profound in all movies. In the case of *Jungle Princess* what was the director trying to convey? What was he trying to say? I told them I hadn't the foggiest idea, that he had trouble ordering his lunch. They laughed at that, but very politely and I got the feeling they thought I wasn't taking them seriously, that I was being something of a dilettante. I excused myself by saying that I hadn't been in the profession long enough to be profound about it. But I will say this about the French reporters in contrast with the English and American and Italian press, they never asked questions about my personal affairs or about my private and family life, except to ask me if I were married and whether I had any children. But they are like that, the French. To them their home and family are sacred. It's their bastion, their refuge, a place to which a man can retreat and throw off the façade of the boulevardier, take off his shoes, browbeat his wife, frolic with his children, and be a dictator or a king, to be loved or feared because this is his home. His. Outsiders are rarely invited into it, if ever. Two things a Frenchman will always give you—good manners and directions to the nearest public toilet. That's about it.

We sailed for home aboard the old *Paris,* a lovely ship, all wrought iron and potted plants and the world's best food. A few years later we were to see her lying on her side in Le Havre, burned to the waterline. The saddest sight. There is nothing so forlorn or so inevitable as the end of the line for these lovely old dowagers of the ocean sea. They sail off alone to some foul knacker's yard, usually in Asia, there to be ripped up, raped and torn to shreds and then forgotten. At that I think it's a better fate than the one they had in store for the *Queen Mary.* Now she towers above the trashiness of Long Beach Harbor like a bedizened whore.

Just a few weeks ago we were sitting at home having cocktails with Mal's sister and her husband, dredging up a few memories, and I happened to mention that we had been on both maiden voages of the *Queen Mary*: when she was first launched, and again after the war, when she reentered the transatlantic service after having served so well as a troopship during those tragic years. She had been refurbished from top to bottom. But the British, with their canny sense of history, had not touched the handrails that ran around the promenade deck. They were covered with initials, carved by the thousands of troops she had carried during those years. She had meant safety and the voyage home to so many sorry ones. She was so fast and so efficiently protected the U-boats didn't have a prayer. And then we spoke of the postwar travelers, the Windsors, Winthrop Aldrich, the International Set, those posturing peacocks, and Molotov, the greatest sybarite of them all, not excluding Gilbert and Kitty Miller, Harrison Williams and his Mona, and then there were the courtesans, both male and female. And of course there was Carine, chief steward, and the *Mary*'s Machiavelli, a right smart cookie.

After about an hour of reminiscing, my sister-in-law, with her eyes all aglitter, jumped up and said, "Let's not go to the Club to eat. Let's go down and have dinner on the *Queen Mary*. I hear they've got three or four restaurants on board that are supposed to be good. You can show us everything and sort of make it come alive. Okay?" And with that we piled into the car and rode down to the harbor.

It was a mistake. One of the worst I've ever made. It seems this was the night the Gay Liberation Front had decided to hold their first Pacific Coast convention and they had decided to make it a fancy-dress ball. The theme was ancient Egypt. They had taken over what had been the main first-class dining room and at one end was a papier-mâché version of Cleopatra's barge complete with slaves, *big* ones. And there were flowers everywhere, great sheaves of them along the walls, on the tables, even hanging from the chandeliers. For some reason it made me think of Forest Lawn, except for the noise, which was deafening, the orchestra beating out a rock version of *In a Monastery Garden* but getting lost among the matronly screams and the incessant chatter and the tantrums. Oooooh, the tantrums!

Suddenly my attention was caught by someone who appeared to be the master or mistress of ceremonies, standing on the prow of the barge beating on a gong trying to get the room's attention. Why, for Christ's sake, I thought, that's my goddam dentist! *My* DENTIST! made up as Nefertiti, queen of the Nile! In a daze, I got out of there and we made our way to the promenade deck. Needless to say, he's not my dentist anymore. But I watch the new one I've got very carefully. I mean, a thing like that can really shake you. But, third time lucky, I guess.

After a while I calmed down. I was explaining lifeboat drill, how the boats were swung out and lowered to the promenade deck where people could get into them, when I noticed it—the marks I mean. They had gone. All those scratches, all those hundreds and hundreds of initials, many of them epitaphs, all had been sanded away, buffed out and varnished. The handrails were just handrails again. On the way home we had dinner at a little Mexican joint, where I got gently stewed on margaritas and melancholia, so I think I'll get back to the thirties.

Immediately upon arrival in California I found myself cast as "Bulldog Drummond" and did two such pictures back to back. The day after I finished the second one I was assigned to a lead in a picture called *Gilded Lily* with Claudette Colbert and Fred MacMurray, directed by the same somber-visaged Wesley Ruggles who had started me out in *Bolero*. It turned out to be a very pleasant engagement, with just two slight flaws. Ruggles was in the middle of a divorce from his then wife, Arline Judge, and was more morose than ever. Also I was convinced that Claudette Colbert hated me. I couldn't imagine why. I hardly said a word to her besides "Good morning" every day. Frankly, I was very much in awe of her, and the putting out of bogus charm is not something I can do. With her it wouldn't have helped anyway. Claudette was much too alert and intelligent. But I'm afraid I magnified it out of all proportion, because the picture turned out to be a very pleasant engagement and most successful financially.

Thereafter I made four pictures in a row without one day off. A Robert Louis Stevenson number called *Ebb Tide,* at my own studio, Paramount, then a loan-out to Universal, then another loan-out to Columbia for a picture with Loretta Young, then back to Paramount for a little gem called *Hotel Imperial.* That one which almost wrote finis to my film career. In it I played a young Austrian cavalry officer, a part in which I felt quite at home. There was a scene that called for me to lead my trusty troop of San Fernando cowboys at full gallop after a clutch of retreating Cossacks. The set was the main street of a small

Austrian town, badly destroyed by Russian shelling.
We were to start out of sight around a corner. At
a given signal we were to come charging through an
archway, go barreling down the street and on out
of camera range. There was quite a wait while the
two cameras were set up, one on the right-hand side
of the street with a wide-angle lens and another on
the balcony just above it, using a much closer lens.
Then we were sent around the corner to wait for
the whistle. We waited for a good ten minutes with
everybody becoming a little restive.

Then we got the signal and away we went with
me in the lead. As I turned the corner I was horrified
to see that they had set another camera on a very
low tripod, smack in the middle of the street. By this
time we were at full stretch with no place to go but
straight ahead. There was only one thing to do—clear
the camera. My mount was a pretty good quarter
horse who could jump, so at the proper moment I
hung my hooks into him and he took off. But as he
bunched for the takeoff the girth broke. I was airborne
with just a saddle between my legs, heading for what
I hoped was a pile of horse manure, only it wasn't.
It was a pile of broken masonry with a couple of
shovelfuls of the stuff sprinkled over it.

I woke up in the Cedars of Lebanon Hospital with
a badly mangled left hand and a three-inch gash in
my skull that took nine stitches to close and a slight
concussion. I spent a week in the hospital and a week
at home convalescing. But as the director, Robert
Florey, so neatly put it, no real harm had been done.
It had been the last day of the picture and the whole
thing had cut together very nicely, so hurry up and
get well because there are a few wild lines we have
to record. A true son of Gaul, the bastard. All in
all, I spent almost a month without having to put
on makeup, thoroughly enjoying my little nest, being
waited on hand and foot by my life's companion even
though she kept dropping snide remarks about some-

body swinging the lead, or as she put it, goldbricking. But I let it pass.

It was during this time that Mal and I decided to build a house of our own. Up until then we had been renting a small house on King's Road, a quiet residential street south of Santa Monica Boulevard. We had been in it for almost eight months, but there was something very odd about it. Not a month would go by without two or three people knocking at the door late at night. They were always men and always slightly bibulous and a little furtive. They would look surprised when I answered the door and would mumble something about wanting to know if Yvonne was there, or Elaine. But most of the time they asked for a female named Arleen. After this had happened four or five times I walked up the street to the next house, which was occupied by Betty Furness and her mother. Now, Betty Furness was a well-known ingenue in those days and we had been friends for a couple of years. She was bright and intelligent. So I told her what had been happening and asked could she throw any light on it.

"All I know," she said, "is that a lot of taxis used to drop people off there. There were always two or three cars out at the curb. If I were you I'd call the agents you rented it from and ask them about it. And complain."

The next morning I called the trust department of the Bank of America, from whom I had rented the house, and did just that, complained. They were most apologetic and explained that the previous tenants had been most unsuitable and with the help of the police they had been evicted. Would I consider a twenty-five-dollar reduction in the monthly rent as compensation for the inconvenience? I sure would. It was that which started us thinking of building a home of our own. We found a lot off Coldwater Canyon, had a house designed, foundations started. But I kept wondering about that Arleen. She must have been a lulu.

I was halfway through a picture with Paulette Goddard in a little over two months after my accident. You think I was a glutton for work? Well, I thought so, too, until I tangled with Goddard. There was the hardest working female I'd ever come across. Wise, humorous, and with absolutely no illusions. If the call was nine A.M. she would be there at eight walking the set and going over her lines. After a ten- or eleven-hour day she would go to her dressing room with her coach, Phyllis Laughton, and put in two more hours boning up on the next day's work. I would get tired just watching her. By the way, Phyllis Laughton is now the mayor of Beverly Hills. After the years with Paulette it must seem like a vacation. As for me, it was the same thing over and over again. Finish a picture on a Saturday, start another three or four days later. I played cowboys, half-baked playboys, aviators, an eighteenth-century English procurer, and once I even played the devil. And I became tired. Tired of all the spurious emotion, of the intrigue, of the flaring temperamental outbursts and the deviousness.

My pet hate was the publicity department. By the beginning of 1939 I had acquired quite a following, including two fan clubs. I took lunch in my dressing room while giving interviews to fan magazines. In those days there were at least twenty-five, not counting the foreign press, who were usually much more cerebral and penetrating. Then you were asked to attend openings and exhibitor meetings. I got out of most of those by having a relative die suddenly. I honestly believe I had more relatives kick the bucket than any individual west of the Rockies. Occasionally I would get a whole week off, and when that happened Mal and I would quickly hop a plane and take a trip somewhere, Mexico City, Vera Cruz, anywhere. We even made it to Panama once. These seemed to be the only times my wife and I were together. And the separations affected her. She was becoming subdued as I became more irritable.

It was at this time that her father died. He had been confined to his home for almost a year following two strokes that had left him almost helpless and, strangely, I was the only person he would allow around him. I got into the habit of dropping in to see him every night on my way home from work, making him a very weak Scotch and soda and perhaps lighting a fire for him in his bedroom. His speech was terribly impaired, so much so that the other people in the house couldn't understand him. For instance, if he wanted a fire to be lighted he would say, "Open the tomatoes." Now this sort of thing called for imagination and Welsh intuition, which I had. But it stumped the other people in the house, who were at that time all women, and his rages were something to behold. So there were always several little chores he had saved up for me by the time I got there. Also, his language became appalling as his frustrations rose. This in a man who didn't normally allow slang to be used in his house. He couldn't think of words like *shoe* or *dish* or *chair,* but he had no trouble at all when it came to swearing. Funny, that. Then came a third massive stroke and that was the end.

It was February, 1939, and I was thirty-two, when I wrecked my left hand for the second time. The studio had put an end to my joy riding out of Mines Field, no more flying except by scheduled airlines. I had become too valuable. So, for something to do at odd moments I had outfitted a machine shop behind our garage and I had everything in it, bench saw, drill press, all-purpose lathe, shaper, planer, the works, and every piece had its own motor. There was only one thing wrong. No room to work a piece of wood longer than three feet. Nevertheless, I was trying my hand at making a small Chippendale end table and was just finishing off an extra leg, just in case, when the damned thing slipped. My left hand went right into the circular blade, which at that time was doing about 750 r.p.m. As a result I found myself in Santa Monica Hospital minus part of my thumb and the tendons all chewed to hell. Luckily, the back of the hand wasn't even touched, so it looks quite normal. Thanks to the excellence of the surgeon who worked on it, the hand recovered 50 percent of its efficiency. I was fortunate that at the time the accident happened I was between pictures so the studio knew nothing about it. If anyone called they were told that I had gone fishing for a few days, so I almost got away with it until I absentmindedly picked up the phone one Friday afternoon. On the other end was dear old Y. Frank Freeman, the latest head of Paramount Studios, the Georgia swamp fox himself, a very devious type, who wanted to know if I could pop around to the studio about six that evening, he had a very attractive proposition for me. I asked him if I could possible make it Monday morning instead, because we were just getting ready to drive to Santa Barbara for dinner.

"Well, I guess that might be all right, son. But it's not going to leave ya'll much time to get ready."

(At that moment, my hand was so bandaged up it looked like a broken leg.)

"Get ready for what?" I yelped.

"You're going to England on Thursday," he said, "and you'll be doing a picture called *French Without Tears,* our top production for Europe this year. It will be directed by Anthony Asquith. You'll have to leave on Thursday in order to catch the *Aquitania* the following Wednesday, so tell your wife to start packing, because she's going with you. We figure she'll give you a little class. So you get in here before midday on Monday and we'll straighten out the details."

In panic, I called my doctor and explained why he had to reduce those bandages to practically nothing by Monday and to write a letter to the doctor on the *Aquitania* explaining everything, including how to re-dress my hand before landing. When I told Mal that we were going she was ecstatic, and then her face dropped. "But, darling, how can you make a picture with your hand in that condition?"

"Don't worry about it," I said. "It's an English comedy, and the only violent thing they do is run in and out of rooms and constantly tap cigarettes. It'll be a cinch. And another thing, go pick up your mother and take her down to the passport office this very instant. Make out a passport application and mark it 'special' and pay the excess. We're taking her with us."

What with having only one hand it took me a full five minutes to untangle her from around my neck, then laughing and crying at the same time, she took off in her car, quite forgetting to put on her shoes. I adored my mother-in-law, and this would be a wonderful thing for her. Normally a gentle and humorous woman, she had become melancholy and quite lost since the death of her husband. Best idea I ever hand. By six o'clock I was in the clinic getting my hand re-dressed, and you know it didn't turn out too badly? If I could just throw or carry a raincoat or something, nobody would notice a thing. Ask and ye shall receive! Monday morning it was pissing rain and I appeared in Freeman's office with a raincoat carelessly draped over my left forearm and everything turned out just fine. I even brought a tear from Freeman's eye when I told him my mother-in-law's condition and how much she meant to me. I walked out of there with her transportation ticket in my pocket also. Nice little performance.

In London we took a flat in the Arlington House, just behind the Ritz, overlooking Green Park. We stayed there for three and a half months. While I worked, Mal and her mother went sightseeing all over Britain and France and had a ball. As for the picture, I enjoyed making it and it turned out to be profitable. By the way, the cutter on it was David Lean, at that time a cheerful, elegant, and enthusiastic character. Then he got hooked up with a famous British actress, and married her. That seemed to take some of the steam out of him because after the divorce, which didn't take long, he's become quite an introvert, they tell me, something of a loner. Pity. But it doesn't seem to have interfered with his success, which has been phenomenal and deservedly so.

It was a lovely summer, theater was good, restaurants were packed, and the gardens were at their best. However, there was an undercurrent. The laughter, I thought, was a touch hysterical. Chamberlain was pussyfooting between London and Munich, people were being fitted for gas masks, air-raid drills were being carried out at odd hours, and all seemingly being treated as a huge joke, a joke I failed to see.

At the beginning of July I decided that Mal and her mother should go back to America, and I would follow as soon as the picture was finished. They gave me quite an argument. But I insisted, and they sailed on the *Georgic* two weeks later. I had made the decision as a result of an evening I had spent with my old regiment in Knightsbridge barracks, where I heard talk that two-thirds of the regiment had been dismounted and sent for tank training, that there were plans for the evacuation of civilians, no leaves longer than a weekend and then only on compassionate grounds. That and Hitler's increased ranting painted, I thought, a very clear picture. They had no sooner sailed when the crisis seemed to pass and things became almost normal. We completed the film in the middle of August, and I sailed on the *Normandie* two days later. It was to be her last voyage.

As we started out across the Atlantic I noticed that she was tracking way north of the normal steamer lanes and that men were covering all ports and windows with black paint. On the third day we began to sight icebergs on their summer drift to the south. The atmosphere on board became more ominous as lifeboat drills were meticulously carried out and the people became more silent. I figured there was not much point in worrying unless they started playing "Nearer My God to Thee." We made New York all right, docking two days late.

Within a week of arriving home I found myself in another picture, Hitler attacked Poland, and my wife told me she was pregnant. To say that life was confusing for the next few months would be an understatement.

Later, when the United States actually went to war, I tried to enlist in the air force, for which I considered myself qualified, but was rejected for active service because of the restricted use of my left hand. Finally I did succeed in being employed as a civilian contract primary flight instructor for the army. I spent all my time between pictures in the Arizona desert in a delightful little community called Salome-Where-She-Danced, which eventually led to two short tours in the Solomon Islands where I contracted a pox called dengue fever, flavored with malaria. When they shipped me home I was not my usual 175 pounds but 142. I wish I looked that way now.

chapter xiii

Cecil B. De Mille was unquestionably one of the greatest showmen the movies ever had. The industry is much the poorer for his loss. He could utilize a camera better than anyone. He had no peer at manipulating mobs or armies. He could stage and plan a battle better than Clausewitz. At spectacle he was the master. But he didn't know a damned thing about acting. A lot of people who worked with him will tell you this, but I am one of the few who can prove it.

It happened early in the forties in a picture called *Reap the Wild Wind,* produced and directed by De Mille. In it there was a sequence where I had to fight a giant squid at the bottom of the sea in a full and authentic deep-sea diving outfit. It was staged in what is known as the Big Tank at Paramount Studios. The tank was almost the size of a football field and about twenty-five feet deep at the deepest part. Down there they had built a marine wonderland: the hull of a wrecked ship, strange and jagged rocks, a slowly moving aqueous forest. And caves, dark and frightening. I won't bore you with the technical details of how we photographed these scenes, except to say that the whole sequence took about ten days to shoot.

Right in the middle of this sequence I was told
that I had to attend a party given by an overrich
and slightly fruity Texan who went under the name,
believe it or not, of Rex de St. Cyr. The party was
being held in honor of a group of Latin American
bigwigs. Don't forget we were at war then and we
needed all the help we could get. The affair was being
sponsored by the Office of Inter-American Affairs,
run at that time by Nelson Rockefeller, I believe.
Due to my knowledge of Spanish I had made a lot
of radio appeals for that outfit, which would then
send the records all over Latin-America to be broadcast by their local stations. I was tired, but there was
no way out, I had to go to this brawl. Because she
spoke no English, I found myself seated next to the
wife of one of the guests of honor. To make matters
worse, they served only champagne, of which I am
not particularly fond. It gives me terrible heartburn
and an even worse hangover, but as a protective device
I drank it anyway. If Mal had been in town it wouldn't
have been too bad. However, she was at Newport
Beach with our two-year-old son in a house I had
rented for the summer.

Finally, at four A.M. the party was finished, and
so was I. Stoned. I got home about five, parked my
car on the lawn (I couldn't find the garage), and
stumbled into the house. I knocked on my butler's
door, told him to awaken me at five-thirty and get
me to the studio by 6:15 A.M. He wanted to know
why I bothered to go to bed. I told him. I wanted
to die for a while. Well, he got me to the studio
on time, and with the help of my stand-in brought
me up to the makeup department, where I promptly
passed out. I came out of the coma about an hour
and a half later as they were putting me into a suit
of long underwear that I wore under the diving suit.
I was still stoned, but now had a terrible headache
and a frantic desire not to let De Mille see me in
this condition. I felt ashamed and I didn't want to
embarrass him. So I begged the prop men and the

diving technicians to put me in the diving suit and lower me to the bottom of the tank before he came on the set. Besides, I wanted that mixture of air and oxygen they pumped down to me. They did it and thereby saved my life. In about half an hour the lack of body weight and that heavenly mixture began to have their effect. I slowly came back to the land of the living. But still mighty yeasty. In a few minutes, De Mille and all his entourage arrived on the set ready to create. He immediately got on the headphones and after congratulating me for being on time and ready to work, explained the action he wanted for the first couple of shots. I vaguely understood him and we got started.

By eleven o'clock I was dying of thirst, so I begged them to haul me up and give me a drink of water. After unscrewing the face plate they stuck a Coke bottle full of the stuff into my mouth. I drank it all. This was the worst thing I could have done. Right here I must impart a word of advice to all apprentice drunks. Never, but *never* drink water after a night of champagne. You'll be just as polluted as you were the night before. But immediately. That's what happened to me.

Somehow, I remained alive until lunch time, whereupon my cronies quickly hustled me to my dressing room and started feeding me their pet cures for a hangover. Lynne Overman, a sweet man who was also in the picture and had been quite a bottle belter in his time, gave me three little black pills which he swore were the source of life. I swallowed them with a little tomato juice. Then John Wayne came in and gave me two monstrous green capsules which he insisted I wash down with a little gin. Finally, just before I was to be carted back to the tank, Bob Benchley came in. He said the only *real* cure was a wineglass full of Worcestershire sauce with a raw egg in it, which he just happened to have with him. By this time I was beyond caring, so I swallowed that too. The rest of the afternoon was a nightmare and best forgotten. But De Mille never tumbled. About five o'clock they called it a day, and when they hauled me up I was horrified to see that De Mille had not left the set and was waiting for me. Now, here I must tell you something about him.

In 1934 or thereabouts, the government had minted a small issue of half-dollars commemorating the original Virginia Dare. De Mille had bought the lot. He awarded them sparingly to people who in his opinion had done something outstanding or above the call of duty. Well, while I was having my helmet unscrewed and praying that they would take my head with it, he majestically called through his ever-present megaphone for complete silence on the set. Counting technicians, there must have been close to one hundred seventy there. In front of everyone De Mille stated that in all his years in Hollywood and in the theater he had never seen a finer or more perceptive day's acting than he had that day. Then he dramatically presented me with his personal Academy Award, a Virginia Dare half-dollar. After a handshake full of sincerity, he and his entourage left the set in columns of threes. I felt like a louse letting him appear a fool in front of all those people who were in the know.

Strangely, though, after reading the foregoing, I'm beginning to wonder: Who did what to whom?

That happened in the early forties and is probably a little out of sequence. I know only that my life seemed to have degenerated into one huge kaleidoscope of faces and scenes and spurious emotions, shallow and momentary friendships, long absences from home working on locations all over the Western hemisphere. When I did get time off it was never more than a week. Finally, in 1948, I rebelled and refused to do a picture I had been assigned to, the first and only time I was to take a suspension in the twenty-one years I spent at Paramount. And with good reason. The movie was a turkey called *Bride of Vengeance*. Can you believe that title? Yet the title they had when they were writing the script,

A Mask for Lucrezia, wasn't bad. The story was about the Borgias and the Duke of Ferrara, a very lush and expensive picture to make. It had the top director on the lot, Mitchell Leisen, Paulette Goddard, and half the contract list employed by Paramount.

But the story? Whew! I can still smell it. To make matters worse, two nights before they handed me the script I happened to see a movie called *Prince of Foxes* with Ty Power, very well done, with practically the same story as ours, only better. I high-tailed it to the front office and spent two hours trying to get out of it. No soap. I either had to do the abortion or be suspended for two months without pay, the time of the suspension to be added on to my contract term. I took the suspension and stormed out. I could afford it. And I went skiing.

At that time there were two reigning queens in Hollywood, both female, each with a daily column in the two leading newspapers and a weekly radio show. They were pandered to and fawned upon to an incredible degree, and to all intents and purposes they ran the town.

One of them was Louella Parsons, top columnist for Hollywood goings-on for the Hearst press and apparently a newpaperwoman from the year zero. By comparison with her rival she was rather kindly and seemingly vague, though with a mind like a bear trap. She never forgot a thing and, by the same token, never forgave anyone who crossed her. But she was never vicious.

The other one was Hedda Hopper, top Hollywood columnist for the L.A. *Times* and an unmitigated bitch. She was venomous, vicious, a pathological liar, and quite stupid. She was a tall and rather handsome woman who at one time had been an actress on the New York stage but who never quite made it to the top row, I suspect because of her infinite capacity for making enemies, never friends. Wise Hollywood hostesses never invited columnists to their parties, because once you did you can never leave them off your list for future parties or they would crucify you.

One delicious gal, Joan Bennett, did fight back at one time. Through no fault of her own she got caught up in some emotional tangle that in any other town would have been passed without much comment. Indeed, most of the Hollywood columnists dealt with her quite gently, but not Hopper, oh no. This vomitous assassin proceeded to write such scurrilous columns on the subject that even craven Hollywood was a mite disgusted. Then on Hopper's birthday Joan, from somewhere, procured a skunk that had been dead for a week. She put it in a shoebox, wrapped it in silver lamé, tied it up with gold ribbon and Christmas decorations. She had it delivered to Hopper by special messenger with a card reading "Happy birthday, dear. Joan." Then she called the trade papers, and a good time was had by all.

I'm afraid the foregoing dissertation was inspired by my own slight contretemps with Hopper on the occasion of my being suspended from Paramount. She had been lying in wait for me for about six years, since I had made a picture with Claudette Colbert called *Arise My Love*. The movie turned out to be a blockbuster and my first real step to stardom. I had received a call from Hopper, who, in arrogant and imperious fashion, told me that I was to appear on her nationally broadcast radio show. I told her that I was facing a week of night shooting and that it would be quite impossible.

She said, "Listen, you limey son-of-a-bitch, nobody, but nobody refuses to go on the 'Hedda Hopper Show.' You show up on Tuesday night or I'll run you out of town and don't think I can't!"

I hung up on her. Stupid woman. She and her goddam hats. But half the town was really terrified of her. Well, came the little incident of my suspension, and she really went to town. I was the worst kind of ingrate, there were vague hints about my background, my sexual proclivities, and on top of everything I was a foreigner. The fact that 50 percent of Hollywood were foreigners escaped her entirely. Anyway, a knock from Hopper was practically an accolade, so it did me no harm. Quite the opposite, actually.

Of course there were a lot of other columnists in Hollywood who were nationally syndicated, half of them pretty good, with intelligence and some imagination. But the other half? Mostly cases of arrested mental development. There was one who was a real doozy, name of Harrison Carroll, an over-age peeping Tom to whom news consisted of anything detrimental or seamy. Above all he loved sickness and diseases of all kinds. To get a mention in his column you either had to break an arm or a leg or have an undercover miscarriage. Terminal carcinoma you got a headline.

The publicity department of all the studios fawned upon these parasites. They'd sit up half the night concocting items that would get their stars or their pictures mentioned by these garbage men. But a few people, the really talented ones, just ignored the columnists. They didn't need them. There's a great similarity between making a good picture and winning important football games. Without a good game plan (script) and a good coach (director), a hell of a good line and tricky halfbacks, the quarterback (star) is going to get smeared and the game goes out the window. And if he's the quarterback in three or four losing games he's soon out of a job. A star cannot help a lousy script. On the other hand, a good script doesn't need a star. It needs a damn good actor, which isn't always the same thing.

It was about this time that I really began to get interested in acting as an art, a profession. Up until then I had looked upon it as a job, albeit an extremely well-paying one. I used to go to the movies maybe once or twice a month. Now I began going once or twice a week, not because I had any favorite stars— most of my enjoyment came from watching the actors in the supporting casts, the true professionals, who provided the salt and pepper, the seasoning, the jewel-like bits worth remembering. People like Frank McHugh, Berton Churchill, Donald Meek, Taylor Holmes. And on the distaff side, Patsy Kelly, May Robson, Una O'Connor, Louise Beavers. And from Europe, Étienne Girardot, Gustav von Seyffertiz, Fritz Feld, hell, there's a list as long as my arm, and they had all been pros from the time they could walk.

There are few things that give me greater pleasure than to watch good acting. It exhilarates me and robs me of sleep. On the other hand, really bad acting nauseates me. But where have they gone? these "soldiers of the king," these dependable flavor makers? I know only that they've never been replaced. Once in a while, if you're lucky, you can catch them on the goggle-box around two A.M. when you're alone and the house is silent. I don't mean to detract from the stars, many of whom were, and still are, brilliant, some of them touched with genius. But the ones who reached the top and stayed there are the actors and actresses who started in their teens and worked at it, the dedicated ones, the professionals. As an interested observer, I believe that anyone with normal intelligence can be a fairly competent actor, and be able to earn a living at it, provided he is to a certain degree intuitive and has normal physical equipment, common sense, and logic.

There are actors who have become stars without that last quality, but these are the fakers, the bogus talents much given to excess in makeup and hirsute adornments and weird infirmities. If a part calls for the use of spectacles they'll always use a pair at least a hundred years out of date. Actors with Shakespearean backgrounds are very prone to doing this, especially if they're English. Such fakery covers a multitude of shortcomings. There is one successful star today, and the type is not uncommon, whose idea of acting is to play everything with a touch of senility. He has done very well at it for forty years.

Then there are the turd kickers, and the *mucho macho* types, and the cigarette actors, all with their shtick, and all of them working. I, as a member of the audience, see very little talent in them. But I see the tide is changing. Now we are being inflicted with expressionless faces, grunts, loose mouths, and tight pants. And the female stars? Ech! You see them in supermarkets, usually in curlers pushing some brat in a shopping cart and looking as if they dressed out of a Goodwill truck. Their cry is that they are being honest, being real, like the girl next door, regular. But their honesty stops when they forget to mention that they're earning a couple of hundred thousand a year that they hang onto while their mother is probably mucking out a chicken coop somewhere in Nebraska.

Goddammit, can't they realize that most moviegoers are sick to death of the dingy sexpot who lives next door and the hairy oaf who's screwing her? They don't want to go to the movies and see their own drab lives depicted over and over again. They go with the hope of being transported by high adventure, by humor and romantic fantasy, to see creatures of another, almost unattainable world, not stained bedsheets and moaning self-pity mouthed by inarticulate louts. They want standards to live by, old ones, preferably, because they are sick to death of the ever-growing cesspool that is confronting them.

But getting back to *Bride of Vengeance*. After the picture was made and shown and reviewed, the ax fell. The critics lacerated it unmercifully, and after five days in release it was yanked, and as far as I know it has never been shown since. Leisen was let out, so was Goddard, so was the producer, and so was the unfortunate leading man who replaced me. Even the assistant director was demoted. The producer eventually migrated to England and is still there, because I passed him on the street. I stuck out my hand to say hello and he cut me dead. This happened at least ten years later, which is one of the things that has proved to me that honesty is not always the best policy. At least in Hollywood.

The pictorial debacle did one thing for me. The studio began to treat me with a little more respect and proceeded to work me harder than ever, but I didn't mind. I'd had two wonderful months skiing and sailing and was in the pink of condition. Another satisfying thing: when you're on suspension no one at the studio is allowed to contact you, which meant no publicity department, no appearances, no nothing. As far as the studio was concerned, I was in purdah for two months. But the pictures I did afterward were better, a little more care was being taken, and my contract was rewritten for the third time. I did two more pictures with Claudette, a couple with Ginger Rogers, and one or two others the names of which I have forgotten.

A few years ago I happened to be playing golf with Forrest Tucker, a much underrated actor whose talent is yet to be appreciated, assuming his rollicking ways don't get to him first, a guy who has really been around. Anyway, we had finished the first nine and were sitting in the grill at Bel-Air having a sandwich. He was browsing through the trades and without looking up said, "I see where Ma Kelly died."

I said, "No! Does it say how old she was? Hell, she must have been ninety."

"No," he replied. "Djever meet her?"

Well, I had, as a matter of fact, early in 1945. Remember my telling you about that gal, Bernadette Conklin, the one who was hired to teach me how to speak American back in '31 at MGM? This is what happened to her.

I had just completed a picture at Paramount, this time I think with Betty Field, and before I could get off the lot I was trapped by the head of the foreign public relations department, a real charmer, Luigi Lusaschi by name. If he turns illegitimate he'll be the greatest con artist the game has ever known. He had had a request, he said, from the State Department, asking if I could be sent down the following Wednesday to Lima, Peru, to help dedicate a new opera house. The war was staggering to a close and we were still buttering up Latin America. I was to emcee the occasion and sort of represnt the theatrical and artistic world of the United States.

"Why me?" I asked.

"Because," he said, "they like you down there. And besides, you speak Spanish and you have your own white tie and tails in which you look beautiful."

I told him I would think about it over the weekend and let him know on Monday. Monday morning came and it was pouring rain, so I called him and said yes.

I left on Pan-American on Wednesday, first stop Mexico City, then on to Panama. As we were approaching Guatemala City two fighter planes appeared beside us and forced us to land. We taxied up to the airport building. Six Guatemalan militiamen came aboard and took off one man. We were kept there for two hours and not allowed to leave the plane. We just sat there and steamed while the gangling militia lounged in the aisle with their guns pointing in all directions. It seemed there was a revolution going on. We were finally allowed to take off, only to find when we got to Panama that I had missed that day's plane for Lima and could not get out until the next day.

I spent the night at the only decent hotel in Panama, at that time called the Tivoli. It reminded me of one of those clap-board administration buildings you can still see at Sawtelle Veterans Hospital. It was hot, sticky, and the food abominable. The next morning, with great relief, I caught a Panagra plane for Lima, where I was met by a couple of men from the United States Embassy. Apparently the occasion was more important than I had thought. Artur Rubinstein had come from New York, Bidu Sayao from Brazil. There was a week of press interviews, with visits to local points of interest, including a side trip to Cuzco, with photographers and politicos all religiously wearing dark glasses. At the end of the week the dedication and official opening of the opera house was to take place, followed by a supper to be given at the presidential palace by President Bustamente. On the big evening there was a reception held in the foyer of the opera house. A glittering affair, the men all in evening clothes and the women breathtaking in their diamonds, dressed with great chic. Peruvian women are stunning anyway.

There was also a most intriguing drink served called "pisco sour." About nine P.M. the roar of motorcycles announced the arrival of President Bustamente. It was time for me to go on stage.

Luckily I speak Spanish and fair French and these two languages combined with the pisco sour made for an absolutely brilliant dedication speech, I thought. After a lot of introductions the performance went on. It was short, consisting of excerpts from *Aida* and *Butterfly,* a Chopin étude played by Rubinstein, until finally—and unaccountably—the orchestra ended the performance with a dirge of Moussorgsky. At eleven o'clock the performance was over and we of the elite repaired to the presidential palace for supper. It was magnificent. The people, the rooms, the gowns, the jewels and, of course, the lovely pisco sour. By now it was midnight, and my plane back to Panama would leave at one. I was panicky. I whispered to one of the aides that my plane was due to leave in an hour. "It is absolutely imperative that I catch this flight," I said. "Can you suggest to his excellency that it would be a great boon to me if I could leave?"

The aide looked horrified and said, "No, that would be most improper. I will call the airport and hold the plane."

President Bustamente, like most Latin Americans, was a great movie fan. He told me that as a young man he had been madly in love with a Hollywood actress named Catherine Dale Owens, but only on the screen, you understand? Could I tell him anything about her? That this dame was probably old enough to be my mother and that I had never met her didn't faze this kid. By the time I got through with her Busta-mente was ready to leave on the plane with me. Finally he noticed that I kept peeking at my watch, and with a rather roguish and conspiratorial leer asked me why. I told him of my predicament, and he immediately in-formed an aide to have the plane held. The aide said that it had been done. The president then presented me with two wonderful pieces of pre-Columbian pot-tery, a couple of bottles of presidential pisco, and sent me off with an *abrazo* and a full police escort. I was swept up to the Gran Bolivar Hotel to pick up my bags and then roared to the airport, right up to the door of the plane. After arranging with the two aides for my bags to be stowed and saying some cheery good-byes, I climbed the steps and entered the plane to face forty people looking at me with raw hatred in their eyes—they had been sitting in this trap for over two hours. And there I stood, this fatuous fool in white tie and tails with my two bottles of pisco under my arm and my pre-Columbian pottery. I wanted to die. One of the passengers happened to be the famous director William Wyler, whom I had met before. To him this night I was a Nazi. All the way to Panama no one spoke to me, not even a stewardess. By a not too strange coincidence, I have never worked in a William Wyler picture.

Upon my arrival to Panama I was met by the two men in charge of all Paramount activities in Central America, who took me back to the tacky Tivoli Hotel. It was still hot and sticky. I told them I would not eat in this morgue tonight; there must be somewhere better. They looked at each other and then looked at me and asked, "Have you ever heard of Ma Kel-ly's?"

I said, "Who hasn't?" It was, at that time, the most raucous bagnio in the New World. It had every-thing: food, music, wine, and, if you will pardon the expression, women. It sounded delightful, so off we went. Being quite well known because of my movie activities, we were given a ringside table immediately and the proprietress herself came over with three of her nymphs, who were really not too bad. One was German and the second one I'm sure was Chinese, but it was the third one who shocked me. She was tall, blond, and a little over the hill. She didn't sit, she just stood there and stared at me. Then with a look both despairing and bitter she hurried through the dancers and was gone. Fourteen years has passed since I had last seen Bernadette Conklin.

In a daze I heard my friends order some food which Ma Kelly said would be on the house. She also suggested that we order some cocktails and a bottle of champagne for the sake of the girls, apparently they got a percentage. Halfway through the dinner a fight started on the floor between some sailors and a bunch of marines. In roared the police, who obviously kept a squad outside the door every night. I said to the Paramount men, "This is where we blow." And blow we did, not paying for the drinks, straight back to Sawtelle, or to give it its local name, the Tivoli. It was a long time before I slept that night. The next morning I caught the Pan-Am plane back to Los Angeles. I had had enough local color.

I have been in New Orleans just once. And for me, once is enough, because being a European originally one has a preconceived idea of America, and always a romantic one. For instance, a European always imagines New Orleans as one big Bourbon Street, Basin Street, and the "blues," magnolias and trumpets, that sort of thing. Well, I was in the town for just two days and a night. I had to see the French Quarter and all the rest of it. Basin Street is now a freeway, just one big fester of concrete. The French Quarter is about two square blocks and looks as if it had been erected for a picture starring John Carroll. And of course, I had to have dinner at Antoine's. There was a line outside a block long. I thought for a moment they were waiting to get into a movie. Production-line seating and a very mediocre dinner. I was then taken to a "typical" New Orleans jazz-box. The ceiling was low, the drinks minute, and the music deafening. The farthest spot from it was the bar. I sat there alone and ordered a Ramos Fizz and stayed there miserably sipping it. Two stools away sat a woman who appeared to be in her seventies, with improbable red hair, cerise cheeks, and oddly orange lips. And she had a hat on. She looked at me and said, "You owe me twelve bucks."

"What for?" I asked.

"Never mind what for. You owe me twelve bucks."

Now I am a peaceable man, so I gave her the twelve and left. When I got back to my table I asked the waiter to look over at the bar and tell me who she was. He looked and said, "Oh, that's the famous Ma Kelly from Panama. She's retired now." Not quite, I thought, not quite.

chapter xiv

When I got back from Lima a book was delivered to my house with a note inside which read, "Read it. Study it. You're going to play it." And it was signed "De Sylva." It was from Buddy DeSylva, at that time production head of Paramount. The title of the book was *The Lost Weekend*. I took it to bed with me that night, but after a dozen pages I fell asleep. I awakened at four A.M. and had another crack at it. After an hour's reading I began to feel a strange uneasiness. The book began to repel me. I got out of bed and went downstairs and made myself some breakfast, all the time brooding about that damned book. Its subject was one I knew very little about. Alcoholism. I could not abide being in the company of people who were drunk; they made me tense and very nervous. I never knew what to say to them. After I finished breakfast I went up to Mal and told her that I was going down to the boat for a couple of days by myself to study the book.

About a year before, I had purchased a beautiful Sparkman and Stephens yawl called the *Santana*. She was fifty-five feet long and the best there was. Because the war was still on and the harbor closed, sailing opportunities were very limited, so most of the time we sat in the slip and had weekend picnics. Occasionally, when I felt the need to get away from people and from the incessant telephone I would spend a few nights on her alone. So peaceful, so simple. Except when Flynn came down to spend a few night on his *Sirocco*. But this was the beginning of the week and things would be quiet, so I could concentrate on the book.

On the third night I drove home, subdued and just a little leery of the project. To begin with, it was unlike any motion picture story I had ever read, downbeat and stark, with not one light moment, about a problem that people treated with uneasy laughter and usually pushed under the rug, alcoholism. Not the social drinkers or the party drunks, but the disease itself, the addiction. Unaccountably, my thoughts went back to the Tennant Canal, to the day when my foot touched that frightening unknown thing on the bottom.

When I got home and sat down to dinner, I said hardly a word. At the very best, I thought, the movie would garner a few huzzahs as a social document. Also, it would call for some serious acting on my part, something I hadn't paid much attention to up until now.

Later that evening, when we were sitting in the library, Mal, who has that wonderful faculty of knowing when not to talk, looked over at me and asked, "How was the boat, and how was the book? Any good?"

"Beautifully written," I said, "but depressing and unrelieved. Damned interesting though, only it's going to call for some pretty serious acting and I don't know whether I'm equipped for it."

She gave me an old-fashioned look and said, "How do you know? Up until now you haven't had many opportunities to find out. You've just been coasting. To me, the story sounds very worthwhile and it will probably cause a lot of comment. Besides, it's a challenge. So stop dithering and get to work on it. Even if it turns out not to be any good you will at least have learned something from it."

"Yes, but if I'm lousy in it, I could very well be through in this racket, which would mean finis to this sybaritic life we've been leading. But for you, my nagging wife, I'll do it and I'll do my damnedest. I'm warning you, though, I'm not going to be very pleasant to live with for the next three months."

"Were you ever?"

The director was Billy Wilder, whom I described for you at the beginning of this book; the producer was Charles Brackett, who also cowrote the script with Wilder. They were known as the Gold Dust Twins, the Katzenjammer Kids and Hansel and Gretel. As far as I know, they had never had a flop. I had worked in several pictures they had written before. One of them was Wilder's first directorial effort, *The Major and the Minor,* with Ginger Rogers. But they were a most improbable pair, Brackett being the erudite scion of an old-line Eastern family that owned a bank in Saratoga, I think. He was a man of great charm and had a gently Satanic sense of humor. They were a well-met pair.

As the starting date of the picture came closer, my worry increased. I had had a copy of the script sent to me two weeks earlier and it was a gem. So much so that the doubts I had as to my ability to do it justice increased. Then I had what I thought was a brilliant idea! Mal's sister and her husband were coming to dinner that night. Why not get fractured and then read the script to them? Get their reaction. I must tell you, I was not exactly what you would call a drinker in those days. If I had two drinks in a month I was overdoing it. I just never thought about the stuff.

Well, the stuff I lapped up that night was something called Old Mammoth Cave, left over from the early days of the war, when it was mandatory to buy two cases of tequila in order to get a couple of bottles of bourbon. By about nine-thirty that night I was done to a turn and figured I was ready. Not that the script had a lot of scenes where the man was "under the influence." Far from it. There were just two, both quite short—and these were the two scenes I intended to parade for my family. The rest of the story, about 80 percent of it, was concerned with his search for the stuff, the terrible physical craving, the degradation and complete moral breakdown. There was also a scene where he had an attack of d.t.'s. Sttangely, these didn't worry me too much. It was the drunk scenes that really bothered me. I was afraid I would overdo them and be amateurish. But not tonight. Tonight I had 'em down pat. Tonight I was lord of the universe, my capabilities endless.

At about ten o'clock we gathered in the library, and I took center stage in front of the fireplace, opened the script and started. It was pathetic, a shambles. In the first place, one of the things I had to do in preparation for the picture was lose about eight pounds so that I could have the drawn and haggard look required for the end of the tale, because they intended to shoot the picture backward, do the last half first. As my normal weight at that time was around 168 pounds, I had gone on a diet of dry toast, coffee, grapefruit juice and boiled eggs. On this night I was down to about 160 pounds, and my six-foot-two frame looked like a buggy whip. So the bourbon I guzzled that night had me quite shook up. The words were fuzzy and I had quite a bit of trouble separating the pages. After about twenty minutes of this my in-laws were practically rolling on the floor in hysterics. Even my dog Cinderella, who was half Great Dane and half boxer and who weighed about seventy pounds, even she got into the act and took a leap at my chest, which caused me to fall on my ass in the red-hot fire. By the time I struggled to my feet my rump was on fire and I felt deathly ill. Somehow I managed to make it to the powder room, get on my knees, and stick my head in the toilet bowl. And there I was, smoking and smoldering at one end and throwing up at the other. Somehow they got me to bed. Mercifully, I slept.

I awakened at dawn feeling like the wages of sin, staggered into the bathroom, and stared into the mirror. I thought of only one thing: "This is the day they ought to start the picture." Wally Westmore could never top what I was looking at. Quietly I weaved my way back to my catafalque. It was six months before I could bring myself to take another drink.

During the ten days before the company left for New York, I became increasingly more snappish and morose, so much so that my wife decided to stay in California with our five-year-old son for the month I would be away. I would have my stand-in stay with me in the suite at the Waldorf and be a sort of general factotum. He was a very pleasant chap, a not too successful small-part actor with writing aspirations, a good companion who later became a very good friend.

When we first arrived in New York I wanted desperately to spend one night in the psychiatric ward of Bellevue Hospital. I was told that was where the really far gone alcoholics were confined until they were sufficiently dried out and could be returned to their families or whatever dismal pads they lived in. Up until now, what little knowledge I had about drunks I had got from watching my friends. I had never seen anyone with d.t.'s, and I don't think many people have. I've never seen a dead donkey either, come to think of it. Without much trouble the evening was arranged. I was taken to the hospital and, after much conspiratorial goings-on stripped, given some hospital pajamas and a threadbare terrycloth bathrobe and assigned to a narrow iron bed. The bed was located near the door of a large whitewashed ward containing about twenty other beds, three-quarters of them occupied. Three tough-looking male nurses who had been alerted to my situation were in charge of the wards. They seemed more like jailers than hospital attendants. The place was a multitude of smells, but the dominant one was that of a cesspool. And there were the sounds of moaning, and quiet crying. One man talked incessantly, just gibberish, and two of the inmates were under restraint, strapped to their beds. Within an hour the attendants had given me a rundown on the fifteen men in the room, and it seemed to me that the majority of them were or had been in the advertising profession. One of them had once been the mayor of quite a large city.

Toward eleven P.M. the attendants went around dispensing small glasses of a cloudy-looking liquid. I asked an attendant what it was.

"Taste it," he said.

I did, and damn near threw up all over the bed. "What is it?" I asked.

"Paraldehyde mixture," he replied. "Calms 'em down so they can get some sleep maybe, and gives us a chance to make a little coffee. This being Monday, we should have a slow night."

After he left me I dozed off for an hour, only to be suddenly shocked into wakefulness by the slamming of the double doors near my bed and the entrance of two attendants manhandling an obviously new inmate. He fought them all the way to the bed at the end of the ward. At the same time he kept up a high, keening wail, and when they got him to the bed he started screaming that it was on fire. They finally got him strapped down, but the screaming didn't stop, and other inmates began growling in the foulest language imaginable. Then from across the room a long ululating howl started, the sound that coyotes make at night in the high deserts of Arizona. Suddenly the room was bedlam. I knew I was looking into the deepest pit.

I struggled into the hospital robe, and not bothering with slippers, slid through the double doors. I had had enough. Somehow, I made it down the two flights of stairs to the main hall. It was after three A.M. and the lights had been dimmed. The two attendants behind the admittance desk were busy with telephones. Like a ghost I made it across the hall, through the front doors and down the steps. I raced down the path and through the gates onto Thirty-fourth Street and then turned toward Second Avenue hoping to find a cab. Only I ran smack into the arms of a policeman. (There was always one patrolling that block.) Vainly I tried to explain that I was a movie star and that I lived in a suite at the Waldorf Towers and that I was lapping up some atmosphere for a movie and that I had to get a cab and go home. Then he saw Bellevue Hospital stamped on the gown and the jig was up. I started to struggle, but he stomped on my bare toes and ran me right back into the admittance hall. After thirty minutes of explanation and corroboration from the chief nurse I was allowed to go home. I never wanted to set eyes on that horrifying place again. But I did. It turned out that the very first scene we made in New York portrayed a ward filled with men with the d.t.'s. It was shot in exactly the same place. The only difference was that it was photographed at dawn instead of three A.M.

For most of the work in New York the cameras were hidden. Holes were cut in the canvas tops of delivery trucks, or from the inside of a huge piano packing case strategically placed on the sidewalk before dawn or from the inside of a vacant store front. Therefore, nobody paid any attention to the unshaven bum staggering along Third Avenue looking for a pawnshop for his battered typewriter, an instance of protective coloring. To them I was normal.

There was one incident on a Saturday morning that could have become quite embarrassing socially. We were shooting a segment of my pathetic search up Third Avenue. In my almost complete exhaustion I was suppose to lean against the window of an antique shop, unshaven, close to tears, my face shadowed and drawn, mouth open and fighting for breath and my clothes looking as if I had slept in a public urinal. The camera was to shoot from inside an ambulance drawn up at the curb. At that moment, two well-dressed women approached with the obvious intention of looking in the window. They saw me and stopped dead.

Slowly a look of shock came over their faces. Then they dropped their heads and hurried away, stopping after a dozen steps to look back. One had a look of utter disbelief, the other an expression that I can only describe as anticipatory joy. The first one was a friend of Mal's. The other was a notorious Hollywood nymph who had once invaded my room in a Mexico City hotel and was politely asked to leave by the management at my request. She never forgave me.

On this Saturday morning I didn't attach any importance to the fact that they had seen me in this condition, figuring that on reflection, they would assume they had been mistaken. Couldn't have been me. Four nights later I got a frantic call from Mal saying there were items in all the columns insinuating that I was in New York on a monumental alcoholic binge and that I had been seen lying in the gutters. She had also received several commiserating calls from "friends." What was going on?

I explained what was going on. That these two women had seen me playing a scene in the street and, not noticing any cameras, had drawn the obvious conclusion. And because the company didn't want anyone to know we were shooting these scenes in New York, nothing had been in the papers.

"Then you'd better *get* something in. And get it in fast," my wife said. "Besides being humiliating for me, it's a dreadful thing for your career. So you'd better *do* something as soon as I hang up which is right now!" Click.

Within thirty seconds I had the unit publicity man on the blower, and ten minutes after that I was talking to the head of Paramount publicity in Hollywood. Talking, hell! I was roaring. I reverted all the way back to my early teens. What with the concentration required for the role, the stringy diet I was on and the odd and leery looks I got from people whenever I went out at night, I was on the ragged edge anyway. Within a week everything had been corrected and the picture went on. After a month in New York the company returned to Hollywood.

Now the real work started, the cerebral part, the part where the thought processes become vocal, where the camera comes so close that nothing can be hidden and fakery isn't possible. Thank God for Wilder and Brackett, Wilder with his prying, probing, intuitive touch of genius, and Brackett with his kindly calm and sociological insight. There was also Charles Jackson, the author of the book, like a bright, erratic problem child, telling me of the horrors he had been through that had let to the writing of it, which only served to increase my morbidity.

There was one amusing thing that occurred, however, while we were shooting the interior of an old Irish bar on Third Avenue called P. J. Clarke's. It had been reborn on Stage Five with absolute exactitude, even to the dusty stuffed cat on top of the telephone booth, and this was the place where I, as Don Birnam, did most of my drinking and rationalizing. For a full week, at five o'clock every afternoon, the stage door would open and a man would walk in and amble right up to the bar and ask for a straight bourbon. It made no difference to him whether we were shooting or not, and without blinking an eye, Howard da Silva, who was playing the bartender, would pour him out a straight shot from a bottle of the real stuff which he kept beneath the counter. The man would then drink half of it, and with a long exhale of pleasure look around and make some inane remark about the weather. Then he would finish the rest of it, plunk down fifty cents, give a painful little smile to the bartender and leave. While he was there, nobody said a word, and when he left we got on with our work as if nothing had happened. The man? Robert Benchley. Who else? Like all expatriate New Yorkers, he was homesick. Besides, it would make for a very quotable anecdote.

But my home life was deteriorating. Life didn't seem to be joyous anymore. Up until this point, with the exception of a few minor irritations, it had been one big buffet. Only now the irritations became problems: my wife without humor, my friends stand-offish. One night, coming home from work I flew into a rage because I was expected to attend a dinner party given by some people I despised. I roared up the stairs, grabbed two pairs of socks and some shorts. I stormed out of the house and rented an apartment in the Sunset Towers. For two weeks I stayed there, eating at Lucy's, across from Paramount, after work and boiling my shorts and socks before going to bed, my wife thinking my depression was a dramatically staged excuse to shack up with some blond Hollywood dame, and not without reason. There had been a few previous peccadilloes, nothing serious, just the normal male revolt against his convenient chains. It was very easy to succumb to in those days. In that town. But in two weeks, when my shorts became grayer, I sneaked back home with the injured attitude that I hoped she had learned her lesson. The household help looked at me as if I had the pox. Ten days later the picture was finished and my wife and I packed the car and took a long drive. All the way to Canada. Our home life came back to normal and I put on ten pounds. But you know, to this day Marie, our housekeeper, still looks at me with a jaundiced eye, and this after twenty-five years.

The trip to Canada turned out to be one of my wiser decisions and I've made very few. On the way up we stopped and played golf at Pebble Beach, stayed a few days in San Francisco, drove through the redwood forest, caught trout in Oregon, and had three party-filled days in Vancouver with some Canadian relatives. The drive home was a joy. We sang old songs, stopped at roadside cafés for coffee and apple pie, and once, while passing an orchard, we climbed the fence and stole a hatful of pears, which turned out to be as hard as iron but we kept them anyway. A week later, at home, they were just fine.

As we got near the redwoods again we decided

to stop for lunch at one of those large wayside restaurants set back in the trees. A long-distance bus had pulled in just ahead of us and the place was filled, so we eased up to the bar for a drink until a table became available. I ordered a rum and Coca-Cola and coffee for my wife. As we sat there sipping, the place began to empty and while looking around I happened to catch the barman polishing glasses and looking at me with a puzzled expresson on his face. Then he put down his towel and eased along to where we were sitting and said, "You on the stage?"

Ah, I thought, the price of fame! Even in this out-of-the-way spot. So, preening a little and in my best affable manner, I said, "Well, I suppose one could say I am, really, although actually I'm from Hol—"

That's all I got out, because he stopped me by saying, "Then you'd better finish up ya drink 'cos it's just about to leave."

And with that he went back to his glasses, and my life's companion staggered off her stool in a paroxysm of coughing mixed with whoops of laughter. With no little concern and much back slapping, I got her seated at a table, whereupon she looked at me with eyes still streaming and croaked, "Whooo, that was funny! Hoo hoo, so *funny!* I'm sorry, darling, but it really was. Oh boy, oh boy!"

I looked at her quite mystified and said that I failed to see the joke, something must have gone right by me. So she explained. In America, outside of metropolitan areas, long distance buses are not called "buses." They are called "stages" by country folk, a throwback to the days when most traveling was done by stagecoach. I had the good grace to laugh.

Soon after returning to Hollywood in 1945 I was assigned to a picture called *Kitty* with Paulette Goddard and directed by Mitchell Leisen, who at that time were still with Paramount. In it I played an eighteenth-century fop, complete with powdered wig, beauty spot, silk breeches, and buckled shoes, who made his living as a procurer and pimp. Immediately following that, opposite Olivia de Havilland, I played a naval lieutenant in the Second World War. Most of the crew on that picture had also worked on *The Lost Weekend*. One Monday morning, the sound mixer said to me, "The sound department ran a rough cut of *Weekend* Saturday night, just checking the sound track. I wanna tell you something. You're going to be nominated for an Academy Award. You can't miss."

I gave him a quizzical look and told him to stop kidding around. At that, he became the tiniest bit belligerent.

"Look," he said, "I'll tell you how much I'm kidding around. I'm willing to bet on it, not that you'll be nominated, that's a cinch, but that you'll get the Award. And I'll make a bet on it right now. Ten bucks and you give me three to one, which is pretty good odds when you consider there'll be five nominees. What d'ya say?"

"I'll do better than that," I said. "I'll give you fifty to one if you're right. Okay?"

"You bet your ass it's okay. Your trouble is, you're afraid to think about it."

He was so very right. I drove home that night in a very bemused state, trying not to think about it, but it kept filtering back. Could this wonderful thing possibly happen to me? To little Reggie? To be acclaimed by one's colleagues in all the cinema crafts, for having given the best performance of an entire year? Against all comers the world over? No! No, stop it! Don't even think about it. Think about the disappointment if nothing happens. Besides, nobody at the studio had intimated anything along those lines, not the director, or anyone in the front office, no even gentle Charley Brackett. But I *had* noticed that I had been getting smiles from people I didn't know, a little more deference from the gang in the mailroom, and an unaccountable query from studio operations wanting to know if I'd prefer a parking slot right outside my dressing room instead of the one I now

had, which was way down by Crosby's room. I began
to add up a lot of other little incidents. Was it imagination? Nah! Wishful thinking. That night at dinner
I was very subdued, and later, when we were reading
the evening paper is the library, Mal noticed that
I hadn't turned a page in fifteen minutes.

"What's bothering you, honey?" she asked.

I looked at her for a moment and then spilled it.
What the sound man had said, the subtle difference
in the attitudes of people on the lot, my sneaking
little hopes, offset by the fact that the front office had
not changed *their* attitude toward me one iota. If
anything, they were a little more offhand than before.

"Listen, darling, if you deserve it, you'll get it.
This is *one* election that can't be rigged, so start hoping and wishing. Even if nothing comes of it, it's not
going to be the end of the world. People learn a lot
from disappointment. To even be considered is quite
a reward. As for the attitude of the front office, you've
forgotten something. Your contract comes up for
renewal in January. They don't want anything to rock
the boat. So go to bed and do a little dreaming."

I kissed her and went upstairs. God, what a wonderful girl she was! But it would be more to my credit
if I remembered that more often. That night I dreamed
but I didn't sleep.

The next three months were absolute hell. I kept
working, but I wasn't really there. I'm afraid I gave
only lip service. Then one night they gave a preview
at the studio for a select audience. A few venerable
actors and actresses, social pontiffs from Los Angeles
and Pasadena, writers of weighty columns, some members of fashionable consulates, and people who gave
parties with tents. There were producers from other
studios and the usual coterie from the Mittel European
community. But there were no technicians, and no
working press. In order to write their reviews they
had to wait until the picture opened officially, in this
case in New York. I sneaked in and took the last
seat in the last row near the door. As the final scene

faded from the screen I bolted. The thing had had the strangest effect upon me. I *had* to have a drink, and I had to have it fast. I ran through the lot to my car, yanked it through the Lemon Grove gate and drove out Sunset to a bar called the Running Horse, which I thought would be quiet. I ordered the biggest Scotch and soda I could get. My mind was in a turmoil. I didn't know whether what I'd done was good or bad, a subject of this kind hadn't been done before. I had no standards, and it had depressed me terribly. It was two A.M. before I got to bed.

The next morning Mal asked me how it had gone. I told her I didn't know, I had left before the lights went up and I didn't want to talk about it. God love her, she never said another word. I went down to the boat that afternoon and it was three days before I went back to the studio, ostensibly to attend to my mail. Miss Logan, my secretary, told me that there were at least two dozen out-of-the-ordinary phone messages that I must answer. I looked them over, and half of them were from people I didn't know but had heard of. I called the ones I knew and they had all apparently seen the picture or had talked to someone who had been at the showing. Their congratulations were profuse, but their manner was strangely hushed. I smelled disaster. Around five o'clock I went in to see Brackett and Wilder and asked them what the reaction had been at the showing. Wilder seemed confused I thought, a little unsure, his comment being that the reaction had been odd, very odd. But Brackett was almost ebullient. We had made, he said, something really worthwhile, a veritable landmark of which we could all be very proud. There it was again, the faint whiff of disaster.

The picture was scheduled to open in New York ten days later and I wanted to get out of town, out of the country. So with the studio's permission, Mal and I flew to Acapulco for some fishing. We stayed there ten days. Acapulco then was not the place it is today, far from it. It had three old hotels and I think about four taxis, but the fishing was magnificent and we didn't want to leave. However, my furlough was about up. I was brown, healthy, and free of depression, so via an old Fokker trimotor and a still-camouflaged DC 3 we waddled back to Los Angeles.

As I drove into the studio the next morning, the usually laconic policeman at the De Mille gate gave me a very large hello, which surprised me until I remembered that Christmas was only two weeks away. His reception was nothing compared to the camaraderie and back slappings I received while walking around the lot. Y. Frank Freeman, head of Paramount, even let me pet the dogs, and there were calls waiting for me from Buddy De Sylva, Brackett and Wilder, as well as the legal department. There was also a puzzling call from the head of the construction department. Then I remembered that before going to Mexico I had asked them if I could have a new toilet in my dressing room, one that worked. It seemed they were not only going to put in a new toilet, they had decided to repaint, recarpet, and refurnish both rooms. All this called for some explanation. It was this.

When Paramount made *The Lost Weekend* and the studio heads first saw it they came sadly to the conclusion that what they had was a well-made, socially conscious documentary that would lay an ostrich egg, that it just wasn't Hollywood. They were resigned to box-office receipts on a par with the collection plate in a Wesleyan chapel. Then the movie opened in New York, and its reception was incredible. Bouquets were thrown at everyone who had the slightest connection with the picture. Most of the comments and critical evaluations of my contribution were so laudatory that I was embarrassed and felt constrained to be apologetic about them when in the company of other actors. Then the movie opened in Los Angeles, and the same thing happened, and suddenly my life wasn't my own anymore. I found myself the recipient of more awards than I ever knew existed, New York

Critics Award, *Look* Magazine, Foreign Press Award (this in the days when there really *was* a foreign press), a citation from A.A. Unwed Mothers of America also got into the act I think, and there was a warm commendation from Joe's Bar and Grill in Pismo Beach. More seriously, the most important thing that came about was the fact that although I had been termed a *movie star* in the usual magazine concept for five or six years, I was now being accepted as as actor with dramatic merit. It was a wonderful feeling.

Then, one morning in March I awakened to the knowlege that this was judgment day, when the morning paper would have the names of the five nominees, five actors who would be in purgatory until the "Night" be thrown on the lawn at any moment. I pulled on a dressing gown and went creeping down the stairs in fear and trepidation, only to be met by the sight of Mal, the cook, the butler, the nurse, and my five-year-old son all sitting in the dining room with their eyes glued on the window, which faced the front lawn. I asked them what was going on, why were they up so early. As one they replied, "Same as you. Waiting for the paper."

"Oh, for God's sake," I snarled. "It's not *that* important and where's my breakfast?"

And without looking around my wife said, "It's on the breakfast room table. You'll have to pour the coffee yourself. Think you can do it?"

With the long-suffering look of a man forced to live with mental defectives, I went in to my breakfast. I was just lifting the cup to my lips when I heard the scramble for the front door, and I froze. There was a moment of silence and then one big yelp of exuberance as they all came barreling through the door yelling, "You made it!" "You're nominated!"

"Look! Right here on the front page!"

"Pictures of the five of you. That's you in the middle!" In silence I stared at myself, I didn't look at the other four, just me. Little Reggie, the tattooed kid, the boy with the horse, the friend of Gillam and

Dunbar. Then I burst into tears. It was March, 1946. I was thirty-nine years old.

The next four weeks were a phantasmagoria that brought me to the point of almost hating the town. With just one picture Brackett and Wilder had made Hollywood pause and take stock, and I found myself being looked upon as an authority on alcoholism. *Me,* for Christ's sake, *me,* a guy who if he took three drinks had to be carted off to bed and given up for dead! But slowly and inexorably *der Tag* came closer. On the day it dawned I knew I couldn't face it and made up my mind not to attend. At breakfast I hesitantly told Mal of my decision. She slowly put down her fork and just examined me. I didn't know where to look.

Then she said, "I know that you're erratic, volatile, and the possessor of a foul temper. But I never thought you were a coward!" Then with a look as cold as a Canadian nun, she said, "You'll go to that ceremony tonight if we have to put you in a straitjacket. And I'm calling the troops right now!"

I think we sat in the fifth row that night. I had hired a mile-long limousine with a liveried chauffeur and the inch-by-inch creep to the forecourt of the theater, the screaming of thousands of bleachered fans, the batteries of searchlights, the inane microphone interviews, the multitudinous photographers with their incessant flashbulbs, the hushed and excited whispering in the rapidly filling picture palace, all of it reduced me to a sheet of quivering harpstrings. My carefully acquired air of savoir faire had quite disappeared. My smile had become a rictus. And we sat, and we sat, through the interminable minor Awards, applauding dutifully each recipient and the endless speeches of acceptance, and inexorably the frightening moment came closer. Suddenly it was upon me. There she stood. The magnificent Ingrid Bergman, who, having won the previous year's female Award, now, traditionally, was called upon to announce this year's male winner.

After announcing the names of the five nominees,

she turned to the man from Price, Waterhouse, held out her hand and said, "And now, the envelope, please!" Quickly she tore it open and unfolded the sheet that held the name. A great big grin appeared on her face. Like a blow to the heart I knew I hadn't won. She was smiling and I'd never even met her. It had to be one of the other four. Then dimly, I heard the words, "Are you nervous, Mr. Milland? It's all yours!"

In the applause that followed I just sat there. I never thought to move until I felt Mal's elbow in my ribs, a blow which I still feel to this day when it's raining. My dear one hissed, "Get up there, sweetheart! Get up there! It's you! It's you!"

I don't remember much of what happened after that. Everything was a jumble of handshakes, microphones, people with notebooks and pencils, and flashing camera bulbs. It was almost midnight before we could get to our car and pull away from the theater and head toward the Restaurant La Rue, which Paramount had taken over in anticipation of winning a few Awards. By God, they were right. The picture carried off four Awards. Otherwise it would have been a wake.

I thought of the sixteen years since I had first seen Sunset Boulevard, in 1930, when all I had was curiosity and not much purpose, when the world seemed one big candy box, and suddenly I hit the chauffeur on the shoulder and told him to go on out Sunset to the bridlepath and stop near Hillcrest. We would come back to La Rue's later.

"But, darling," cried my wife, "you mustn't. They're all waiting for you back there!"

"It's all right, dear," I replied. "There's something I want to do first. It'll only take a couple of minutes."

When the car stopped at Hillcrest I got out, and with the golden Oscar in my hand, I walked to the edge of Sunset and looked down at the lights. They seemed very bright that night. After a few moments

I quietly said, "Mr. Novarro. Tonight they belong to me!" Then we drove to La Rue.

The next six or eight months seemed a maelstrom. In May I made a picture called *California* in which I played a trail boss leading a wagon train of settlers to California, perhaps *wagon master* would be a better term. Pro-pro Barbara Stanwyck played opposite me, and Barry Fitzgerald was in it too. But strangely the leading heavies all seemed to be English. Perhaps it was because of the director, the masochistic Australian, John Farrow. The movie took three months to make, and in the middle of it I was notified that I had won the Grand Prix Award at the very first Cannes Film Festival. First prize was a choice of paintings, an ugly one by Picasso or a study of fishing boats by Othon Friesz. Brilliant me, I chose the one by Friesz. Also my contract was rewritten and I became the highest salaried actor then on the lot. There were many other emoluments and privileges. Great deference was shown in nightclubs and restaurants. The mere whisper of an endorsement brought showers of gifts, lawn mowers, a new kitchen, carloads of soap and cigarettes, etc., etc., most of which we gave away. Next England decided to hold the first Royal Command Film Performance. It was to be the first big gala after five years of war, and London was girding for it. My invitation, when it came, was most impressive, all covered with seals and ribbons.

Then Paramount decided this would be the ideal time to open *The Lost Weekend* with a series of "premieres" in all the capitals of Europe, sending Adolph Zukor and myself to attend each one. It turned out to be the labors of Hercules all over again. We sailed from New York early in October on the *Queen Mary,* itself a very gala trip. This was her maiden voyage after being used as a troopship for five years.

The week in London was a caldron of excitement. The dresses and jewels to be worn by the visiting notabilities on the "Night" were minutely recorded in the press. Every meal seemed to be a public event. Claridge's, where Mal and I were staying, was positively festive! On the evening of the Command Performance itself, London put on the closest thing to a riot since the days of Titus Oates. In one interview I referred to it as the Battle of Leicester Square, and it was by that name that it was known for the rest of our stay. Then came Cardiff, the capital of Wales, where I was given a roaring welcome and the key to the city. Hometown boy makes good! All my relatives showed up, half of whom I'd never heard of. God, there must have been a hundred of them. I don't think anyone in the world has more relatives than I, except perhaps a few shameless Portuguese.

Paris was a replay. A testimonial banquet given by the French theatrical community, a reception at the Élysée Palace given by Georges Bidault, then Premier, and the memorable night when I danced with Mistinguette at a bash given at the old Lido. She must have been close to eighty. I didn't see much of my wife during the daytime, because it was the year Christian Dior burst upon the fashion world, and the financial scars were deep indeed. Then Rome, Nice, and the long hop to Stockholm, a different kettle of fish entirely. The city seemed to consist solely of earnest bearded types, all belonging to cinema art groups, which seem to thrive in a cold climate. They feed you six or seven times a day and as far as I can remember it was always the same thing. Smoked reindeer meat and aquavit, a murderous combination. My own breath used to awaken me in the middle of the night.

On my return to London I noticed this dull heavy ache in my upper stomach that only went away when I ate or drank something. My disposition became that of a dyspeptic badger. My friends became quite concerned and insisted that I see a doctor. One of them arranged an appointment with his personal physician the next morning and no arguments! So, at ten A.M. I presented myself at the chambers of a Mr.

McNaughten in Harley Street, London's fabled street
of medics. Specialists all. The difference between doc-
tors and specialists in England is that a doctor charges
you two guineas a visit and a specialist charges you
ten. A doctor is always addressed as "Doctor," but
a specialist insists on being addressed as "Mister."
Ultimate snobbery.

My car deposited me before a quite lovely Georgian
house about three stories high, with a door that was
painted a dark shiny green. Set into the lintel were
three discreet brass plates giving the names of three
physicians who had their consulting rooms there. Mine
apparently was the most important, because he occupied the ground floor. I yanked on the old-fashioned
brass bell pull and was admitted by an elderly retainer
type dressed in a dark blue uniform with brass buttons.
He brought me into a small, beautifully furnished
waiting room. For about ten minutes or so I perused
the periodicals lying on an ancient, well-polished
mahogany drum table. They consisted of *Country
Life, The Field, The Sphere,* and several copies of
Punch, the latest issue being not much younger than
the table it sat on. Suddenly I heard the well-bred
hiss of a door being opened. I turned, and there,
dressed like Florence Nightingale and right out of
Rebecca, stood Mrs. Danvers! Suddenly I wanted
to run away! I wanted to go back to my lovely life
as a movie star, with an Academy Award and a suite
at Claridge's. But her eyes had me pinned. Then she
spoke. "Mr. McNaughten will see you now."

With the skin between my shoulder blades crawling,
I passed her and found myself in one of the most
beautiful English drawing rooms I have ever seen.
The walls were paneled and painted a soft white.
The floor was parquet, dark and glowing. There were
Oriental rugs and a small white marble fireplace with
a gently burning coal fire. There were books with
rich bindings, Chinese screens, and at the far end
of the room was a bow window that looked out on
a small sunken garden. In the window was set a leather-

topped mahogany desk. Behind it stood a huge man of almost seventy years dressed magnificently in a black morning coat, striped trousers, and a winged collar, with a stock made of heavy black silk and a pearl tiepin. He was gorgeous. He was Mr. McNaughten.

After a very perfunctory introduction he seated himself and said with professional cheeriness, "Now, what seems to be the trouble?"

I began to tell him, when suddenly he stopped me and said, "We must get all this down."

He thereupon opened the center drawer of the desk. Pushing aside a motley collection of tongue depressors, surgical clamps, and an old rubber stethoscope, he hauled out a ledger that had all the earmarks of the original Domesday Book. I sat there for at least half an hour while he asked questions about my previous illnesses and aberrations while his pen spluttered and scratched. Then he closed the book and told me to take off my clothes and throw them over a chair. All except my shorts and socks. He proceeded to tap and peer and sound every bone, crevice, and cavity he could find. And all he ever said was "Hmmmmm." Then he rang a little silver bell and in slid Mrs. Danvers.

"We need a specimen from this young man," he said. "Do we have anything?"

She thought for a moment and replied, "Yes, I think I can find something."

Oh, no, I thought. They can't mean it. Not here in this lovely room. Not while I'm standing here on this beautiful Chinese rug. Not here in front of God and everybody! But they did, because in she came with a small glass jar with a metal screw cap on it. She silently handed it to me and I squeaked, "I can't, I can't!"

"Good God," he said, "why not?"

I threw a fleeting glance at Mrs. Danvers. "I just can't!"

Mr. McNaughten looked at me and said, "Why not? Did you go before you came in here?" And then, "I see . . . Nurse, would you leave us, please?" After she left he walked behind one of the Coromandel screens where there was a small washbowl and turned on both faucets and then stuck his head around and said, "Now try."

Trapped, I started to unscrew the top on the jar and I noticed something printed on it. It said, "Crosse & Blackwell. (Raspberry)."

I was now fully dressed and waiting while Mr. McNaughten laboriously wrote out a prescription. He told me to have it filled at the chemist's shop on the corner. He also said that I should take a spoonful dissolved in warm water before each meal and that his fee was ten guineas. Just as I was leaving the room he called from his desk. He was very much afraid that I had the beginnings of an ulcer. By God, I thought, I've finally made it! I'm a success! Me, little Reggie, with an ulcer!

I hied myself to the druggist on the corner. He looked at the prescription and in a supercilious tone said that he might have it ready by five o'clock that afternoon. With a derisive snarl I snatched the prescription out of his hand and left. Now, there is a drugstore, one of a chain, in Piccadilly Circus called Boot's. It is much frequented by Americans because of its efficiency and its large and comprehensive stock. They had an American prescription pharmacist whom I knew slightly. When I gave the prescription to him and asked, "How long?" he looked at it and said, "About five seconds."

He walked to a shelf and took down a short squat tin, put it in a paper bag, and said, "That'll be six shillings, please." When I got back into the car I took the tin out of its bag and read the label. It said "Bisodol"!

Three days later we sailed for home and the pain disappeared.

chapter xv

It was toward the end of July in '72, and a bunch of us were sitting under a huge carob tree in a botanical park just east of Cape Town. We were waiting for the sun, and there was a decided nip in the air. South Africa, down at the tip, can be pretty unfriendly weatherwise. And otherwise. We were trying to finish a picture being produced by a South African company, and the project smelled of disaster.

Although the basic idea in the script wasn't bad, it was bitched from the start because on the ludicrous casting of the two juvenile leads, two young men who were supposed to be my sons. One of them was a young American from somewhere in West Virginia whose only claim to fame was that he had once played an inarticulate Indian in a TV series about the old West. He was about twenty-five years old and was supposed to play a diplomatic troubleshooter hooked in with the CIA. The other actor was a plump young German Jew with black curly hair and rosy cheeks, whose almost nonexistent English was straight out of the Katzenjammer Kids. He was about nineteen years old and was playing the part of a test pilot for NASA. Needless to say, he was a friend of the

producer. Need I go on? My part was what is rever-
ently called a "cameo" and was to be completed in two
and a half weeks entirely in the Cape Province. Then
I'd fly back to France, where I'd just spent three
months doing absolutely nothing and fighting the
beginnings of boredom.

It had been almost twenty years since I had left
Paramount. Twenty wonderful and exciting years, until one morning everybody woke up to find that Hollywood was a graveyard. The place had priced itself
out of the market. Unemployment in all the motion-
picture crafts was almost 60 percent. That didn't
mean that pictures were not being made. They were.
But not in Hollywood. They were being produced
in every corner of the globe where financing could
be found, and actors were becoming vagabonds again
and taking their pay in all kinds of wild and woolly
currencies. One actor I know made a picture in
Australia and took as payment a carload of kangaroo
skins. He intended to ship them back to the States
and make them into throw rugs and fur coats for chic
skiers in Sun Valley and Vermont. It didn't seem to be
a bad idea, until his crates were opened on the dock
by the customs people, several of whom fainted from
the ungodly stink. It cost him eighteen hundred dollars
to have the skins carted off and burned. I was more
fortunate, or perhaps crafty would be a better word.
I always managed to have my salary deposited in
an American bank *before* I started a picture, so I
always got paid. None of those profit-sharing schemes
where you have to hire a battery of lawyers to try
and find the profits, and if they are successful the
profits are eaten up by their fees. My system worked
very well except in England, where they hit you for
about 70 percent income tax. After you've paid expenses all you end up with is a free trip.

But it was a good life, and we made many friends,
because Mal always traveled with me and she has
that facility. It's a quality of hers that sometimes
drives me up the wall. She insists that there is some

good in everybody, and that's the way she leads her life. But I could gladly strangle some of the people with broken wings that we get stuck with. I was intolerant as a youth, and then came forty years of increased understanding laced with some compassion. But now, in my sixties, I feel that shitty selfishness sneaking back. I can't be bothered anymore. Time is getting short and I have a lot to do.

"D'ya know something? Actors today are a bunch of whores." The speaker was a damn good actor named Cameron Mitchell, and he was sitting with his back against the trunk of the carob tree, morosely watching an aged baboon quietly masturbate. We somnolently flicked our eyes in Cam's direction, waiting for his dissertation, because he's a guy who can really dissert. After a few moments of nothing, John van Dreelen, a brilliant Dutch actor, said with a touch of asperity, "Well, don't just let it hang there, Cam. Please explain, because your remark affects me personally and I'm afraid you may have a point, which is upsetting."

"Well," said Cam, "as a for instance, look at the five of us sitting here. Five pretty good actors, competent, adaptable, and, let's face it, each of us blessed with a touch of talent, an instinctive knowledge of what to do with a part without having to go through a lot of psychiatric delving in order to get a scene done. Directors look upon types like us as insurance. Yet we are all lacking one thing. Integrity. Artistic integrity."

"Now just a bloody minute . . . !" This from Tony Dawson, an intense English actor I had last worked with under Hitchcock in *Dial M for Murder,* about fifteen years earlier. "Are you implying that we accept a part, slough it off, then take the money and run?"

"Hell, no. I'm not implying that. You weren't listening. What I meant was that when we are offered a part, and there are a lot of actors just like us, we ask about four questions. How big is the part, what's my billing, where do we shoot it, and how much do

I get paid? And if the answers are satisfactory we pack our bags. In this particular case, I didn't read the script until I'd flown twelve thousand miles and was waiting for a connecting plane in Johannesburg. By the time I got here it was too late. Once we accept the script, we do our best, but we hardly ever concern ourselves about its artistic merit. The only thing that seems to matter is that we are working. Different actors, different reasons. With most, the reasons are economic. In my own case it's that I have an incurably itchy foot. Some guys just want to get away from their wives. Steve Boyd, here, just wants to make enough money fast enough to buy a horse farm in Ireland and walk away from all this slop. And look at Milland. Here's a guy who they tell me is really loaded, got an Academy Award, married to a beautiful dame, and the proud possessor of two good hair pieces—what's *his* reason for being in this bomb?"

"It's very simple," I replied. "I've never been in South Africa before."

"There y'are, ya see? A whore just like the rest of us. And it isn't only us! Look what's happening back in Hollywood. Guys like Fonda selling aspirin, and floor tile, powder for cleaning kitchen sinks or some such. And then there's MacMurray, a guy who probably has the first dollar he ever earned, doing a TV pitch for a bus company. And here's the topper: Larry Olivier, *Lord* Olivier, if you please, doing a TV spiel for a cheap camera! And they don't even give him billing, for Christ's sake!" Sulfurously, Cam turned back to watching the baboon, who was now lying on his back with his feet in the air, completely spent. "We're *all* whores, only with us it's a difference in degree." And then he shut up.

I guess he'd had trouble with his coffee that morning, being a rabid coffee hound. I'd spent a few evenings in his room at the hotel in Stellenbosch after work, just chewing the fat, and I counted seven different coffee-makers, all electric and each a different make and design. I said, "D'you travel with all these?"

"You bet your ass I travel with them. Different countries, different coffee, so you have to adjust. Good coffee makes up for the lousy food you run into."

We spent the rest of the day on our toes waiting for breaks in the cloud cover, and when one did appear jumping into a scene and racing through it with some semblance of credibility before the sun disappeared again. Hectic.

On the bus going back to the hotel that night I fell to musing over our conversation about TV commercials and suddenly realized that I missed them! Don't misunderstand. Not the 90 percent that are the epitome of bad taste and that drive people away from a product, but the little jewels that make up the other 10 percent. Like the one featuring a fellow who looks a little like a bloated Stan Laurel and who used to do a thing with a two-way medicine cabinet, advertising a shaving soap or a deodorant or something in the toiletries line. The commercial began with a Milquetoast type opening the medicine cabinet in his bathroom. Just as he was reaching for something, the back of the cabinet would swing open as if from the apartment next door, and there would be Moonface, all warmth, saying, "Hi, guy!" and then going into a ludicrous, uninhibited spiel for whatever he was supposed to be pushing. Milquetoast would just look at him all agape and then turn into the camera and call out despairingly, *"Mona!"* Sounds like nothing, right? But to a watching actor, this guy was a joy. I saw him later on some talk shows, booked probably because of his commercials, and he was brilliant, so many-faceted. Then there was the marvelous commercial about some Italian spaghetti or sauce or something, where the pitchman kept forgetting his lines. Wonderful satire, done with great treachery. Then there's that lovely, fruity bird who insists that Western Airlines is "the *only* way to fly." They should announce the *commercials* in cases like this, and not the dreary programs they support. Did you ever see the one Brenda Vaccaro did for Kodak,

I think it was? Pure talent! And the little covered wagon drawn by a team of six that gallops under the rug and then emerges only to disappear into a crack under the kitchen sink, closely pursued by a bemused and life-size mutt. And those wonderful pen-and-ink commercials for Raid. I think theatrical stars with their rather patronizing manner touched with condescension run a very poor second to the TV-commercial pros. And I don't think the stars help the product, mainly because the public can't bring itself to believe that Loretta Lovelace actually gets down on her knees to wax the kitchen floor. Or that Fred MacMurray would actually ride the bus to Victorville—although on second thought, and knowing Fred, I have to admit he just might. So, as Cam Mitchell said, whoredom is a matter of degree.

Two days later I finished my part in the picture and began the involved machinations for getting out of South Africa with my finances and personal possessions intact, while the rest of the cast forlornly packed for a miserable two weeks of shooting in the wintry South Atlantic on an almost derelict whaling ship, or factory ship, as they are called. The boat was about five hundred feet long and had been lying to a hook about two miles off Cape Town for at least two years. It should have been lying two *hundred* miles off shore, because its stink was everywhere. After a morning session at the Standard Bank in Cape Town and a frustrating hour at the offices of Alitalia, I found myself free to depart on the three P.M. plane for Johannesburg, so I hailed a cab to take me back to Stellenbosch to pick up my bags. On the way I told the driver to stop at the dockside where the hell ship was now moored. As we approached, I could see that the cast and production crew were all on board and lining the rail, watching their baggage being hauled up in nets. The weather had deteriorated, and everything was made more depressing by a cold, driving sleet. I got out of the cab, and, daintily side-stepping the puddles, walked to the dockside. I smiled up at the rail twenty feet above me, wished them all bon voyage, and shouted such gaieties as, "My regards to Admiral Byrd, and don't forget to bring me back a Kee-bird." They didn't say a word. They just looked at me with still faces, and the looks were filled with vitriol and sulfur. But I realized, pleasantly, that there was no hate in their faces, just a barely discernible death wish.

At that moment France Nuyen, who was playing the Tondeleyo part, piped up with, "Tell me please, what is a Kee-bird?"

And relishing the moment, I said, "When you're far enough south to see the Pole, you'll find a bird sitting on top of it, and he'll keep sending out the same plaintive cry—'Keeee-*rist*, it's cold!'" There was a two-second silence, and then a half-eaten fried-egg sandwich hit me right in the mouth. I backed off grinning and said, "There's still time if any of you want to jump ship. The plane doesn't leave till three o'clock." But not one of them would have entertained the idea. They had given their word, and all their moaning, groaning, and bitching was just a protective veneer, like Napoleon's soldiers singing the "Marseillaise" as they advanced into the Russian winter. They would do the job asked of them to the best of their ability, and none of the puking petulance or outrageous demands for personal attention and impossible comforts demanded by so many so-called stars. These were pros of solid honesty and more talented than most of the masquerade. There are many of them, the very marrow of the profession, and you will meet them in all the odd corners of the world. People to whom friendship is not just a word but something of real worth, something given only where there is respect. They are the well-paid gypsies, the Whores of Stellenbosch, and I'll meet them again up some dark Brazilian river, or washing out their socks and shorts before going to bed after a day's work in some unused African gold mine. I'll be glad to see them, and I will be at ease.

The thousand-mile flight from the Cape to Johannesburg was uneventful, but the eleven-hour drone from there up the length of Africa and across the Mediterranean to Rome was frightful. To begin with, they had forgotten to put any water aboard the plane, and there was a hundred and seventy people back in economy, half of them children who howled the whole night through. There was no ice for the drinks, and the only water we could get came out of the toilets. So the twelve gilded passengers in first class had to make do with unchilled South African wines and warm gin. We landed at Fiumicino airport, in Rome, in a state close to catatonic, and after four hours of unbelievable disorganization I finally took off for New York, where I arrived only two hours late. I had just enough time to catch an American Airlines 747 to Los Angeles, where I was greeted by the news that my baggage was still in Fiumicino. By that time I didn't give a good goddam, and I went to bed for three days. So much for whoredom. But I've finally figured out what's so attractive about it. It's variety.

chapter xvi

Looking back on the exciting and tumultuous twenty years or so since Paramount and I parted company, I would like to recapture and describe some of the daft and lunatic episodes that have touched me. The trick is to do it without laying oneself open to a suit for libel. Nowadays we suffer from an over-abundance of lawyers with an underabundance of principles. And a lot of them are hungry. And as my granny used to say, "The truth can always hurt, be careful with it."

Well, anyway. I was sneaking around down at the marina the other day, quietly casing a couple of boats that were for sale—I was temporarily "on the beach"—when I bumped into this actor, a quite well-known leading man and the only guy I can honestly say is queer for women. Really insatiable. Except for one occasion, which I'll try to describe.

After all these years I finally realized that the only thing I ever wanted to be in this business was a director. And through devious finagling and by as-suming horrifying financial liabilities I've succeeded in directing six pictures—none of them outstanding but none of them lost money either. In each one I've had to play one of the leading roles and also help write the script, while serving simultaneously, as the physical producer; since in cases like this it is impossible to separate your allegiances, the picture inevitably suffers. All right, then why did I take on so many jobs? Very simple. It was the only way I could get a job directing. If I were some bearded hippie from CCNY in sweat socks and dirty sneakers, it'd be a lot easier. But enough of the sour grapes, let me get back to our libidinous Thespian.

The occasion was my second directorial venture. The first one had exceeded expectations, and the man who had given me my first chance, Herbert J. Yates, wanted me to direct another picture as soon as possible. Only this one had to be made in Europe; being married at the time to a gal from Lower Slobbovia, Yates had a lot of in-laws who were eager to visit their relatives over there, and the picture would enable him to write off their expenses against the production. This I found out only after the picture was halfway completed, otherwise I would have gone up like a Roman Candle. Yates was a tough little monkey, president of Republic Pictures, president of Consolidated Film Labs, and also one of the pioneers in the plastics industry, of which he owned quite a hunk. He was a mean, ornery, tobacco-chewing little runt, but his word, as far as I was concerned, was pure gold. He ran his studio with an iron hand, and his employees both feared and respected him. Once, when he went to the hospital to be operated on for gallstones, the word around the lot was that with Yates, the stones would probably turn out to be rubies. It didn't work out *quite* that way, but close. They removed eleven fair-sized stones, and Yates had them polished and set in platinum and used them for a dress set. Shirt studs, vest buttons, and cuff links, and he was seventy-six years old at the time. Between us we practically stole a screen play that Paramount had been trying to lick for five years and that had preparation charges of almost 180,000 dollars against it. We got it for $10,000. Five weeks later, with help from a couple of alcoholic screen writers, I got it into shape so that it would stand up as a fairly good foreign-intrigue picture that would probably get its cost back and show a small profit. Then up and away to Europe to shoot the epic.

There I was, doing the same three jobs, producer, director, and playing the leading heavy, with three key men in the camera crew, a chief electrician, a set designer, head construction man, and a unit manager. The rest of the crew we would hire in Europe. I don't intend to identify the country we shot this picture in, except to say it was one of those places where the toilet paper has to be roughed up pretty good before you can use it. Otherwise you could get a nasty chafe. It was also a country of no national character, no national architectural style but I mélange of everything. I mean, England looks English, France is French, Italy is Italianate, and Spain looks Mexican. This country looks like a grab bag. Even its household furnishings were in the worst possible taste. When the style wasn't heavily Gothic it was revoltingly Victorian. So you may wonder why we chose this as the country in which to make our picture. Well, in the first place it had hardly ever been photographed, in the second place its labor was cheap, and in the third place its location was ideal for our story.

And then our troubles started. The studio we had rented had been built by an Italian company back in the early twenties, and the floors of the stages were of wood so warped and buckled that trucking shots would have been impossible. So there was nothing to do but refloor two of the best ones, not too long a job. Then the cameraman and the chief electrician took a closer look at the lighting equipment and found that 70 percent of it was quite unusable. Practically every condenser was cracked, and the cables looked as if hungry Hottentots had been chewing on them. The outcome was that we had to fly in about five tons of equipment from Rome and Paris, and you can be sure those mackerels didn't send us their best. Then we hired a four-man English sound crew, together with their equipment. They promptly went on strike the third day they were there, demanding better working conditions and something called hardship money because their food and accommodations were not what they had been used to. You bet your ass they were not what they had been used to. Just about three times better, if you ask me. But there was nothing for it but to pay them. There was no point in flying them back to England, because the next lot might be worse. I'm afraid the honest British workingman died in World War I. There are a few left, but they practically have to go into hiding if they're caught actually working as if they liked it. I could go on like this for pages, but the hell with it.

Set construction started the day after we arrived, the plans and designs having been drawn up in Hollywood, and the local workmen and carpenters went at it like beavers fourteen hours a day. In the two weeks it would take to put up the first couple of sets I planned to go out and shoot exteriors. But when we got to our first location we found that the mobile generator hadn't shown up. It was stuck on a hill four miles away with a broken drive shaft that would take five hours to fix. I conferred with the cameraman, and he figured he could shoot most of the stuff that day with reflectors, so I yelled for my first assistant, who came trotting up. No, I shouldn't say that. He came up on the *double,* snapped smartly to attention, and said, "Sir!" He was awfly militry. He had on a double-breasted dark blue blazer with deep vents at the side and a multitude of brass buttons, at least four on each cuff, and the ubiquitous brown suede shoes. I noticed that his buttons were regimental—17/21st Lancers, I think. I explained to him the trouble with the generator and that he had better get the reflectors unloaded as quickly as possible. At that, a rather glazed look came into his eyes, and in a slighty panicky voice he said. "Well, actually, sir, we have a slight problem there."

"Problem, what problem?"

"Well, you see, knowing that you had ordered the generator out first thing, I naturally assumed you wouldn't be needing any reflectors, so I didn't lay on any transport for them." I just goggled at him. "But not to worry, sir. There's a phone at the police post just down the road, and I'll pop in there and call the studio and we'll have them out here in less than two hours."

And with that he took off. On the double. Leaving me with a case of the trembles coming on. I found out later that his only previous experience as an assistant director had been on some cartoon commercials for television. He was back in ten minutes with the information that the stuff would be there within the hour. I asked him if he had been in the army during the last set-to and he said that he had. I asked him what regiment. "Artist's Rifles, sir." Well, that figured. Within a week he was gone.

One day, when I was about halfway through shooting the exteriors, I got a sort of nervous call from the set designer, one of the best in his line, whom we had brought from Hollywood. He wanted to see me in my hotel that night as soon as I got in from location. I didn't think much about it, so I said okay, meet me in the bar. About nine o'clock he drifted in, looking, I thought, a little shifty. I asked him what he'd have, and he said he'd like a double Scotch. Which surprised me, because he hardly ever took a drink. After he'd had a couple of swallows I said, "All right, Frank, what's on your mind?"

He took another swig and then he told me. "Now, there's no holdup with construction. As a matter of fact, the main set, the interior of the mansion, is practically finished, and it's one of the best things I've ever done. All four rooms lead into each other and are connected by a long marble loggia sort of thing, so you can get one long trucking shot of people going from one room to the other. Even the fireplaces are two-way, so you can shoot through them if you want to. As a matter of fact, it's going to take us as long to tear it down as it did to build it. These guys over here did a hell of a job. Built like a brick shit-house."

"Then what's your problem?"

He took a long breath and without looking at me said, "The problem is, we can't furnish it."

I looked at him with complete astonishment. "You'd better explain that," I said, "because you just lost me."

"Okay, I'll try. This is a city of about two million people, right? Well, I've searched it from end to end. Nothing. I've been in every department store, every furniture shop, and every antique store—only they're not antique stores, they're junk shops. I've tried hotels and apartment buildings, and I've come up with one couch and two chairs that are usable. We need ten times that much. As far as wooden pieces are concerned, quite hopeless. Of course, if we were shooting *Bleak House,* the crap I've seen would be ideal. But this is a picture of glamour and excitement, filled with rich, attractive people who screw at the drop of an eyelid. No, I'm afraid you'll have to start thinking about renting the stuff from Paris and Rome. The insurance will be frightening, but that's the only way out, as far as I can see. These sets are too well done to be ruined by filling them up with crap." And with that, he stuck his nose back into his drink.

His point was valid, and something had to be done about it. This called for some devious thinking and my Celtic mind began to take over. . . . After all, this was a big city, and there were a lot of large villas about. Some of them could rightly be called palaces, and they were inhabited by people of taste, jet-set expatriates with a lot of loot, whose current social leader, a rich, handsome, and rapacious woman of close to fifty years, had decided to give a soirée for the company two nights later so that the leading lights of the local scene could meet us vagabonds. The fact that there were four pretty big stars in the picture, three of whom were men, didn't hurt a bit. Also, the local luminaries were all dying to appear in the film one way or another, and since I would be needing a lot of dress extras . . .

At this point Frank came up out of his drink to get some air and said, "By the way, I forgot to mention it, but the Standing Ovation just flew in."

I looked at him. "Who you talking about?"

"Oh, hell, you know who I mean, Hot Rocks Herbie, Love's Leading Laborer, your romantic lead."

"But what the hell is he doing here now? He's not due for another week."

Frank shrugged. "I got the idea that he had to get out of town fast. I think his wife caught him again, and you know what *she's* like."

I certainly did. At the age of seventeen she had been runner-up for the title of Potato Queen of Idaho, one of the prizes being a six-week contract at one of the lesser known studios, which seem to make a business out of this sort of thing. The practice was that if the kids showed any talent their contracts would be sold to a major studio, where they usually got lost in the traffic. Some of them made it, but not this one. She had talent, but not in the acting line. She was also quite volatile and, to the eye, a magnificent creature.

I asked Frank to call Lover Boy's room and tell him we'd like to come up if it was convenient. It was. He had just finished taking a shower when we got there, and he was sitting on the edge of the bed mixing an Alka-Seltzer, looking very forlorn. He was a big, good-looking guy, I imagine about thirty-three years old at the time, and without a mean bone in his body. But, boy, was he weak! He could be talked into anything. He reminded me of nothing so much as a big Labrador. After the preliminaries I asked him what had happened, what was he doing here a week early? And this was his story.

"Ray, baby, you're not going to believe this, but it's the absolute gospel truth. My wife was back in Boise visiting her folks for a week, and I was at loose ends. Then, about three nights ago, Doris Stein invited me up the hill to one of those big bashes she throws. Now, I like Doris, and it's one of those houses where you can't get into much trouble. She always has a nicely mixed bunch. I behaved well, like someone from Wilmington, Delaware. Anyway, during the course of the evening I found myself being kind of monopolized by a long-limbed number with horn-rims who had just graduated from Oglethorpe and it was her first visit to California. Now I was on my best behavior, because up at the Steins' you never know quite who people are. This one had first cabin stamped all over her, although for an Oglethorpe graduate she sounded quite naive. Around eleven-thirty I started to yawn and said I'd better leave, that I had some studying to do. She asked if I'd mind driving her down to her hotel, if it wasn't out of my way. She was staying at the Beverly Hills. I said I'd be glad to, that I lived practically around the corner. On the way down the hill she happened to mention that she was having quite a problem getting to sleep since she'd been in California. I said, 'Why don't you take a sleeping pill with half a glass of beer? That'll make you sleep.' She replied that she was afraid of sleeping pills, that people sometimes got mixed up and forgot how many they had taken. I told her that I had some at home that were foolproof. You *couldn't* forget how many you had taken. They were French, quite harmless, absolutely no hangover. The only problem was that they needed about half an hour to take effect.

" 'That's very kind of you,' she said. 'Are you sure you can spare a couple?'

" 'Of course,' I replied. 'But I'm not going to give you a couple, just one, and I'll tell you how to use it, because they're new and a little different.'

"In about ten minutes we were at my joint and I took her into my private quarters, which is a combination bedroom, den, and library, with a bathroom-dressing room leading off it. I told her to sit down while I went into the bathroom and got the sleeping

pill. I came back and told her, 'Now, listen. These
are not pills you just swallow. They're called Sup-
poneryl, and they're suppositories. You insert them.
Know what I mean?'

"She nodded in a sort of scared way and said,
'I . . . I think so.'

"I took one out of its plastic wrapper and showed
it to her. I don't know why her eyes popped, they're
no bigger than a thirty-thirty cartridge and not even
as long. 'Now look,' I said. 'They can't possibly hurt
you. They're just wax, and your body heat melts them
once they're inside you.'

"She looked a little windy for a couple of moments
and then asked if I'd mind if she went into my bathroom and tried to do it. 'You said it would be half
an hour before they took effect, and you could take me
right to my hotel.'

" 'Sure,' I said. 'Go right ahead.'

"It was about five minutes before she opened the
door, and she stood there looking kinda sheepish.
Then she held out her right hand, and in it was just
a glob of wax. 'I tried, but it just wouldn't go in,
and then it all melted in my hand. I'm sorry.'

" 'That's all right,' I said. 'I'll get you another
one and you can have a second go.'

"Then she looked at me in kind of an embarrassed
way and asked if I couldn't possibly help her—I would
be more or less acting like a doctor. I looked at her
for a moment or two and thought, Well, well, *well!*
What sort of a gig is this? But the dame was actually
blushing. She was on the level!

"So I shrugged as nonchalantly as I could and
said, 'Okay, honey, take down your pants and pull
up your skirt and lean over the back of that couch
close to the light.' Boy, if Jules Stein ever finds out
about this, I'll be barred from Universal for life! I
unwrapped another magic bullet and was stabbing
around trying to find the hole and thinking, This dame
is really tense, and wondering at the same time how
any guy with ten years of medical training would

ever choose to be a proctologist. At that moment
the suppository found its mark, and I gently shoved
it home with my middle finger. Right up to the big
joint. And with that the bedroom door opened and
my wife walked in.

"For five seconds it was a real stop-action shot,
a perfect frozen frame. And then I bolted. I mean,
in a situation like that what the hell could I say?
I jumped in my car, which was still at the curb, and
headed for Phoenix, where I caught a plane for New
York and another across the Atlantic. And here I
am. If my wife calls, tell her you haven't seen me
and that I'm not due for ten days."

Weakly I asked him if he'd left his work permit
at home. He said he'd just got it that day and it was
in his passport in the glove compartment of his car.
By this time Frank was in the bathroom throwing
up, pretty close to apoplexy. When things calmed
down a little, I told Hot Rocks that he wouldn't have
to work for at least a week but that there was a party
on Saturday night and that I was going to need him.

"Anything, Ray baby," he said. "Just keep me
close to you 'cos I think I'm accident-prone."

The reception, party, soirée, call it what you will,
was held on Saturday night in an edifice that looked
to me about as big as the Escorial, and which had
probably at one time been the home base of this huge
and now scattered family. The place was literally
a museum. No matter where one looked the eye was
met by elegance. There was boulle and marqueterie,
Louis Quinze and Louis Seize, Italian Renaissance,
eighteenth-century English, Empire, the lot. Suddenly
I felt a terrible blow in the side. I turned and it was
Frank, the set designer, his eyes sticking out like hat-
pegs in a chapel.

"*This* is the stuff we need! *This* is what our sets
scream for! I don't care how you do it, but somehow,
some way, you've got to borrow it. If we can't borrow
it, we'll steal it. But we've got to have it!"

I thought for a few moments and said, "Frank,

calm down. Everything is possible. It so happens that I'm sitting at the head table next to the dame who owns all this, and in my wily way I'll start the ball rolling."

Frank looked a little dubious and said, "I'd be a little careful if I were you. She looks like a barracuda to me."

"In that case," I replied, "if the reaction is at all favorable, we'll throw Hot Rocks at her and tell him that if he doesn't swing it we'll send for his wife. That should do it."

And do you know something? It worked! Sunday afternoon Frank and the trucks backed up to the mansion and loaded what we needed—and on Monday morning the sets were dressed. Beautifully. Just to be on the safe side, after each scene had been shot I had the camera run about a hundred extra feet of that aspect of the set and kept on doing it until I had all three sets covered. That way I could always fall back on "process" shots just in case something went wrong.

I'm a realist if nothing else. I knew Hot Rocks was fast out of the gate, but where would he be at the end of ten furlongs? My perspicacity proved itself eight days later, when our boy showed up for his one big scene in these particular sets. He looked as if he'd been drawn through a knothole.

"You sick, Herbie?" I asked.

He looked at me as if he were peering up from a dungeon. "I'm at death's door, you bastard. I've got to know something. On the level, how much longer are you gonna need this furniture?"

"About another week. Why?"

Slowly his head moved from side to side, and he groaned, "I'll never make it."

His reprieve came four days later, on Friday night, when his wife suddenly showed up. Saturday afternoon a fleet of trucks appeared at the studio, and in three hours the sets were bare. It seems that Hot Rocks had told our aging Medusa, who owned the stuff, that he was separated from his wife, which of course technically he was, by about seven thousand miles. When our Boise belle showed up on the set, his goose was cooked. But 'tis my belief that Hot Rocks was beginning to fade in the stretch, which was quite understandable in a way because the bloom had been long gone from our local lollapaloosa. In spite of her, we still managed to come up with a creditable effort, helped in no small way by some damned good process work after we got back to Hollywood. Let there be no misunderstanding regarding the aforementioned incidents. They all happened. Down to the last syllable. Of course, I've had to juggle some things slightly, and leave out some even wilder and wackier sequences.

Before I leave this foreign episode, though, I do want to mention the night when the city government decided to give a testimonial dinner thanking us for reactivating the motion-picture industry in their country. Our leading lady, who by the end of dinner and two dozen toasts was a little out of sync, decided to respond in border Spanish. I think it was a speech she had given to the Ladies Aid Society in Tijuana nine years previously. It might as well have been in Erse. There was loud applause, which puzzled me because 90 percent of the audience spoke English better than she did—a necessity, since the native tongue was unintelligible to the rest of the world.

There were also two pillars of wisdom and strength in the picture, both actors and both elderly. One was sixty-eight years old the day he started the movie, and the other was eighty-one the day I asked him to swim almost a hundred yards in a tidal river mouth literally festooned with used contraceptives, it being a very Catholic country. His remark when we pulled him out was, "Funny time of the year for jellyfish." He only had one eye. The left one had bothered him, so he'd had it taken out. God, I'm going to miss this racket.

chapter xvii

Picture making isn't always goofy. The discipline and organization in a large and successful film studio can be awe-inspiring. Studio craftsmen and technicians can build anything, from a castle to a cargo ship. They can reproduce hurricanes and monsters, disembodied dreams and ghosts. They can turn ugliness into beauty and make swans look like pelicans. It is usually much easier to make a good picture than it is to make a bad one, because the good one inevitably has the one indispensable element, a good story. When you have that, you don't need stars, just good actors.

Stars cannot help a bad screen play, but they're a must when it comes to getting the thing financed. It seems that bankers can only calculate and are incapable of dreaming. Otherwise how can one account for the dreary list of disastrous remakes of some wonderful old pictures? The most shocking example is MGM's remake of Frank Lloyd's classic *Mutiny on the Bounty*, a picture that was as near perfection as any film could be, a film that wasn't even twenty years old! If it were re-released today it would triple the box-office take of the original run, and it might even bring back the hordes of moviegoers who have given up in disgust because of the scurrilous filth that is prevalent. But such was the paucity of ideas, the barren and callous thinking of the men at the studio helm that the remake practically bankrupted MGM and ended its career as the bellwether of the industry. A more recent and much more galling example of the conceit of individuals stupid enough to think they can improve something that's already perfect is the case of Columbia's remaking *Lost Horizon,* Frank Capra's gem. I was fortunate enough to see the original version a few months ago, not the blotched-up abortion one is likely to see on television but the picture as Capra meant it to be shown. I tell you, I was like a child waking up on Christmas morning, I was so overwhelmed by the joy and the adventure of it, the pure escapism, which is what pictures should be all about—that is, if they expect you to pay your own way in. And do you know that some birdbrain actually did a remake of John Ford's *Stagecoach?* I was one of the unfortunates who saw it. But who am I to carp? I was once inveigled into a remake of *The Awful Truth,* which turned out to be a fizzle of the worst kind, for which I still haven't been paid, and rightly so. And that was over twenty years ago. I'll bet you that right at this moment there is a fool sitting on some gilded toilet in Bel-Air planning a remake of Ronald Colman's *Random Harvest!* Mark my words. But the prospect isn't *all* bleak, I see some signs of intelligence creeping back, films by people who really love the medium. The greatest drawback in making pictures is the fact that film makers have to eat.

You know, actors are wonderful people to be around, especially in the shank of the evening, when the squares have all gone home and they don't have to be *on* anymore and the girdles can be let out a notch or two. Actors are so many-faceted, so intuitive, so basically intelligent, and, almost without exception, humorous. And by country-club standards, very moral. Of course there are exceptions, and the entire profession suffers as a result, because the exceptions are nothing if not volatile. When they do a little ex-tralegal banging, it is done with flair and panache. Why waste time on half-measures? If you're going to be hanged you might as well be hanged for a sheep as for a lamb. This is what is called "living a full, rich life." And it's surprising how many of these wild and woolly ones end up being mentioned in the New Year's Honors List. But that isn't what this chapter is about. I want to talk about talents all actors have, of which the general public isn't usually aware.

I remember one night, in the early fifties I think it was, when we were sitting around up at Charlie Feldman's house, on Coldwater Canyon. It was around midnight, and the party had been a pretty big bash. As a producer, Charles Kenneth Feldman had made some of the best and some of the worst pictures ever to come out of Hollywood. He also owned a large talent agency and consequently was pretty well fixed financially, in spite of which he was well-liked and had a touch of elegance. About half the guests, those who were working, had left soon after dinner, which was normal procedure in Holly-wood, and reasonable, when you consider the working hours. (I still awaken at the crack of dawn.) There were about twenty of us left, and things had quieted considerably. Burton, who was kind of new in town at that time, had finally stopped sonorously spouting *Titus Andronicus* and had meandered into one of the guestrooms, flopped on one of the beds and fallen fast asleep. No one had been paying much attention anyway, with the possible exception of Clifton Webb, who had been casing him with a furtive and rather contemplative look. Burton didn't realize it at the time, but there was an American actor there that night who could have given him cards and spades when it came to Shakespeare. Yes, right there among us shirtless ones, the canaille, the unenlightened, the money grubbers. His name was Edmond O'Brien, and his only trouble was that, by English standards, he didn't *look* Shakespearean—which to me was an asset. By God, he had the genius to make Shakespeare come alive, to humanize it. Very few actors can do this. Most of the time their only concern is to say all the words, and in so doing they forget the sense. After seeing most of them I leave the theater with the feeling that I've been staring at a painting of John the Baptist. There are exceptions, of course. I think Maurice Evans doing Macbeth, or Lear, is just about as good as Shakespeare can get, and I'll go to see Olivier in almost anything. Almost, I said, because that guy can get a little gouty too.

Anyway, getting back to Charlie Feldman's pad, that night there was a guy fooling around with the piano. His name was Sam Browne, and he played the piano like someone floating around in a lily pond. He was thin and very tall, probably a lot of Watusi in his ancestry and a lot of Lee Sims in his fingers. Leaning on her elbows in the bend of the piano was the beautiful Dorothy Dandridge, looking a little sad this night as she listened to Sam, who had slid softly into Brahms' "Lullaby." Quietly, she began to hum along with it. Suddenly, from across the room, in a sweet, light baritone, came the words. A fellow about forty years old walked over and joined her and they did the thing together, he with the lyrics and she vocalizing behind Sam in a high, thin soprano. Wise Sam Browne barely intruded. When they finished my eyes were wet and I was breathing in little shudders. I looked around to see if anyone noticed, but there was no need to be embarrassed; all of us were in the same boat. The guy's name was Frank Ross, one-time husband to Jean Arthur and a highly respected film producer, a man who had sunk every dime he had and all he could borrow to make a picture he believed in. And he made a lulu. Called *The Robe*. I had known Frank for almost twenty years, and to me he was always a producer, a serious and somewhat introverted man. It had completely slipped my mind that in the early thirties, when I was playing my first lead with Jean Arthur in a picture called *Easy Living,* that Frank had been around, that he was the one who tried to calm me down, to help my nervousness. He had been a singer with the big bands, and *his* problems had been worse than mine. Now it all came back. He had been out of context for almost twenty years. But he would never sing for me again. I think it embarrassed him. Producers are not supposed to be able to sing.

Then there was the time when I attended a meeting of the full membership of the Screen Actors Guild, held in the Hollywood Legion Stadium, and up in the ring presiding over it was the best president the Guild ever had, Ronald Reagan, now governor of California. He had a tough job directing the traffic that night, what with calls to the barricades by a lot of coffeehouse characters, wailing about the violence outside studio gates. Hell, the only violent activity *I* ever saw outside a studio gate was over at Republic one morning, when Vera Hruba Ralston lost her skate key. Meanwhile, back at the Legion, the ring was beginning to look more and more like an all-in wrestling extravaganza. Becoming a little wearied by the tedious platitudinizing, I climbed up to the topmost row of seats and sat down next to Gary Cooper. Now Gary never said much at large gatherings, but he did an awful lot of listening, and he was nobody's fool. I've always been of the opinion that there was a lot of Will Rogers in Coop, but he was much more diffident, a shy man really. This particular evening he was sitting with his feet up on the chair-back in front of him, with a large sketchpad on his knees. A few of the sheets were lying on the floor between us. I reached down and asked if he minded my looking.

"Go ahead, Commando," he said, "but don't flash 'em around."

I looked at the first one rather casually and saw that it was covered with just suggestions of human figures, a head caught as it looked over one shoulder,

the expression fierce and hateful, an arm extended
with the finger pointing, a man sitting in a chair with
his head sunk between his shoulders. None of the
figures was clothed, and they were all done on rough
paper with a soft lead pencil. Not more than a dozen
lines to each, but they showed tremendous power.
Then I looked at the other sheet I had picked up
and stopped in sheer amazement. It was an impression
of the entire arena and the people in it. The rawness
of George Bellows was in it, and some of the hopeless
lyricism of Winslow Homer, and in the angry faces
a reminder of Goya. This was not just the idle sketching
of a dilettante, this was professionalism of a very
fine order. Typical of someone who couldn't even
draw a box, I was in awe.

I said, "Coop, did you ever do this for money?"

And without looking up, he said, "Yeah, I guess
you could say that. One time, back in Montana, I
used to do cartoons for the local paper. Once in a
while a few ads for the sporting goods store."

"But where did you learn?"

"England."

"England?"

"Yeah, I went to school there for a while, when
I was a kid."

By the time the voting was over and the meeting
had broken up, almost an hour had gone by, and
it had taken me all that time to worm out of him
that his father, who was a judge, had taken a six-month
sabbatical to study English courtroom procedure and
had taken Coop with him, put him in school, and
then decided to leave him there for a year. I've
forgotten the name of the school, but it was a private
one and it obviously had a good art teacher. I know
it had a talented pupil. As we were leaving the meeting
I asked Coop if he would consider giving me the
sketch of the arena, saying I'd really love to have
it.

He looked at me, grinned, and said, "Yeah, you

can have it, but don't ask me to sign it. And have it fixed, that lead is pretty soft and it'll smudge."

That was twenty-odd years ago, and it's about fifteen since I last saw the sketch. Now that my wife and I have become gypsies again, it's probably stored with the rest of the accumulation of forty years. But I imagine Coop's widow Rocky has a lot of his stuff squirreled away somewhere, and the sketches would be well worth looking at again.

Very few people know that Randolph Scott, before he got sidetracked, started out as an accountant. Now he's back at it again, only this time the money he's counting is his own. Between that and playing golf he's got no time for acting anymore. And there's George Montgomery and the wonderful furniture he makes. He's truly an artist at it, and if he ever made carpentry a full-time occupation, Baker, Heritage, and big-time companies of that ilk would find him serious competition. But he's too much of an artist about it, he has to examine and correct and help polish every individual piece his little operation turns out. I've only got a table of his, and it is beautiful. I envy people like this, people with extracurricular talents, because I have none. At least, none that would enable me to live in the manner to which I have become accustomed.

And now the time has come when there is snow on the roof, or what's left of it, and I find myself using my arms more when I have to get up out of a chair. And I notice that young girls hug me a lot more than they used to, and they give me great big smacking kisses when they say good-bye. They'd never have dared do that twenty years ago. But it works both ways; girls don't bother *me* so much anymore, either . . . althought I *did* see a little number the other day that brought back a slight twinge. In case you're interested, Niven, she works in that dress shop next to the African Queen in Beaulieu. I'd like a full report.

I've noticed something else since I've graduated

to playing fathers and grandfathers. The work seems to be easier. I don't have to deal with that youth syndrome anymore, whether the wattles are waggling, and the constant and dreary effort to appear dashing. Acting at last is becoming enjoyable, the fear and the fright are leaving me, and the contentment is leaking in. I noticed it first when I was approached to do a little picture called *Love Story,* which I think I'll tell you about. It's an odd little saga.

At the beginning of December, close to three years ago, I was starting rehearsals for an eight-week tour of *Front Page.* Opening night was to be on December 15 in Palm Beach, Florida, preceded by eight days of rehearsals in New York. Toward the end of November, just as I was beginning to get my mental attitude in shape to face New York, I got a telephone call from Howard Minsky, a guy I hadn't seen in twenty years. He had been in distribution for Paramount, and now, it appeared, he was going to produce a little picture in New York with Paramount money and the Paramount production head's wife, Ali McGraw, and a kid called Ryan O'Neal. He'd like very much if I would play the boy's father and do it sans peruke, the whole thing to be shot in New York and Boston.

I said, "Howard, I'd love to do it for you, but I'm afraid it's out of the question. I'm opening in *Front Page* at the Palm Beach Playhouse on December 15, and there's no way I can get out of it. It's two weeks there, two weeks in Lauderdale, a week in Coconut Grove, a week in Atlanta, and two weeks in Toronto. There's just no way."

He came back with, "Look, there is a way. I've done a hell of a lot of phoning the last couple of days, and I know all about your tour and all about your rehearsal schedule in New York. Now, on this tour you don't work on Mondays, and your last performance on Sunday nights is over by eleven-thirty. We can have a car waiting at the stage door of whatever theater you're playing in and have you at Lauderdale airport in time to catch the one-thirty A.M. Eastern Airlines plane to New York. You'll get in at four-thirty A.M. and be in bed by five. We'll have a car pick you up at the Waldorf Towers at eight-thirty and you can be on the set by nine A.M. That'll give you a good three hours' sleep, and I promise not to work you after five P.M. On Tuesday mornings we'll only work you for a couple of hours, and you can be on the mid-day plane for Florida in plenty of time for the evening performance. You don't go on till the end of the second act, anyway. Now, you know I need you—otherwise why the hell would I go to all this trouble? I can have a script over at your house in half an hour. Just read it and call me right back. Okay?"

Okay, Howard. I was tired of just listening to him. Well, the script arrived within the hour and I read it. He was right, it was a little picture. But it made me cry. I gave it to Mal and she read it and *she* cried and said, "I think you ought to do it, if it isn't going to be too rough on you. I've got a feeling about it."

I had a feeling about it too, parboiled exhaustion.

Twenty minutes later I called Howard back and told him he had a deal, but what about my rehearsals in New York? I'd have to have some days off or have a guy on the set to rehearse with me between takes.

"That's all taken care of, Ray baby. I've already talked to them, and they've agreed to let you rehearse between six P.M. and midnight." Fade out.

And that's the way it went for eight weeks. No slipups, not major ones, anyway, though there was one Tuesday when I narrowly escaped missing my entrance. We were playing in Coconut Grove at the time, and the temperature had been twelve below zero in New York, and the plane was an hour and a half late taking off from New York. Ten minutes after we were airborne the cabin heating system packed up, and we arrived in Lauderdale deep-frozen. I got to the theater midway through the first act, to be greeted by Allen Jenkins, who was playing one of the reporters, with the statement that I walked like a man with his feet froze.

"Why the hell shouldn't I?" I said. "They *are* froze."

With all the hectic running around and the continual worry about making the curtain, I'm afraid I became a little antisocial, which was great for the part. For the rest of the tour I was the perfect managing editor, "Walter Burns." But there's a little more to the chronicle of the making of *Love Story,* and it has to do with the near-destruction of a brilliant individual. Just before they started shooting, someone got the idea that it might be a good thing for Erich Segal to write a short novel based on his script. When the book hit the stands it took off like a rocket to the moon, and for the time it was on the best-seller list it outsold the Bible, made Erich Segal a millionaire, and guaranteed that when the picture came out it would be a gold mine. And it came to pass. And then they started in on Segal. The self-appointed arbiters of literary quality, the TV "personalities" whose only claim to fame is an ability to talk endlessly about nothing, the late-night talk-show hosts who rang in every author they could find who wore a flannel shirt and sandals. The downgrading was almost paranoid. Segal had committed the cardinal sin: he had written a fantastic commercial success and he hadn't spent ten years in a garret doing it. And to make matters worse, he was a professor at Yale! And before that at Harvard. Why, the bastard even took baths and ran in the Boston Marathon every year! They really lit into him, those dull, ponderous pundits. But strangely, I don't recall any *professional* critics behaving in this manner. On the whole they were very fair and saw the effort for what it was, a story about two young people sadly passing by. The fact that Segal had written another picture a couple of years before called *The Yellow Submarine,* which caused few ripples and sank slowly to the bottom, was never

mentioned. That would have made him a quondam
failure, which would never do at all. He had to be
brought down, and they've almost done it. He finally
quit the Eastern seaboard and went to Europe, where
he took a job teaching at some obscure German college.
Now I read that he's quit that job, too. I saw it only
the other day in that disgustingly anti-American blatt
called the Paris *Herald-Tribune*. It was just a one-liner,
no reason given, so it must have been a good one.
Segal's young yet, and brilliant. There's plenty of
time for him to confound those strung-out boors.
I only met the guy once and talked to him for less
than an hour, but that's the way he impressed me.

There was something else in the *Tribune* just yesterday that gave me a hell of a chortle. I've got it right
before me as I write this. It reports that Marlene
Dietrich fell into the orchestra pit the other night
at the conclusion of one of her performances. At
her age that's not hard to do. I did it once before
I was thirty. But at seventy-two years of age, it's
not the falling in that's hard, it's the getting out. I
know if *I* had been in the theater that night I'd have
stayed until the a-frame got there just to watch the
hauling out. According to the paper, Marlene told
the audience to get out and go home, that she was
quite all right, not hurt a bit, that she had been through
bombings and bombardments, had tramped through
battlefields and never got a scratch, and that she also
received the Congressional Medal of Honor. It is
to be hoped she was misquoted because, while she
was honored by the government for entertaining the
armed forces, the only way this individual could have
got the Congressional Medal was to have picked it
up in a hock shop. It is a medal given only to soldiers
for deeds of great bravery and heroism, above and
beyond the call of duty, and the awarding of it is
carefully and jealously weighed. I bring the item up
only because this kind of statement is the sort of
thing that gives actors a bad name, and frankly, I've
met very few actors I didn't like. I've been an "inter-

ested observer of the passing parade" all my life. My main fault is that I see the faults and foibles first. It is a quality that tends to make one cynical.

But if there is cynicism in me it has been engendered by disillusion. Most of my pedestals stand empty and the world seems filled with predators, so that I have come to the conclusion that my perennial nostalgia is not for a place but for a *time*. A time of good manners, of elegance and modesty, of honor and pride and self-respect. Many of these qualities remain with me only faintly, but I remember them and know that if I can recapture and polish them I shall be safe. The few people today who seem to display kindliness and good manners are cabinetmakers and the postman. Another cheerful troop are the men who deliver the milk in the morning. It seems that when I was a young boy everyone was like that. Of course, there were always a few sour apples, but they were a necessary leavening—one just couldn't have everyone going about with the big "Ho, ho, ho!" Life would be a big bloody bore.

In moments of retrospection, which are becoming more frequent of late, I have felt needling touches of guilt because—let's face it—I've had a most wonderful life and as far as I can see have done very little to deserve it. Oh, I've pitched in and worked hard and been cooperative and accommodating, but I've even enjoyed that. So why have I been so blessed? I've been presented to kings and queens, met presidents and princes, master criminals and legendary concubines. I have been patronized by kept husbands and propositioned by rich wives, and in a few instances by rich husbands. I have been paid fabulous sums to frolic with and to make bogus love to the most beautiful women in the world, which on one or two cases turned out to be not so bogus. Overall, a joyous existence, but threaded through it, deep depressions and peaks as high as the stars. It is only now, when I have arrived in my sixties, that I experience sad disappointments and bothersome annoyances. In earlier days the "sad disappointments" would have plunged me into the depths of depression, in some instances with suicidal overtones, convinced that God had forsaken me. And the "bothersome annoyances" meant raging fury, revenge in its most horrendous forms, the first of which would be castration with a rusty knife. My life in those days was one long saga of agony and ecstasy. Volatile? You bet!

It's only when I lie in bed in the early hours before dawn that I let my mind dwell on the punishments I would like to inflict and the kindnesses I would like to perform. But I've got to stop all this attic searching because I must leave for Johannesburg on Friday. A new picture, new people, a new place. And who knows?—maybe one or two of the Whores of Stellenbosch will be there. By now it must be quite obvious to you that my life is still filled to the brim and it's going to stay that way. I've got a lot of things to do.

Addio.